Personal Goals
and
Work Design

Personal Goals and Work Design

Edited by

Peter Warr

MRC Social and Applied Psychology Unit
University of Sheffield

JOHN WILEY & SONS

London · New York · Sydney · Toronto

Library of Congress Cataloging in Publication Data:
Main entry under title:

Personal goals and work design.

Based on papers presented at a conference held in York, England, in August 1974, sponsored by the Scientific Affairs Division of NATO.

Includes indexes.
1. Job satisfaction—Congresses. 2. Psychology, Industrial—Congresses. 3. Work—Psychological aspects—Congresses. I. Warr, Peter Bryan, ed. II. North Atlantic Treaty Organization. Division of Scientific Affairs.

HF5549.5.J63P368   301.5'5   75–4568

ISBN 0 471 92095 9

Photosetting by Thomson Press (India) Limited, New Delhi and printed by The Pitman Press Ltd., Bath

To
Harry Kay

Contributors

PAUL M. BONS   University of Washington and US Military Academy, West Point, USA

ALBERT CHERNS   Loughborough University, England

T. G. CUMMINGS   Case Western Reserve University, Cleveland, USA

LOUIS E. DAVIS   University of California at Los Angeles, USA

FRISO DEN HERTOG   Philips Gloeilampenfabrieken, Eindhoven, Holland

PIETER J. D. DRENTH   Free University of Amsterdam, Holland

DAVID ELLIOTT   The Open University, England

FRED E. FIEDLER   University of Washington, Seattle, USA

GEORGE H. HINES   Massey University, Palmerston North, New Zealand

GERLOF HOOLWERF   Free University of Amsterdam, Holland

RALPH KATZ   Massachusetts Institute of Technology, USA

LORNE M. KENDALL   Simon Fraser University, British Columbia, Canada

EDWARD E. LAWLER III   University of Michigan, USA

TERENCE R. MITCHELL   University of Washington, Seattle, USA

ANDREW M. PETTIGREW   London Graduate School of Business Studies, England

JOHN ROWAN   Consultant social psychologist, London

PAUL F. SALIPANTE   Case Western Reserve University, Cleveland, USA

HENK THIERRY   *University of Amsterdam, Holland*

JOHN VAN MAANEN   *Massachusetts Institute of Technology, USA*

LEOPOLD S. VANSINA   *International Institute for Organizational and Social Development, Kessel-Lo, Belgium*

P. J. VAN STRIEN   *Groningen University, Holland*

PETER B. WARR   *MRC Social and Applied Psychology Unit, University of Sheffield, England*

With cartoons by AREND VAN DAM, *Free University of Amsterdam, Holland*

Editor's Introduction

In his observations on *The Condition of the Working Class in England in 1844*, Friedrich Engels wrote: 'Man knows no greater happiness than that which is derived from productive work voluntarily undertaken. On the other hand, man knows no more degrading or unbearable misery than forced labour. No worse fate can befall a man than to have to work every day from morning till night against his will at a job that he abhors. The more the worker feels himself a man, the more must he detest work of this kind—the more acutely is he aware of the fact that such aimless labour gives rise to no inner spiritual satisfaction. Does he work from any natural impulse, or because he enjoys the tasks that he performs? Of course not. He works for money. He works for something which has nothing to do with the tasks that he has performed. He works because he must'.

It is thoughts of that kind which reflect the motivation for this book. People are deeply affected by their work; some enjoy it enormously, others undertake it reluctantly, most are in between. Is it possible that work can be designed in ways which meet both organizational requirements and the personal goals of employees? The possibility certainly exists, but the aim is not easily achieved. This book sets out to review some of the issues and techniques which have recently attracted attention in several parts of the world.

The book itself is one of the outcomes of a conference held in York, England, in August 1974. The meeting was sponsored by the Scientific Affairs Division of NATO, and its 87 participants came from 13 countries: Australia, Belgium,

Canada, Greece, Holland, New Zealand, Norway, Swaziland, Sweden, Switzerland, United Kingdom, United States of America and West Germany.

The conference dealt with psychological and related approaches to the quality of working life and examined ways in which this might be improved. It examined research, practice and potential from three standpoints—issues of understanding, value and change:

Issues of understanding. Here we asked questions such as: What is the present level of work satisfaction? What is known about attitudes to work? What do people want from work? How are societies' views of working life changing? How adequate are our conceptual frameworks and methodological approaches?

Issues of value. These covered questions like: What organizational features are ethically desirable? To what extent should work be designed to promote psychological well-being? How do researchers' and consultants' value-systems correspond to those of other people in organizations?

Issues of change. How can we achieve what is desirable? What in practice can researchers and consultants do to change organizations? What factors prevent recommendations being followed? What organizational tactics yield most substantial improvements?

These three kinds of issue are naturally interdependent, and discussion moved from one type to another. The conference included orthodox sessions for the presentation and discussion of papers, but much of the time was spent in small discussion groups. These were mainly scheduled for specific times on the conference programme, but participants were in addition invited to lead unscheduled discussions at different times with small groups of people interested in a particular topic.

There was thus considerable social interaction throughout the conference, of a kind which is difficult to capture in a book of proceedings. This book summarizes what happened through the inclusion of revised versions of the papers presented in the formal sessions. Most speakers have rewritten their contributions to take account of comments and discussions which arose from their presentations. The chapters of this book are therefore based upon, but not identical to, the papers delivered to the conference.

In addition to the conference presentations themselves (Chapters 1 to 14), three members were asked to review the conference as a whole (discussions as well as formal papers) in an attempt to bring together themes which they personally thought to be important and interesting. These conference reviews (Chapters 15 to 17) deal with issues of understanding, value and change respectively.

The conference presentations were selected to give coverage of different approaches and emphases. It was particularly interesting to learn how people from different countries had their own biasses and concerns and to see how different disciplines brought their own viewpoints into the arena. In addition to the wide range of countries represented, the participants varied considerably in their professional background. Membership included psychologists, sociologists, social scientists, engineers, economists, managers, teachers and consultants. These different emphases will be noticeable in the chapters which follow.

It is usual to say about books based upon conferences that they contain some interesting chapters but lack a common theme. Throughout the planning stages of this meeting and book I have been very conscious of the need to balance diversity against narrowness. The quality of life at work and the possible influence upon it of researchers and consultants is no simple topic. It must be approached through several disciplines, methodologies and illustrative studies. This book does that, and I hope that readers will look especially hard at chapters which raise questions which are not orthodox ones for their own professional group.

I have found it helpful to think about two main ways in which people differ in their outlook on the topics covered in this book. The first dimension of difference is in terms of 'thinking big' or 'thinking small'. With regard to issues of understanding, this difference may emerge as one to do with the scope of the system which we should study: can we look at individuals, or must the unit of analysis be a group, a technological system, a socio-technical system, or society as a whole? Similarly, the difference may be in the depth of understanding which is thought to be desirable: should we devote our limited resources to limited understanding of certain situations or should we require more complete and complex explanations and models? In terms of change, there are related differences in thinking: should we try to initiate small changes, perhaps to reduce dissatisfaction of a few employees, or is that too narrow or superficial an approach? Should we try to alter a whole system, perhaps attempting to influence the initial design or total operation of production systems, or is that impracticable and overly idealistic? Also, in terms of value issues the thinking big or small dimension is represented by variations in compartmentalization of value systems. Should we approach organizational change as a separated part of our lives, viewing the ethical issues as being restricted within the situations we are studying? Or should we see conditions within an organization as a reflection of a more general political condition which may or may not be desirable?

Those several strands of the dimension of difference from 'thinking big' to 'thinking small' are of course distinguishable from one another, but it is my hunch that they are in reality moderately intercorrelated: people who tend to 'think big' in one sense tend to 'think big' in others. In reading this book you might like to consider where each author might be placed upon the several strands of the dimension. And where do your own preferences lie?

The second dimension of difference is a familar one in all disciplines. Its nature is well captured in terms of a range between 'tough-minded' and 'tender-minded' approaches. The tough-minded commentator is one who looks for hard data, controlled experimental designs and statistical sophistication. He is concerned about scientific method and the need for strict interpretation of evidence. His more tender-minded colleague might agree that such requirements are appropriate in limited situations; his own preference is, however, for an understanding through personal experience, greater reliance on hunches, and an explicit recognition of the complexity of dynamic systems. The tough-minded investigator is likely to accept that his own approach limits the field of enquiry, but he tends to argue that in the present state of knowledge such a limitation is both necessary and desirable.

Conference participants clearly varied in the extent to which they were tough-minded or tender-minded, just as they differed in their tendency to think big or think small. Many people managed to tolerate some degree of ambiguity, finding benefit in movement from one outlook to another without denying the validity of other approaches.

Such an orientation is perhaps the appropriate one for readers of this book. It may be helpful to view each of the contributions in terms of these two dimensions of difference, while keeping an open mind about the advantages and disadvantages of the different approaches. There is no one road to better working lives.

The success of a conference is measured partly in individual terms, the degree to which personal aims are met, and partly in social terms, to do with the general atmosphere and tempo. This particular meeting appeared to go well, and for this thanks are largely due to members' willingness to undertake formal or informal roles in the discussion sessions and elsewhere. Much is also owed to my secretary, Karen Thompson, and my wife, Patricia, for invaluable secretarial and administrative assistance. The 87 participants and their families will recall the important part which these two played in making the conference a success. We were of course also indebted to the Scientific Affairs Division of NATO for their sponsorship. In a fundamental sense, however, the meeting and this book would not have been possible without support and encouragement over many years from Harry Kay, now Vice-Chancellor of the University of Exeter. I should like to dedicate this volume to him.

PETER WARR

CONTENTS

xiv

Cartoons by Arend van Dam

1

Social Change and Work

Albert Cherns,
Loughborough University, England

The Value of Work

Christian civilization traces its descent from its Hebraic and Hellenic parentage. From the former it learned that work was the common lot of man, a punishment for disobedience, symbolizing his fall from grace, his expulsion from Paradise. From the latter it learned that work was an activity fit only for slaves.

It is a long journey from Ecclesiastes to Samuel Smiles, from 'What reward has a man for all his labour, his scheming and his toil ... There is nothing better for a man to do than to eat and drink and enjoy himself in return for his labours' to 'As steady application to work is the healthiest training for every individual, so is it the best discipline of a state. Honourable industry travels the same road with duty; and Providence has closely linked both with happiness'. Work, as Orwell pointed out, could be performed voluntarily: 'Throughout the spring and summer they worked a sixty hour week, and in August Napoleon announced that there would be work on Sunday afternoons as well. This work was strictly voluntary, but any animal who absented himself from it would have his rations reduced by half'. Tom Sawyer has a more realistic view: 'Work consists of whatever a body is obliged to do, and play consists of whatever a body is not obliged to do'.

Work, then, may be perceived as a burden, as a punishment for ancestral sin, as an unwelcome intrusion into the spiritual life, as the yoke and stigma of a 'working' class; or as man's true vocation, as ennobling, as the service he owes to his fellows or to his God, as his principal means of contact with 'reality' or his environment, as a drug to deaden the pain of thought, or a way of filling and ordering time. Most of us manage to combine some of these views at different times and in different places. Hence it is a brave or a foolish man who would pontificate about the place of work in a whole society, or about the attitudes to work of a whole people.

On the other hand, we are aware of change and should seek to identify, understand and explain it, not forgetting that changes can affect different groups in society in different ways, bringing different definitions of what is to be included in 'work' to different people. We often tend to obscure issues and to confuse ourselves by talking of 'work' when we mean 'employment'. The value we attach to employment—having a job—naturally tends to increase when employment becomes scarcer and to diminish when it becomes more abundant. But the value we attach to our work—what we do in employment—is not necessarily affected in the same way. When, on the other hand, the need for people to carry out traditional types of work diminishes, change may come less immediately in our beliefs about work than in our definitions of what constitutes it. Such a situation arises in the 'post-industrial society'. This term was invented by David Bell, to describe the situation now developing in the USA where less than 40% of employees work in productive industry and where values which sustain a high level of productivity at the expense of personal leisure and comfort are no longer required.

Some 10 years ago an editorial article in *The Economist* argued that modernization of Britain's industrial structure required that people employed in declining industries should be forced or urged out of them to create the 'pool' from which new developing industries could create their labour force. Since they would thus be forced out of work for no fault of their own and to serve the interests of the community as a whole, they should receive an adequate wage for the job of work-pool member, not unemployment pay based on subsistence considerations. Recently we have heard more of the structural argument that the comparative affluence of the majority is built on a system of stratification which inevitably produces the exploitation of a minority. The claims of the latter are therefore for recompense, not charity. These arguments, though from politically very different schools, bear more than a surface resemblance.

We should therefore be aware of the wide social and cultural influences affecting beliefs about, and attitudes to, work. We also need to take care to distinguish between beliefs about and attitudes to work and beliefs about and attitudes to employment. Finally, we need to remember that different groups and classes are affected unequally.

Forces Making for Change in Society

Technology

In trying to understand changes in society and culture we tend, because it is the most obvious and dramatic, to think of technology as the principal source of change and to think of it as if it were in some way outside society. Now it is of course true that new technologies have wrought immense changes. But there has never been a time without technological innovation. What has characterized Western society since the industrial revolution has been its growing acceptance of innovation and its readiness to pay the price. This was not always so. Nor should we take for granted the uses to which technology has been put. We tend unthinkingly to subscribe to a kind of technological determinism which has two main features: first that technology is an independent factor outside society, and second that it has its own logic. Together these make us the prisoners of a development unable to resist the inexorable logic that what can be done will inevitably be done. It comes as a strange idea that society can choose its technology and what it will do with its technological capabilities and, even stranger, that this is largely what political processes are, or should be, about. Indeed one of the forces making for change in cultural attitudes to work is the revaluation of technology brought about by wider recognition of its unreckoned costs, the negative consequences of an unheeding embrace of all it offered.

The search for outside sources of change is in any event mistaken. Opportunities for change are always present in the environment; the significant feature is what our culture predisposes us to make of them, how the structural elements of our society are differentially affected by the power shifts that would be involved in and caused by their use. We have experienced for the last 200 years the dominance in our societies of the groups whose interests were served best by the adoption of industrial technology, and who possessed the power to take the necessary decisions.

If technological policy has been widely based, the sum of many decisions taken by many people, population decisions have been so dispersed as to be unrecognizable as a policy. Yet population change has been one of the most powerful of all factors influencing attitudes of all kinds and not least those towards work and employment.

Population

The long history of human development with its very slow rate of population growth until modern times suggests the operation of negative feedback. Migration, removing part of a population from the competition for resources, has been a continuous feature. The work of filling the many empty spaces has taken hundreds of thousands of years, and within territorial areas, the Malthusian famine-type regulator appears to have been a comparatively rare event. Populations have found ways of restricting population growth by means of a wide range of techniques, some sophisticated, some horrifying. Babies thought likely to grow into weaklings in ancient Sparta were exposed on hillsides; old people in many tribal societies are reported voluntarily to seek death. Birth-control techniques have ranged from physical and pharmacological methods of abortion to the adoption of social norms calculated to restrict family size. Of these, late marriage, particularly of women, has been a recurrent feature. The common modern Western pattern of marriage at around 24 or 25 for men and 2 to 3 years younger for women obviously meets the requirements that the man has had the opportunity to complete his education and training and establish himself adequately in his work life to support a family, and that his wife should have as long a child-bearing period ahead of her as is compatible with the amount of education and training felt necessary for a woman. But this modern Western pattern is shifting; women are tending to marry slightly older and the age gap between husband and wife is diminishing.

The time scale for the processes of population growth is a long one. This is best exemplified by the phenomenon known as the 'population transition'. Most populations at most times have been fairly static or have grown very slowly. Births and deaths have balanced. After war or pestilence, births have exceeded deaths until the losses have been restored. The sudden spurt of population beginning with the Industrial Revolution in Europe was brought about by a gradual lowering of the death rate, lengthening the expectation of life without a concomitant decline in births. The reduction in the death rate had multiple causes: better nutrition, more efficient distribution of food, improved sanitation eliminating some of the most lethal communicable diseases, and finally, improved medical knowledge and methods of treatment.

Some 50 to 100 years after the death rate started to decline, the birth rate began a similar trend. In the meanwhile several generations of children had reached maturity in greater numbers than ever before, having survived in unprecedented proportions the dangerous first years of life (especially the very first year). When the birth rate finally dropped to near replacement level the population had grown, as in England and Wales four-fold in 110 years (Appolla, 1962; Marsh, 1958). This phenomenon is described as the 'demographic transition'. It is currently occurring in most of the undeveloped world. However, both birth rates and death rates start there from a far higher figure than in Europe before the transition, and through the importation of sanitary methods, modern medicine and disease control, better obstetric help and more efficient transport of food to threatened areas, the drop in the death rate has been far more precipitous. As a consequence, the rate of growth is anything up to twice as fast as the most rapid experienced in Europe.

Two questions present themselves: Why did birth rates tend to decline with lowered death rate? And why the lag between the two? We do not know, but we can surmise intelligently. Behaviour in these as in other respects is influenced by social norms. As we grow up we acquire attitudes and expectations about the kind of life we shall lead. We learn that people have families of three, four, five or eight children or whatever, and from the way people talk we learn the reasons. In societies with high death rates we learn that children frequently die, as some of our own siblings may have died, that property is left to sons, that people expect to be provided for in their old age by their surviving children, that children are needed to work on the family farm, or in workshops or cottage industry. During the early days of the Industrial Revolution in Britain urban families often depended upon the earnings of their small children in the mills and factories. Children were economically desirable or perhaps essential, and the costs of feeding, clothing and educating them were low.

Now the death rate begins to fall. The need for large families declines. But there is no disadvantage attached to them. Disadvantages begin to mount as living standards rise, as education becomes compulsory and extended, as children consume more than the value of what they produce now that their labour is no longer required. Large families come to stand in the way of a desired higher standard of living. When that happens, family size begins to decline. The transition period varies; in Europe, as we have said, it took two generations and even then affected different classes and regions unevenly. Other attitudes and values change. As welfare provision extends to cover necessities for the old, not only is the need to have children to provide for you removed, but the responsibilities of those you do have are reduced. With rising levels of living, the economic role of the family is diminished, rising provision of formal education reduces the family's role in education and socialization. Fewer children means a shorter child-bearing period for women and promotes their return to the labour force after their child-rearing responsibilities are over. A higher proportion of families have no dependent children at home as parents live longer as well as having fewer children. The constraints upon divorce are weakened. In Western society, as the sanctity of the family has been eroded, other living patterns have been tried, tolerated or approved. Ecological considerations begin to influence attitudes towards population limitation. The unmarried state is no longer seen as evidence of failure or irresponsibility or faint heartedness but as a legitimate option. Nor does it any longer imply the assumption of celibacy, particularly when contraceptives are effective, widely available and socially sanctioned. Homosexuality becomes tolerated and homosexuals then demand not mere toleration but acceptance. Society has turned towards values which encourage a low birth rate, weakening the institutions which protected it and establishing and strengthening institutions which reduce it.

It looks as though a general liberalization in the laws governing personal status is likely to lead towards lower birth rates. How far such liberalization can run ahead of public attitudes is another question with which we shall have to deal later. Nor can we ignore the restraining influence of religion. 'Be fruitful and multiply' was God's injunction to Adam and many of the laws of Judaism were directed towards this end. The Christian emphasis on the sanctity of marriage and the family helped to maintain population levels in hard times. It is notable that the forms of religious expression now finding favour among the Western societies emphasize mystical withdrawal and contemplation, a gentle monasticism not excluding or prohibiting sexual relationships but undermining the energetic impulse to engage in them, and certainly discouraging established patterns of family life.

Thus over the last three generations the whole shape of the population has changed. A drastic reduction in the birth rate leavened by successive 'bulges', together with the extended life expectancy of those reaching maturity, has produced a population distribution in more advanced countries in which the ratio of dependent old to population of working age has greatly increased. Simultaneously the statutory school-leaving ages have tended to rise and a larger proportion of young people remain in education beyond the school-leaving age. The tendency for women to marry early by historical standards, to start their child-bearing career earlier and to have fewer children has provided a large reservoir of women workers. The most notable statistical change is in the ratio of men to women in work.

In Britain, for example, between 1951 and 1972 the working population grew by 1.3 million, all women. In fact there were 1.4 million more working women and 45,000 fewer working men. The number of married women working increased by 2.5 million while the number of unmarried working women dropped by 1.1 million. In 1972 women constituted 36% of the working population. This proportion is expected to continue to rise strongly and to reach 38% by 1986. Meanwhile the proportion of the whole population 'economically active' remained stationary at 46%. Cultural symbols and themes based on the norm of work as the activity of the male breadwinner cannot long survive real changes of this kind. In many ways the world of work is still a man's world as we are constantly reminded by the proponents of sex equality and women's liberation; change may be slow in coming but it is unquestionably on the way and its implications are enormous. What are the changes in our view of work that have come about through its increasing feminization? A central feature of working-class culture was the acquisition of masculinity through work. Much work was physically heavy and demanding, holding your own in a man's world was the school leaver's aim and to attain it he often had to endure a *rite de passage*. His position in the family as a contributor to its economic welfare with its concomitant due to deference and special treatment was established. Today his sister may earn as much as a typist, his work is usually less physically demanding and the work *milieu* less aggressively male.

We can only sketch here the consequences for work of population changes and the value changes associated with them. Changing attitudes to women's work, to adolescents at work and to retirement are obvious. The effects of migration are equally obvious; the 6 or 7 million foreign workers in Europe or the Commonwealth immigrants in Britain make clear the association between developments in the world of work and social, political, especially international, and economic policies. As demographic change affects work, so does change in work affect population. With movements across frontiers partly open we have all the uncertainties of a partly managed open system.

Education

A society with fewer dependent children can afford to keep them dependent longer. This is not the sole reason why children are kept longer in school and why more stay beyond the legal minimum. Our technological society has become more complex, requires more and higher-level skills to manage it. Society's opportunities are open principally to the skilled and the functionally literate and numerate. The opportunities for those who have only youth and strength to offer have diminished and those which remain carry low prestige. Longer and higher education engender higher expectations from life and from work in particular. However, reality seldom meets rising expectations, and much of the dissatisfaction with work reported among young people owes its origin to this fact.

Popular education, even mass literacy and higher education for ever-growing proportions of the population, does not necessarily lead to an ever-broadening democratic basis of political mobilization; it does lead, however, to a broad base of recruitment of political élites. Meritocracy is as possible as participatory democracy. Political centralization, in particular centralized planning emphasizing collective as opposed to individual goals, affects cultural views of work, putting deliberate valuations on certain kinds of work as they lead towards the current goals of the planning apparatus.

Educational changes both follow and lead technology. The present vogue for 'continuing education', 'recyclage' and so on, recognizes that the rate of technological change renders specific skills quickly obsolete. And technology is coded knowledge, the product of education; a high level of material technology is the product of materialist values in education, as a high level of religious technology was the product of spiritual values in education.

Media

While we should never ignore or underestimate the capacity of the political system to set work goals and place political valuations on work, other influences are as powerful. No technological innovations have affected our lives more than the strides in the technology of communications, and none has had more influence on attitudes and values. In particular the immediacy of the mass media enhances and amplifies variance and deviation. It is the unexpected, the outrageous, the new, the protesting, the law-breaking, the custom-breaking, the norm-transgressing that feed the media; what they transmit back is the interest, the excitement, the attention that far more often acts as positive than as negative feedback. Through this process the pace of cultural change which could formerly be measured in generations has accelerated towards instability. Superficially the media may appear to be agents for cultural homogeneity, presenting similar fare similarly packaged to all. However, the fare itself is far from homogeneous and the media offer a selection of experiences presented from the instantaneous seat in the grandstand denied even to those geographically close to the event. Many competing interpretations of events, styles of life, questions, answers, opinions are all available, however improbable, however provocative, bigoted, ignorant or malicious, all given the weight of television 'coverage', fragmenting rather than binding the audience. Television pundits, commentators and interviewers reap the benefits of familiarity and wittingly or not promote their interpretations in place of those who occupy representative, elective or official posts.

These tendencies accelerate but do not initiate the decline in authority in our societies; that has a far longer history than the mass media. One of the most powerful sources of this decline is to be found in the demographic changes we have already discussed. As families have fewer children they become more valued, the child-oriented culture that results emphasizes the freedom to develop as against the duty of obedience; as the ever-present possibility of death recedes the consolations of the church lose their salience. The authority of the church has declined with the decline of infant mortality, certainly with the decline in the size of family. In Catholic countries family size has declined more slowly, and infant mortality likewise; Catholic authority has also weakened less and more slowly. This does not of course prove the thesis; Catholic authority has after all been exerted to maintain larger families by proscribing artificial means of birth control.

Decline in authority means decline in the acceptance of authority. In modern societies this has been especially marked by changes in the basis of such authority as receives acceptance. Ascribed authority has everywhere weakened in favour of achieved authority.

The Directions of Change

Scholars have generally perceived change as a one way street. Societies become more complex and more highly differentiated. Maine (1905) traced the trend for societies as they develop over time to shift the basis of rights and obligations from 'status' to 'contract'. Tonnies (1955) detected a similar shift in the nature of personal relationships from Gemeinschaft to Gesellschaft, from community to association, Durkheim (1960) traced the shift of the basis of solidarity from 'mechanical' to 'organic'. Parsons (1968), although disclaiming any inevitability in development, describes five polar 'pattern variables' along which societies differ. They are:

Affectivity — affective neutrality (otherwise known as expressive—instrumental orientation)
Ascription — achievement
Universalism — particularism
Specificity — diffuseness
Self orientation — collectivity orientation

Modern societies display the tendency for people's activities, especially their work, to be instrumental rather than expressive, for the basis of status to be achievement rather than ascription, for universalistic norms, for specificity of expertness and for personal goals as the object of endeavour rather than, say, national prestige or glory. The force of these distinctions is seen if we contrast this with the notion of an English Gentleman, the amateur who without shedding his coat could effortlessly defeat the professional. Similarly, the cult of the amateur, scorned by the Fulton Committee on the Civil Service, represented a set of values congruent with the pattern variables of an earlier society.

We readily assume that the values of present day society are more appropriate to the attainment of present day goals. No doubt this should be the case on the basis of structural functional analysis and if we could with advantage treat societies as wholes. In fact we are obliged to recognise that different groups in society have different and conflicting goals and that values which lead to the attainment of one goal may hinder the attainment of another.

While, then, we can detect changes which appear to affect all societies we note first that these trends do not proceed at the same pace or in the same way in any society, and that they appear to be the outcome of the capacity for differentiation and choice brought about by technological advance, not least in the field of population. They are also outcomes of other forms of knowledge than the purely technological. We constantly need to remind ourselves that technology is not an independent variable outside society, that it is a form of knowledge and like other forms of knowledge is used in different ways. Other ideas have power, that is to say we can use them to change things. If we decide to use them in education we stimulate value changes which in turn initiate political change, change in the basis on which organizations rest, shifting the pattern variables and thus the point of balance between the options present in every society. Eisenstadt (1973) identifies these options as Liberty vs. Authority; Stability and Continuity vs. Change; Rationality, e.g. technology vs. Cultural Orientation, e.g. religion. A choice of Liberty as against Authority for example implies the move of pattern variables from ascription to achievement, diffuseness to specificity. A choice of Change in preference to Continuity implies a change from affectivity to affective neutrality. A choice of Rationality over Cultural Orientation implies a change from collectivity orientation to self orientation, and so on. But we should be naive to believe that 'modernizing' inevitably means a shift towards liberty, change and rationality. None of these is necessarily implied in the adoption of modern technology; the cultural capacity for choice and for combining the incompatible is greater than we often assume.

As societies grow in wealth and complexity, two phenomena occur. With improved methods, particularly in agriculture, fewer people are needed to produce the same quantity of goods. More people are available to undertake the more specialized activities that the new methods demand. The first stage of division of labour in society is sex and age. A second stage now occurs in craft specialization. Highly specialized craftsmen require for the exercise of their skills some kind of 'central place' to which their clients can come and where the materials they require can be obtained. The medieval town which arose partly to meet this demand created the need for more crafts to operate and maintain the civic infrastructure and to satisfy the needs of city dwellers. Also a craft gave to him who acquired it that certain independence still possessed in some degree by the craftsmen of today.

In peasant farming and craft business the family is the economic unit. The hired help, the domestic servant and the craft apprentice acquire the status of temporary family member. In the early days of the industrial revolution this essential pattern was changed, but not completely. More factory work was 'put out' to the weavers for example, but the loom in many cases belonged to the factory owner. Whole families, too, were employed in the mills, workplace was separated from dwelling place, but work life was only partially separated from home life. The 'dark satanic mills' were an outrage to human dignity but they did not essentially disrupt the family structure nor remove from it the functions it traditionally performed. This occurred partly as a consequence of the social reforms aimed at eliminating the worst features of the factory system which forced small children out of the factories and into the arms of child minders, and partly because the more sophisticated technologies began to require a literate workforce which could be provided only by removing the responsibility for educating children from the family and assigning it to the new schools.

Since then we can trace the progressive separation of functions from the family, the growth of more, and more specialized, institutions with the accompanying fragmentation of life space. With advancing technology, jobs became more specialized and esoteric; the exact nature of what a person 'does' is known to comparatively few; work becomes a specialized area of life.

When we speak of the advance of technology we should always be careful to note that this advance is at best patchy. Even in the most developed countries, primitive technologies exist alongside the sophisticated; in the most modern plants, many service tasks are still performed as they were decades ago. Any generalizations require constant qualification. While Marx pointed to the alienation of the worker caused by, or indeed synonymous with, the expropriation of the product of his toil by his capitalist employer, his alienation from the process of production was the outcome not of capitalism *per se*, but of extreme scientific management philosophies which can occur under other forms of ownership than private capitalism. Nor do advances in technology which remove many of the objectionable features of work necessarily reduce, let alone eliminate, either form of alienation. This is partly because of the spotty effects of technology already mentioned, but, equally important, because of the customary failure to grasp the opportunity which advanced technology offers to design work around humanistic values.

Societies have used the benefits of technology to provide a safety net over which styles of life independent of work can be indulged in or experimented with, but they have not used them to make working a less alienating experience.

They are now in the paradoxical situation that the social value of work has declined as its economic value has risen.

The Unevenness of Change

Change within societies

Because education and modern technology both have uneven effects on developing societies, they may deepen the divisions between their modern and their traditional sectors. Change, we need constantly to remind ourselves, is not all one way, and, as Goldthorpe (1971) has pointed out, we are prone to introduce historicism through the back door, replacing a crude Marxism with another brand of technological determinism. Especially when discussing the post-industrial society this leads to a theory of the inevitability of the convergence of politico-economic systems. In the case of the under-developed countries we may indeed observe the weakening of tradition in the advanced sectors of the economy and its simultaneous strengthening in the traditional sectors. In a paraphrase of Eisenstadt (1973) it is suggested that change and expansion are most probable when:

(a) Societies become more specialized.
(b) Symbolic systems develop away from the primordial symbols which give identity to the society.
(c) Different units begin to use different symbols.
(d) In both centre and periphery socioeconomic differentiation produces strata or classes.
(e) The functions of the centre become more differentiated than those of the periphery.

Change between societies

This emphasizes the point to be made—that change drives a wedge between economic sectors, political centres, social foci and then affects them unequally. Change encourages diversity which may or may not be divisive. What is certain is that we should not assume that change of whatever origin will have similar effects on orientations and attitudes to work of different groups and classes or in different industries and organizations. Even when change appears unambiguously to point in a single direction further analysis may reveal substantial differences under the surface. For example, smaller families, more wealth, more economic freedom for the young contribute to the development of a youth culture familar in all developed countries and emerging in the developing ones. But although youth cultures in different countries share a number of symbols—hair, rock music, drugs, gear, opposition to adult authority—the content may range all the way from a patriotic nationalism to a pacifist internationalism, from a militant new left to a quietist oriental mysticism. Whether we look across countries or within them we see how technological developments have created new discontinuities which are specific to cultures and whose consequences are equally specific.

What differs is less the technology than the adaptation to it. In all developed societies the nature of work has been changing. Fewer are employed in primary industry and their productivity has been raised by the progressive application of machine power; nor is this any longer balanced by an increase in employment in secondary (manufacturing) industry. More and more are however employed in service (tertiary) industries and in government, education and welfare services (the new 'quaternary' sector). With mechanization, the economics of scale previously experienced in manufacture become available in some aspects of service industry, making standardized performance readily available and comparatively cheap, while rendering more specialized custom-built service to the expensive luxuries. Thus societies have come to be more homogeneous in many respects; local flavour is harder to detect and local differences are further reduced by the mass media. Paradoxically the range of individual choice has been increased; mass markets and cheap processes make available a wide range of colours and shades of the same basic product. By teaming up products which previously were not regarded as 'going together' we can each 'do our own thing' by ringing changes on a few simple basic themes. One outcome is that while major lines of social cleavage have continued, the graduations on either side of the line are less obvious. Hence in some respects we can see social stratification as consisting of a multidimensional space in which an individual's location on one dimension may be a poor indication of his location on others, while in other respects there appears to be a clear dividing line between classes. These different viewpoints are both correct, their salience depending upon whether you are selling shirts or parliamentary candidates.

If societies use the opportunities provided by technology in different ways which relate to their social and political character, can we discern the convergences and divergences, can we forecast those effects which will be the same and those which will be different? Especially in regard to work, where after all technologies are rapidly transferred across national boundaries, is there not an inevitably high degree of convergence in the outcomes? It has long been noted that a technologically advanced plant in Britain may employ anything from 50% to 200% more workers than a similar plant in the United States. Decisions in French firms are typically more highly centralized than in their British equivalents, despite their technological similarity. Union postures in these three and in other countries differ widely, as do the ideological assumptions underlying those postures.

Is Culture then the Determiner?

I am not saying that technological change is used by societies only to reinforce their existing ways of doing this and that. If the logic of technology is a self-fulfilling prophecy, that logic is after all culturally determined. That view, though seductive, is too 'closed system' in its implications; you do not have a completely free choice of technology nor of how to use it. Because the technology itself is a cultural artefact it embodies cultural assumptions about the people who are going to operate it. When a developing country imports a steel mill, it imports all the things that go with it. It may be used to employ a great many more people than necessary, but it does have its own logic of management.

The agenda of issues facing developing countries is so formidable that questions of quality of working life appear very small indeed if not hopelessly idealistic. Poor countries desperately need to create employment. The overriding aim is that their people should have a working life of any kind; the quality of that working life appears no more than a frill, to be introduced when luxuries can be afforded if that happy day ever arrives.

This generally held notion is, however, a mis-reading based on false historicism. Because industrialization was accompanied in the past by a widespread decline in the quality of working life, it has become accepted that the price of industrialization is alienation as well as dense urbanization. Yet neither of these is an inevitable consequence of industrialization. Furthermore, the present symptoms of dissatisfaction in advanced countries appear to be largely associated with steps taken to advance the efficiency of work organizations. Again the ills are seen as part of the cost of efficient operation. Costs they are, but paradoxically uncosted; necessary costs they are not. Newly industrializing countries need no more follow the road of 'scientific management' than they need begin their industrialization with the James Watt steam engine.

Indeed the principles of scientific management and the organizations based upon them stand in the way of rational industrial development, demanding a labour force trained in alienation, imposing social costs on a social infrastructure unadapted to provide them. Such organizations imply a particular kind of family structure, organized around the daily absent wage earner whose schooling provided by a particular kind of educational system equipped him with the skills of compartmentalizing work from non-work, work from play, work from social life, work skills from social skills. Industrial countries are paying the price for this in the problems which beset virtually every social institution.

Many of these problems have been self-inflicted by the choice of industrial technology. In the case of Western industrialized countries, choice was available, but this was not recognised; we did not realize that what was brilliantly successful and profitable in the short run might pile up enormous costs and dis-economies in the not-so-long run. Have developing countries, then, a choice in the matter? In principle, certainly: there may indeed be only one way open once the technological decisions have been made, but there is not merely one way of industrializing, one way of organizing work, one way of achieving a technological objective. In principle, there are many options open, before the technological decisions have been made.

Most planners at national or regional levels are not themselves technologists;

for their technological decisions they depend on specialists, most of whom have been trained in a cultural context which has evolved together with the technology it embodies. Their solutions to technological problems are based on the unvoiced assumptions of a society already geared to the use of advanced technologies with their attendant values, their advantages and disadvantages. Most of these features are not problematic for the planner; his options are limited in advance in ways he is at best only dimly aware of. The technologist trained in an advanced country who applies in developing countries the scientific values and technological solutions of the advanced countries is, of course, made daily aware of the limitations hindering his work. He adapts as far as he can to the social and political climate; he learns new ways of doing things; he may enlist the aid of anthropologists and sociologists to assess the acceptability of his proposals or even examine their likely effects on the life of the people concerned. And in small-scale projects he may indeed be influenced in the choice of technology by their advice. While anthropologists' advice about small-scale community projects may be precise and relevant, social science recommendations on large-scale matters tend to be vague and general and of very little use to the planner or technological adviser who needs something tangible to put into even the crudest cost-benefit analysis. On the other side the sociologist has little or no grasp of technological considerations which would enable him to propose alternative solutions or indeed to realize that there are technologically feasible alternatives.

Is there a way out? I believe that there is and that it lies along the lines of what may be called 'socio-technical assessment'. Coining a new phrase solves no problems. Much work is required before this concept can be realized in action. The theme is this. Every objective needs to be seen in socio-technical terms, to become a socio-technical objective. In most of Western society, premature fragmenting into social and technical objectives is encouraged by the separation of political systems from technical organization. In this model the social objectives are set by the political system; the means of attaining them is handed over to the technocrats. Unfortunately, the quality of life in such a society is determined more by the means characteristically adopted for achieving ends than by the choice of the ends themselves. If we choose technically-dominated modes of solving social problems or attaining social objectives, we inevitably acquire a society in which the machine dominates the man. Paradoxically, by subordinating the technical to the political, we subordinate man to the machine.

If, on the other hand, we take technical considerations into account in determining social objectives, we are still importing with the technical considerations a whole raft of assumptions and valuations that go with the technology. We must begin by rigorously analysing the social assumptions underlying the structure of societies and the images we have of these structures. We will then perceive that our societies are socio-technical systems with socio-technical objectives. To fully recognise the costs and benefits of socio-technical options requires a new form of socio-technical assessment, based on the skills of people who have acquired the capacities to understand both the social and the technical characteristics of these systems.

Without this socio-technical assessment the developing countries are importing the quality of working life of a people along with an imported technology. When a country imports a steel mill or a textile factory or an oil refinery, it imports a number of jobs designed by the engineers of the steel mill, textile factory or oil refinery. One of the problems arising from this has long been recognized: the industrial skills needed to cope with these jobs may be lacking. Solutions have included the temporary appointment of expatriate staff, more minute division of labour, or the proposal to utilize 'intermediate technologies' based on the availability of existing skills and on the assumptions of a plentiful and cheap but lowly skilled supply of labour.

Problems of Prediction

See-saws

There are three kinds of prophet: optimists, pessimists and cynics. For the optimist the best is yet to come, that of today which will survive is the progressive. Liberty, equality and fraternity, the liberal, social, democratic values will triumph; the Victorian belief in progress had deep roots, but was accompanied by a rate of technological and social change faster than any experienced before. The voices of the pessimists were hushed though not silenced. For the pessimist the best was in a past golden age from which we have sadly declined. We have become soft and weak and undeserving. For that we shall be punished and the instruments of our punishment will be our own children. Pessimism which has roots no less deep than those of optimism has become more vocal and more strident in recent years, reaching its apotheosis in the pronouncements of the doomsayers of the environment.

To the cynic there is nothing new under the sun. *Le plus ça change, le plus c'est la même chose.* You can't change human nature. Change is a see-saw or perhaps a cycle. Cynics have their mystical side, the Yin and the Yang, the Yogi and the Commissar, the elaborate cycles of growth and decay.

The trouble with prophets is that their unit of analysis is too big. Mankind, Civilization, History, the Dialectic, are just not manageable. From them it is easy to abstract progress, decline, inevitability, repetition. From far enough away tides are a twice daily repetition. Over a year they fluctuate from spring to neap and back again. Over the centuries the mean level rises then falls again. But the man in the surf feels the pull away from the shore *and* the rush towards it. Furthermore, he feels them in different parts of his frame. He is literally pulled this way and that. If he avoids being tumbled over and over he may be landed by an incoming tide or swept away by a receding one, but the forces he experiences are nearly equal, impetuous and contradictory. So it is with social change. Changes of different magnitude and in different direction affect the same people at different times and different people at the same time. The same force for change may make the young more free and the middle-aged less; the rich, richer and the poor, poorer.

We are accustomed to thinking of our times as characterized by a growing informality, in dress, in manners, in forms of address and so on. But we are also accustomed to seeing ours as the age of bureaucracy, the most formal of organizational types. This paradox may be only apparent; bureaucracies enshrine universalistic rather than particularistic values; people are treated on the basis of category rather than individuality. Universalistic values remove those distinctions which depend on the recognition of people's particular statuses. These cannot be disguised in small societies, but are less detectable and acceptable in larger societies where the relationships between individuals tend to be one-dimensional; customer–supplier, neighbour, kin, colleague, drinking companion, employer–employee, etc. Broad class distinctions remain but within classes formality declines with increase in societal scale.

As formality between classes lessens and bureaucracy grows, social mobility increases. Geographical mobility in particular reduces the possibilities of geographical separation and segregation. The kind of informality which takes its place is shallow and impersonal, replacing social distance with psychological distance. Here we have a clue to the 'privatized' society, the inward focusing of emotional ties on wealth and home described by Goldthorpe et al. (1968) in their studies of the 'affluent worker'. Both the formality of bureaucracy and the new informality are impersonal.

This has been treated at some length as a good illustration of how easily we may be misled into perceiving as universal a trend which is partial because it is one manifestation of something that lies beneath it. I want to remain with it for a moment because it takes us a step nearer work. Goldthorpe and his colleagues showed that 'privatised workers' were likely to have an instrumental orientation to their work life, obtaining their expressive satisfactions outside it. If the trend is towards greater privatization, then surely we must expect an increase in instrumental orientations. But is it? We also observe a trend towards communalism with manifestations ranging from the hippy commune to encounter groups. Back to the surf. Both are happening at the same time to different people and possibly to the same people at different times. Perhaps then the one universal trend in social change is towards diversity, towards an increase in the number of options brought about by technology. And yet, as we say that, we simultaneously remember that technology has often reduced diversity by making standardization so much more effective and its products therefore cheaper and more available so that we get a wider range but more standardization within the range. Still newer technology with computer control may reduce standardization to comparatively small components leaving wide design choices to the individual.

We all possess a model of a traditional society in which fashions are diffused downwards from the top, slowly enough for the hoi-polloi to be adopting what the élite was discarding. Of course even the most traditional of large scale societies was polycentric; different sets offering leadership in different activities.

However, generally speaking diffusion was downwards from the top. Today the picture is more confusing. The centres of diffusion, the 'early adopters', may be on the periphery, or even near the bottom. Fashions in dress and behaviour, in popular music and art diffuse upwards from the young and often from the working class young. The middle class, middle-aged may get there last of all or may never arrive.

All this makes the life of the prophet hard. He can aim his prophecies at a greater distance, confident that by the year 2000 or whatever, no one will remember what he said, or that something he said will come true and be remembered while his false prophecies are forgotten. But for the serious prophet who wants to help people anticipate tomorrow so that they can plan for or against it, the search for indicators is becoming acute. What is available? We are certainly not an unmeasured society. Our political temperature is taken daily by pollsters. Our activities and possessions are all assessed and converted to pounds and dollars and marks. Our prospective wants are sampled by the marketeers. These 'measures' are, however, uncoordinated and largely unrelated; each is made for a particular purpose. And, indeed, any suggestion that they should be linked introduces the spectre of a central file containing the minutest details of our lives, our beliefs and our actions. Nevertheless, a great deal can be quarried from the data that exist. The problem is that what can be deduced are essentially short term probabilities.

Spotting winners

It is possible to make reasonably accurate predictions of purchasing behaviour, preferences for leisure pursuits, choice of family size and so on. Some predictions may be upset by sudden unanticipated critical events like a large discovery of oil in a hitherto unexpected area or a deliberately engineered shortage of the same commodity. But even these events take time to produce their effects. What we have so far proved unable to predict are the revolutionary trends in society. Who predicted the various youth phenomena of the last 12 to 15 years? Or the changes in the public tolerance of obscenity? Or the emergence of 'direct action' in frustration with bureaucratic, if democratic, processes? Who can predict today how significant they will prove to have been in 20 years' time? Looking back we can now detect the early signs that such change was on the way. It is fashionable to point to signals like the play *Look Back in Anger*, for example, which explained the frustrations of the university educated but culturally limited product of the working class, or to the obsession with 'ugliness' in certain forms of art, or the break up of the formality of construction of the novel and the poem. The weakness of this form of retrospective forecast is clear. We say that the antecedents of present day events and styles were bound to become dominant, to win. How do we know? They won, didn't they? Is there, then, any better way of detecting the trends which will survive? Could we have known at the time that the post-war New Look, the revolutionary reaction against functionalism in dress, would prove to be a romantic retrospect, whereas the land girls' and service women's workaday trousers would become well nigh universal feminine wear in the early 1970's? Perhaps we could. There is a parallel in organic growth.

Gesell and Amatruda (1945) describe the 'synergized behaviour trait' of an infant picking up a tiny pellet by precise pincer prehension. They trace it back to earlier skills now superseded; radial raking, synchronized with a new adaptive adduction of the thumb, brings about a simple scissors type of grasp. This and its evanescent successor skills give way to new developments which incorporate elements of them, pick up and combine with other nascent skills, and eventually produce the final trait to which they have all contributed essential elements but in which they are each unrecognizable.

If social processes follow a similar pattern they are going to be exceedingly difficult to detect and unravel; also the potentialities for pathological development may be many times greater. Emery and Trist (1972) looked at the emergence of social processes in a way somewhat similar to the approach of Gesell and Amatruda. They see social processes beginning as 'intrusions' unrecognized for what they are. We have to live for some time with the future before we recognize it. As these intrusions command no resources—the energy they need is met parasitically—they appear to be something else. They share with other processes parts which may continue to play traditional roles, eventually emerging as a fully fledged new system. The parasitic period has weakened the traditional system on which it has fed. After symptoms of intrusion, which however may only represent passing observations, we next observe 'mutual invasion', but our awareness of what is happening is limited. Emery and Trist go on to point to the possibilities of content analysis of new movements, linguistic usage, etc. as signals of emerging phenomena.

What has been said, and quoted, indicates both the enormous complexity of identifying and analysing those social traits which will enter into new combinations in the future and the variety of possible futures which may succeed one another. The danger of drawing on the embryological analogy is its inherent teleology. Behaviour and change are seen as future-oriented; each manifestation is a stage towards a completed development. In social processes there are no stages, each manifestation is a complete though transitory present. We might comb the present for hairs pointing to the future and look for signs in, say, artistic productions, yet we must remember that while the strange behaviour of the sculptor who leaves holes in unexpected places, or the poet who ignores grammar and sense, or the painter who decorates his canvas with a smudge may indeed be the precursors of anarchic movements in education and elsewhere, they are intended to say something of relevance to today; they are complete in today's terms, their meaning is not what will emerge in the future.

It is equally important to recognize that there is not one today any more than there was only one yesterday. To the extent that the future is implicit in the present, so the present is implicit in the past. And no two countries have the same past.

Thus when we comb today for signs for the future we should not over-read those which apparently point towards convergences. Social and technological change will not necessarily make the world a homogeneous place. Certainly production technology tends to make industrial plants in different parts of the world bear considerable similarities in their social systems. A closed-system, technologically-determinist viewpoint would predict total convergence of their social systems. Open-system thinking reminds us of the different experiences, beliefs, orientations and attitudes that people in different countries and in different parts of the same country bring to their work. Social systems have options in the ways in which they use apparently identical technologies. And social change affects people and different groups of people in different ways. Greater 'permissiveness' in society may stimulate children who have experienced a permissive education to welcome or demand more permissiveness in the work place, and simultaneously provoke other workers who are tortured by the removal of many of their cultural landmarks to seek a reassuring discipline at work.

Thus we mis-read if we conclude that all workers everywhere are going to demand participation or workplace democracy or any other form of increased involvement and reduced formality and discipline. Indeed, we can predict that the faster the pace of social change that has been experienced the deeper the wedge that any change will drive between different groups in society and between different generations.

The speed of change can polarize society more than its tardiness. We can expect great resistance to fundamental change in the workplace. We cannot be certain that this change will come, but we can be certain that we have the technology and the knowledge to make it possible. As we try to introduce it we may see ourselves as the bearers of the future but it is one among many probable futures. It is the one we want because we place a high value on the development of people's capacities and we know that the values of autonomy and interdependence, redundancy of functions rather than redundancy of parts, are those which are needed for survival in turbulent environments. But we cannot be sure that they do not also promote that turbulence.

Because work has been the lot of most men and its products are essential, the organizations which have arisen to get it done have become our leading cultural institution. The Jesuits claimed that if they could have a boy in their hands for his first seven years, he was proof against other influence thereafter. In the same vein, if we could make over industry to new values we could safely leave the rest of our cultural institutions to follow. Industry is a sensitive indicator of cultural change, not of the zephyrs that blow across the social landscape but of the strong dominant winds of change.

Our work organizations embody the values of their designers, often the values of the designers of the organizations from which they are descended and the values of the designers of the technologies which shaped them. The machines of the industrial revolution required some skill and often much strength to operate; their successors, in eliminating the need for the latter largely reduced the former. Since the workers who moved into the new industries were untrained, unskilled and mostly illiterate, the more decisions could be taken by the machine, the more reliable the product. The problem was one of human error. The more the machine controlled the behaviour of its operator, the better. Thus production technology enshrined the concept of man as an unreliable machine to be controlled. It still does and the assembly line represents its apotheosis, but not all industries have assembly lines, although even the traditional craft industries like shipbuilding and construction have adopted many of its features. Process industries have removed the man from the production line itself but have often left him as an adjunct to the machine, its nursemaid not its master. Still the first response of the designer to a source of variance is to programme the machine to eliminate it; his values, although unrecognized by himself, are those of the industrial engineers in the days of F. W. Taylor. Thus our industry embodies the values of an earlier age and in this respect acts as a conservative force.

If, however we are alienated from our work and adopt an instrumental value towards it, then naturally it must be designed to be proof against our uncaring errors and an exploitation of the rewards it offers. The vicious circle is complete. Our attitudes to work are a product of the way in which work is organized; the way work is organized is a product of our beliefs, values and attitudes to work. And this circle lies within the larger one I have described: industry is the leading part of the social system, its values dominate those of other parts which are fashioned to serve it; our educational system labours to produce people with the right attitudes to fit its demands.

Let me draw together the threads of the last few paragraphs. We chase an illusion when we look for the impact of social change on attitudes to work. Our changing experience of work is as much a part of social change as any other. A moment's thought will reassure us of this. A powerful agent of social change is technological change; the first area of our lives affected by technological change is our place of work.

Thus the meaning of technological change and its effect on attitudes and values towards work will differ from culture to culture. The possibilities of predicting social change were considered earlier, and the view was favoured that changes manifest themselves early in artistic, literary and symbolic products. It would make a fascinating and valuable study to examine the treatment over time in different cultures of the symbols concerned with work, their different and changing meanings and associations. Supposing we examine the use of the words for 'participation' over recent years. We would find at least two quite different meanings. In the Mitbestimmung sense it is used to describe formal systems of representation. In the 'workplace democracy' sense it describes the delegation of responsibility and control to working groups. In between, it is used to describe a whole range of formal and informal consultative procedures. Why has the first use been dominant in West Germany and Yugoslavia, the second in Norway and the third in Britain? Is it because representative democracy is new in Yugoslavia, recently restored in Germany and vitally precious in both, while democracy is familar in Norway which is sufficiently small and culturally homogeneous for democracy to be possible? Britain has a long tradition of representative democracy but has deep class divisions. And what should we expect in France where according to Crozier (1964) free collaboration is easy within strata but constrained to the utmost formality between strata?

The impact of technological change on cultures depends on '. . . the extent which any given system of social stratification and organization is capable of continuous expansion and differentiation, so as to minimize the monopolistic, freezing, and ascriptive tendencies of holders of power, wealth and prestige' (Eisenstadt, 1973, pp. 38–39). If social mobility is high enough, and the criteria of status and prestige flexible enough to let new groups move into new centres of power, prestige and influence, a whole range of new cultural patterns of accommodation to technology become possible.

Scenario

If predicting the future of work is so difficult, what can we do? Surprisingly enough we may be more able to influence it than to prophesy about it. Action research is the new positivism. And one of its tools is the scenario, the design of a possible future.

Organizations remain the most persuasive aspect of communal life. And while the structure of an organization reflects to some extent its functions and purpose, as the design of a building reflects the life and activities of its occupants, the same limitations apply. Function varies more than structure. What are the possibilities then of major structural change? And what would be its effects? Organizational structures, like scientific management, exist to prescribe and control behaviour, to limit the range of the human activities within them. They accustom us to produce behaviour according to a particular kind of rationality. Realizing this, organizations have recourse to pathetic, patented attempts to elicit 'creativity', divergent thinking, synectics and what not. But the behaviour constraints we acquire in organizations are learned too well; we use them outside organizational settings where they are less appropriate and adaptive. It is not only an affectation for the creative artists and writers of our society to shun organizational life. Change in organizations aimed at replacing their constraining influences with liberating ones would do more than any other change to engender imaginative and original solutions to our wider social dilemmas. A few tentative models of learning organizations exist; their success could even lead us to a learning society.

References

Appolla, C. (1962). *The Economic History of World Population*, Penguin.
Crozier, M. (1964). *The Bureaucratic Phenomenon*, Tavistock.
Durkheim, E. (1960). *The Division of Labour in Society*, translated by G. Simpson, The Free Press.
Eisenstadt, S. M. (1973). *Tradition, Change and Modernity*, Wiley.

22

Emery, F. E. and Trist, E. L. (1972). *Towards a Social Ecology*, Plenum Publishing.
Gesell, A. and Amatruda, C. (1945). *The Embryology of Behaviour*, Hamish Hamilton.
Goldthorpe, J. H. (1971). Theories of industrial society, *Archives Européennes de Sociologie*, volume 12.
Goldthorpe, J. H., Lockwood, D., Bechhofer, F. and Platt, J. (1968). *The Affluent Worker*, Cambridge University Press.
Maine, H. S. (1905). *Ancient Law*, Routledge.
Marsh, D. C. (1958). *The Changing Social Structure of England and Wales*, Routledge and Kegan Paul.
Parsons, T. (1968). *The Structure of Social Action*, The Free Press.
Tönnies, F. (1955). *Community and Association*, translated by C. S. Loomis, Routledge and Kegan Paul.

2

Cultural Influences on Work Motivation

George H. Hines
Massey University,
Palmerston North, New Zealand

The expansion of multinational corporations, coupled with the rapid growth of communications and transportation links among nations, is creating new challenges for behavioural scientists to explain the nature of work motivation. The problems are very apparent in developing countries, which must simultaneously resist the often-ethnocentric perspective of geographically remote headquarters of international companies and the temptation to become dependent upon overseas-developed techniques set out in prestigious textbooks and by expensive consultants. The impetus of organizational development theory, with its stress on the inevitability of change and the uniqueness of each organization (French and Bell, 1973), has helped an awareness that well-accepted theories of work motivation may not have universal application. As a consequence, applied psychologists and sociologists are faced with renewed responsibility to include cultural factors when investigating the field of work motivation. Behavioural scientists are not redefining the world in a more complex way—rather they are discovering that the world is more complex than they had recognized (Feldman and Moore, 1965).

A brief example from New Zealand illustrates the need to take cultural factors into consideration when evaluating a motivation-based situation:

Employee absenteeism was being discussed by senior managers of the international division of a large American company. The New Zealand

Managing Director was asked for the annual absenteeism rate of his company and he responded 'sixteen percent'. 'Right, six percent', was the acknowledgement. 'No, six*teen* percent', the New Zealander corrected. The North American Vice-President collating the information interrupted the company Chairman who was engaged in another conversation and asked 'What would you say to an absenteeism rate of sixteen percent?' The Chairman looked incredulous, replied 'Impossible, you can't operate a factory on more than seven percent', and returned to his original conversation.

The remedy finally decreed for the absenteeism problem, when the New Zealander could convince senior management to take him seriously, was based on improvement of staff amenities, including new sports fields and a remodelled cafeteria. A selection of staff training handbooks from the corporate head office was also forwarded to the New Zealand company, with instructions to provide better induction for employees. These recommendations were neither capriciously given nor lightly received. They were based on the assumption that the employees concerned would be absent less frequently if they could develop a closer identity with the company. Better working conditions and delineation of opportunities for advancement were deliberately noted as being consistent with motivation theory (Herzberg, Mausner and Snyderman, 1959). Unfortunately for the company, the measures outlined above did nothing to reduce the absenteeism rate. It could also be added that the annual labour turnover rate was approximately 180%, with productivity well below the desired level.

It might appear that the company described above has uncommonly poor management. However the average annual absenteeism rate for companies drawing upon the same labour pool is 12 to 14% and labour turnover ranges from 110 to 300%. The key to understanding the root of the problem is the knowledge that New Zealand has full employment, a condition that strongly influences popular feelings about work. While frequently described in economic terms, full employment is also a socio-political policy and as such contributes to the cultural influences in New Zealand society. The values, assumptions and factors affecting mobility and class structure are part of the cultural system. In full employment, when an individual can walk across the street and get a similar job at the same rate of pay as now, work motivation acts differently than in conditions of high unemployment.

The New Zealand cultural, economic, technical, and political environment contains in microcosm most of the elements of work motivation present in broader form in other industrialized nations. In a sense, New Zealand can be termed a developing country, as it is primarily dependent upon agricultural exports while attempting to expand its industrial base. Most of the work force is employed in urban industry, which includes a broad spectrum of manufacturing, commercial, professional, and service activities. With a population of only 3 million, diversified industry, a common language, and a relatively high standard of education, New Zealand provides an excellent testing ground for the validity and relevance of work-motivation theory. Geographical isolation, despite effective communication with other countries, gives New Zealand a buffer against the more transient influences that flow through North American and European business. At the same time, there are unique features of New Zealand society that permit useful comparisons, as follows.

(1) *Full employment.* As previously stated, New Zealand has extremely low unemployment rates. Full employment is a political policy followed by both major parties and immigration quotas are adjusted accordingly. Unemployment is maintained well below 1% of the total work force. As an illustration, in mid-1974 in Wellington there were almost 4000 more job vacancies advertized than workers available to fill them.

(2) *Company size.* Company sizes are relatively small, with the average firm having less than 20 employees. Personal contact between manager and employee is frequent and there is a tendency for supervisors to work alongside those being supervised. Social relationships tend to be based on friendship and informality.

(3) *Egalitarianism.* There is no formal class structure in New Zealand and the conventional wisdom is that 'Jack's as good as his master'. While titles are used and are acknowledged as signs of accomplishment, artificial deference based on class differences is minimal (Hines, 1974b). Government legislation is closely scrutinized to eliminate 'class' elements that would distinguish between the socially or economically privileged and underprivileged.

(4) *Social welfare.* Medical and hospital services are provided by a system of national health care. Medicines are available free through doctors' prescriptions presented to chemists. Although some company health insurance schemes exist for optional treatment and surgery, they are not widely considered as a fringe benefit.

(5) *Tax structure.* The tax structure acts as a barrier to the acquisition of great wealth and to the establishment of a financially advantaged segment of the population. Personal income tax reaches 50% on income over approximately US$7800.

Until recently most research on work motivation had been conducted in the northern hemisphere in cultural and economic conditions quite different from those prevailing in New Zealand. In 1970 it was decided to conduct a wide-ranging national study in New Zealand, taking into consideration factors of social equality, the multiracial nature of the society, and the minimal unemployment rates. Among the objectives of the research programme were the following:

(1) Assessment of the motivation theories of Herzberg *et al.* (1959) and McClelland (1961) in New Zealand conditions.
(2) Collection of large-scale motivation data to permit cross-cultural comparisons.
(3) Examination of the relationship between work motivation and socio-cultural factors in New Zealand society.

Data were collected from over 15,000 respondents in a wide variety of work settings. The population included a number of stratified random samples of managers and employees; males and females; European New Zealanders, Maoris, Pacific Islanders, and non-Polynesian immigrants; all education levels and private and public organizations. The measurement techniques included interviews, questionnaires, projective tests, objective psychological tests, observation, and unobtrusive methods. Most of the research was conducted in a field environment. The results reported in this paper deal primarily with cultural factors in work motivation; the remainder of the research findings may be found elsewhere (Hines, 1974c).

The Herzberg Motivator-Hygiene Theory

According to the Herzberg model, only motivators (achievement, recognition, responsibility, growth, advancement, and the work itself) can lead to job satisfaction. Hygiene factors (company policy and administration, supervision, salary, interpersonal relations, and working conditions), on the other hand, are held to be incapable of motivating behaviour. Studies conducted in New Zealand fail to confirm the Herzberg theory (Griew and Philipp, 1969; Hines, 1973e). The major findings indicate that interpersonal relations on the job and supervision are critical factors in job satisfaction and are in themselves motivating elements. Workers in many interviews stated that the opportunity to work with friends was a primary factor in remaining at a particular company. In addition, it is apparent that a good supervisor will do much to attract employees (through reputation spread by word of mouth advertising) and to keep them from leaving the company.

When workers can change jobs easily, without concern about loss of status, wages, or pension rights, affiliative needs become more important in the work environment. In New Zealand it is possible to hold constant a number of variables (security, wages, working conditions, and to a large degree, company policy and administration) through shifting to jobs that are highly similar. The Herzberg motivators can also be kept reasonably constant because for specific types of work (especially skilled and semi-skilled) union awards specify many facets of growth, advancement, responsibility, and the work itself. The main variable factor is the human element. New Zealanders prefer to work alongside friends. They also prefer to work for a person they respect as an individual. There is widespread exchange of Christian names by supervisors and employees, emphasizing the personal, informal nature of work relationships (Hines, 1973g). When the 4-day, 40-hour week was introduced into New Zealand companies in 1972 as a means of improving job satisfaction, the scheme failed to take hold in many organizations. A study of the reasons for failure revealed that in many cases, individuals who had initially favoured the scheme subsequently rejected it when they found themselves with different days off from their workmates. In other words, the presence of friends on the job was a motivating influence to stay at work; absence of friends made the job unattractive (Hines, 1973d).

In New Zealand the ability to change jobs almost at will and the special relationships that exist between manager and employee appear to have a strong influence on work motivation. These cultural factors cast doubt on the cross-cultural validity of the Herzberg formulation. By implication, the Herzberg-derived techniques of job enrichment in which motivators are manipulated to enhance work performance seem likely to require different approaches in New Zealand.

The McClelland Need for Achievement Theory

Research on achievement motivation was conducted through the employment of a projective technique (the traditional Thematic Apperception Test) and a self-report (the Lynn Questionnaire). When there proved to be a high correlation between the two measures (Lynn, 1969; Hines, 1973c), it became possible to use the Lynn scale in large population studies. The results were in general supportive of the McClelland model (1961). Specific findings included the following:

(1) Entrepreneurs, engineers, and salesmen have higher achievement motivation levels than managers (Hines, 1973g).
(2) Significant differences were found in the need for achievement scores of different Pacific Island populations (Hines, 1973a).
(3) Engineers and accountants with high achievement motivation levels placed in work situations that feature close supervision and inadequate opportunities for recognition tend to have high labour mobility rates (Hines, 1973f).
(4) Effective performers in voluntary organizations, public relations positions, and behavioural science-oriented work tend to have low need for achievement (Hines, 1974c).

The research was not concerned with the development of need for achievement, but was limited to exploration of the relationships between achievement motivation and various work factors. On the basis of the New Zealand findings, the most useful information that was derived dealt with the effect of culture on individuals with varying levels of achievement motivation. American immigrants to New Zealand, for example, tend to have a high need for achievement, while British immigrants are characterized by a high need for power (Hines, 1974a). New Zealand university graduates with majors in business studies who emigrate from New Zealand, on the other hand, show high achievement motivation levels (Hines, 1973b). Greek achievement motivation tends to persist, whether found in Greece, the United States, or New Zealand (Hines, 1973c). If a society fails to provide adequate perceived outlets to meet achievement needs, there appears to be a tendency for the high achiever to emigrate. The same would seem to be true for an organization that is deficient in need fulfillment opportunities. These findings support the research of McClelland

and Winter (1969) and clearly demonstrate the interaction between social-cultural environment and achievement motivation in terms of work behaviour.

Relationship Between Work Motivation and Sociocultural Factors

Research evidence lends strong support to the conventional wisdom that in New Zealand the social (affiliative) motive is an extremely strong influence on work behaviour. As a social welfare state, it is logical that New Zealand would develop individuals whose primary concern is for other persons. Universal health care, free education, and government pension plans cater to individual needs and lessen the responsibility of citizens to compete against others for access to these resources. Protection of domestic industry is provided by strict import controls on competitive products. As an illustration, no woollen goods may be imported. Products like petrol have one fixed national price that eliminates effective competition among oil companies. The dominant cultural motive as it relates to work is for cooperation, rather than competition (McDougall, 1973).

On a primary level it could be argued that New Zealand should be a natural home for worker participation in management. There is evidence that employers and employees already discuss mutual problems (Hines, 1973g) and the cultural background is one of shared concern. The lack of strong competitive pressure, however, is a two-edged sword—while it may encourage cooperation, it can also lead to a lack of drive for excellence and to abdication of a sense of responsibility. Empirical study reveals that substantial numbers of New Zealand workers—perhaps as many as one-half—do not wish to participate in decision making in the work situation. The implication is that many individuals, who have grown accustomed to relying on society to provide essential needs, have no desire to move from a passive to an active psychological state (Hines, 1974c). This is consistent with the affiliative motives to be with others, to interact with them, to be accepted by them, but not necessarily to share responsibility with them. Many New Zealand workers are extremely conservative and passive, so resistant to the sharing of responsibility that they may change jobs to avoid it (Hines, 1974c). In such circumstances, introduction of participative management programmes could be a serious mistake.

The research evidence from New Zealand is still cursory, but it does provide a number of potentially valuable clues. There is little question that cultural influences significantly affect the nature of work motivation, even to the extent of casting doubt on the cross-cultural validity of well-established theories. While this contention is not new to most behavioural scientists, it is unwelcome news to many practising managers. It is psychologically more comfortable to believe that there are theories of universal applicability than to learn that one must apply a theory with great care in each cultural situation. While the professional literature overflows with reports of well-designed, cross-cultural studies and excellent books on comparative management are continually adopted in university classes, the manager in many developing countries seeks simplistic solutions. In New Zealand, for example, only one manager in 25 has had any formal exposure to industrial psychology and less than 8% feel that a psychologist has any useful skills to offer to business (Hines, 1972). The reluctance of managers to accept the relevance of behavioural science to work situations is a further cultural factor that must be taken into consideration.

Implications for Action and Research

There is little in the New Zealand work environment that cannot be found elsewhere in the world. Similarly, there are no startling revelations in the research reported in this paper. There is, however, one important lesson revealed by the research programme that should be clearly noted: if cultural influences had been ignored in evaluating the evidence, it would have been impossible to produce coherent, useful interpretation. Schuh (1974) has demonstrated how cultural grounding of research instruments can help to reconcile theoretical conflict and to improve payoffs in cross-national comparisons. In most studies of work motivation, cultural elements are implicitly held constant and no attempt is made to determine the philosophical, ethnic, or theological assumptions of the respondents. Yet few nations have sufficiently homogeneous populations to warrant global analysis. One approach to improving research methodology is to define culture objectively and to collect this information simultaneously with data on work motivation, thus allowing more comprehensive analysis (Roberts, 1970).

Unless personal motives are evaluated within the cultural context, it is likely that interpretations will be incomplete, if not erroneous. If jobs are to be designed to permit attainment of individual and organizational objectives, accurate information on work motivation is essential. Basic assumptions must be continually challenged, especially those that are based on research conducted in a different culture or sub-culture. Replication is required. Although psychologists and sociologists preach about the inevitability of change, they appear to believe that research findings, once published, are immutable. If culture changes, research evidence changes with it. The plan for action is clear. Behavioural science researchers should adopt organizational development philosophy for their professional disciplines; probing, challenging, diagnosing, and intervening are as necessary in professional psychology and sociology as in business management. The complexities of cultural influences on work motivation cannot be ignored; in an increasingly interdependent world, such knowledge is essential.

References

Feldman, A. S. and Moore, W. E. (1965). Are industrial societies becoming alike? In A. W. Gouldner and S. M. Miller (eds.) *Applied Psychology*, The Free Press.
French, W. L. and Bell, C. H. (1973). *Organization Development*, Prentice-Hall.
Griew, S. and Philipp, E. (1969). Workers' attitudes and the acceptability of shift work in

30

New Zealand manufacturing industry. Research Paper No. 12. Wellington: New Zealand Institute of Economic Research.

Herzberg, F., Mausner, B., and Snyderman, B. B. (1959). *The Motivation to Work*, Wiley.

Hines, G. H. (1972). Management attitudes toward industrial psychologists: A cross-cultural study. *Australian Psychologist*, **7**, 123–130.

Hines, G. H. (1973a). Motivational correlates of Pacific Islanders in urban environments. *Journal of Psychology*, **83**, 247–249.

Hines, G. H. (1973b). Achievement motivation and conservatism factors in the emigration of New Zealand university graduates. *New Zealand Journal of Educational Studies*, **8**, 19–24.

Hines, G. H. (1973c). The persistence of Greek achievement motivation across time and culture. *International Journal of Psychology*, **8**, 284–289.

Hines, G. H. (1973d). The four-day work week: Blessing or curse? *Company Director and Executive*, **7**(72), 27–29.

Hines, G. H. (1973e). Two-factor motivation theory in cross-cultural perspective. *Journal of Applied Psychology*, **58**, 375–377.

Hines, G. H. (1973f). Achievement motivation, occupations, and labour turnover in New Zealand. *Journal of Applied Psychology*, **58**, 313–320.

Hines, G. H. (1973g). *The New Zealand Manager*, Hicks, Smith & Sons.

Hines, G. H. (1974a). Achievement motivation levels of immigrants in New Zealand. *Journal of Cross-Cultural Psychology*, **5**, 37–47.

Hines, G. H. (1974b). Sociocultural influences on employee expectancy and participative management. *Academy of Management Journal*, **17**, 354–359.

Hines, G. H. (1974c). *Management and Motivation*, Wiley.

Lynn, R. (1969). An achievement motivation questionnaire. *British Journal of Psychology*, **60**, 529–534.

McClelland, D. C. (1961). *The Achieving Society*, Van Nostrand.

McClelland, D. C. and Winter, D. G. (1969). *Motivating Economic Achievement*, The Free Press.

McDougall, G. H. G. (1973). Marketing: The issues for New Zealand. In G. H. Hines (ed.) *Business and New Zealand Society*, Hicks, Smith & Sons.

Roberts, K. H. (1970). On looking at an elephant: An evaluation of cross-cultural research related to organizations. *Psychological Bulletin*, **74**, 327–350.

Schuh, A. J. (1974). An alternative questionnaire strategy for conducting cross-cultural research on managerial attitudes. *Personnel Psychology*, **27**, 95–102.

Winter, D. G. (1973), *The Power Motive*, The Free Press.

3

Research-Based Strategies for Improving Work Life

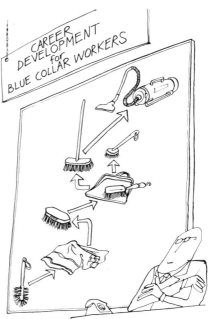

T. G. Cummings and Paul F. Salipante
Case Western Reserve University, Cleveland, USA

Increasing concern with the quality of work life has created a need for well-conceived work improvement strategies based on knowledge rather than intuition. Our discussion concerns the development of research-based strategies for improving the conditions of work. The essential question is how to merge scientific knowledge into a coherent framework for action which is effective and feasible at an organizational level. Our ideas have evolved, in large part, from a comprehensive review of empirical studies concerning job satisfaction, industrial organization, and productivity (Srivastva *et al.*, 1974), and we present some of its findings to demonstrate how current knowledge can contribute to the development of work improvement strategies. The discussion which follows is divided into three sections: the first deals with knowledge required for strategy development; the second reviews current research relevant to this knowledge; and the third presents implications for organizational change and research.

Knowledge Required for Stragegy Development

Using research to improve the quality of work life requires a method for transforming knowledge into organizational action. Given a policy-level decision to improve work life, research can inform decision-makers of alternative strategies for meeting their objectives. The development of alternative courses of action requires three kinds of related information. The first involves

32

the identification of action levers, variables which can be manipulated to create desired changes. For example, the expansion of a machining job to include preparatory tasks may result in increased satisfaction. Without knowledge that a specific change can produce the expected results, it is impossible to formulate a valid strategy.

Hence, the identification of effective action levers is a necessary condition for developing work improvement strategies. It is not, however, a sufficient condition. The context of the organization and the way its members experience work changes also influence the effectiveness of those changes. Since action levers must be manipulated in a particular organizational context, a second condition for effective change is knowledge of those factors upon which valid changes are contingent. It may be, for instance, that job expansion is successful for young workers but not for older ones. To the degree that certain changes are contingent upon such contextual variables, it is imperative to take these contingencies into account when manipulating certain action levers. The third necessary kind of information related to strategy development concerns general understanding of change processes. Since the manipulation of action levers concerns changes that directly affect workers, work improvement strategies require knowledge of how organizational members experience, and react to, changes in the conditions and content of work. Continuing with the job expansion example, it may be that expansion is more effective when workers participate in deciding how to expand their jobs. Understanding the processes that affect change in work settings is essential for manipulating any action lever.

The three kinds of information discussed above provide sufficient knowledge for a decision-maker to formulate a successful quality-of-work strategy. Identification of the causal effects of action levers provides a scientific basis for making specific organizational changes. Knowledge of the contingencies that must be met for the changes to be effective, combined with an understanding of the processes by which the action levers can be manipulated, enables the decision-maker to develop an action plan tailored to his organization.

Applying Research to Strategy Development

Let us now look at how current research provides information on each of the three areas of knowledge. We have reviewed approximately 550 studies published since 1959 on job satisfaction, industrial organization, and productivity. These studies represent an exhaustive search of three sources of literature— Psychological Abstracts, Sociological Abstracts, and Employee Relations Abstracts. All articles or books representing the following two types of field studies were included: (1) innovative work experiments, in which action levers were manipulated by an organization and attempts made to determine their subsequent impact; (ii) correlational studies, relating two or more variables (e.g., job level with satisfaction) across individuals or organizations, but only at one point in time. In addition to this literature search, direct requests were made to organizations for reports of their own projects of change.

Action levers

The identification of action levers requires information about those changes in the conditions and content of work which results in positive outcomes. Since we are concerned with drawing valid causal inferences, organizational studies in which work was restructured under quasi-experimental conditions are especially relevant for this purpose. The review included 57 work experiments. An in-depth analysis of the studies revealed nine identifiable action levers, each of which is listed below with an example:

(a) Pay and reward systems—introduction of marginal group bonus.
(b) Autonomy and discretion—freedom of employees to determine their own work methods.
(c) Support services—assistance on demand from maintenance experts.
(d) Training—training all operators for all tasks in a department.
(e) Organization structure—reduction in the number of hierarchical levels.
(f) Technology—breakdown of long assembly line into smaller units.
(g) Task variety—inclusion of preparatory and finishing tasks in machining jobs.
(h) Information and feedback—introduction of weekly quality control records.
(i) Interpersonal and group processes—increase in the amount and kind of interaction among group members.

Changes in the action levers resulted in positive outcomes in five criterion variables. The criterion variables and an example of each are as follows:

(i) Costs—direct labour costs per unit.
(ii) Productivity—increased number of units produced.
(iii) Quality—average rate of rejects.
(iv) Withdrawal behaviour—absenteeism.
(v) Attitudes—job satisfaction.

Examination of the experiments showed that different sub-sets of the action levers were manipulated in certain identifiable ways. This made it possible to categorize the studies into four distinct change orientations. Each orientation can be thought of as an organizing principle for formulating a particular work improvement strategy. Change orientations include:

Socio-technical groups—this involves the structuring of work around self-regulating work groups that perform relatively whole tasks. Specific changes involve increases in autonomy, task variety, and feedback, with parallel modifications in pay systems, technology, and group processes.

Job restructuring—this includes the expansion of individual jobs on both horizonal and vertical dimensions. The former involves increases in task variety, while the latter concerns increases in autonomy.

Participative management—this approach increases the amount of participation by workers in those decisions that directly affect their work lives. The primary action lever is autonomy.

Organization change—this orientation entails changes in the formal structure of organizations and in mechanisms which increase the amount of feedback.

Table 3.1, taken from Srivastva *et al.* (1974), summarizes the action levers that were manipulated and the results that were obtained for those studies in each of the change orientations. (In the table, the action levers are referred to as independent variables, and the results as dependent variables.) The findings reveal an overwhelming number of positive outcomes. Since most of the experiments change more than one action lever, it is not possible to determine which particular change resulted in a specific result. Examination of the action levers across all of the change orientations does suggest, however, that increases in autonomy, task variety, and feedback are important factors in producing positive outcomes. Before we can devise work improvement strategies based on these results, however, we must have some confidence that these findings are valid.

The work experiments were thus evaluated in terms of internal and external validity. Since internal validity is concerned with whether or not the experimental changes did in fact produce an observed effect, it is the minimum condition required for causal inference. Evaluating the studies for internal validity revealed that most of them were, from a rigorous experimental perspective, less than ideal. Lack of control groups, time series data, and statistical tests restricted the validity of many of the findings. While the internal validity of any single experiment may be relatively low, the relevant issue is the validity of the studies considered as a set. Since the set showed no systematic pattern of threats, we can have considerable confidence that the action levers did, in fact, produce valid results.

External validity refers to the generalizability of findings. Evaluation of external validity showed that the experiments included a relatively heterogeneous set of populations, research settings, and measurements. This suggests that the action levers' effects are not confined to specific industries, organizations, personal attributes, or work environments. Unfortunately, there is one limitation to the generalizability of findings. The action levers might have interacted with special experimental arrangements to produce the positive outcomes reported. The unusual conditions that exist in many work experiments—the extra attention paid to workers during the experiment, for example—make generalizations to non-experimental settings questionable.

Examination of the validity of the experimental findings revealed that the action levers were effective in producing desired outcomes over a relatively wide range of populations and organizational settings. Since the work experiments comprised only a small part of our review, the question arises as to how consistent these findings are with the correlational studies which form the majority of research conducted in this field. While correlational studies are cross-sectional and cannot be used to demonstrate causality, they can supple-

Table 3.1 Summary of experimental studies

	Independent Variables: A summary of the percentage of field experimental studies that manipulated a particular variable									Dependent Variables: A summary of the percentage of field experimental studies that produced totally positive results				
	Pay/reward systems	Autonomy/discretion	Support	Training	Organization structure	Technical/physical	Task variety	Information/feedback	Interpersonal/group process	Costs	Productivity	Quality	Withdrawal	Attitudes
Socio-technical/autonomous groups (n = 16)	56% (16)	88% (16)	31% (16)	44% (16)	19% (16)	63% (16)	63% (16)	63% (16)	75% (16)	88% (8)	93% (15)	86% (7)	73% (7)	70% (10)
Job restructuring (n = 27)	14% (27)	92% (27)	22% (27)	33% (27)	14% (27)	22% (27)	79% (27)	45% (27)	4% (27)	90% (10)	75% (20)	100% (17)	86% (7)	76% (21)
Participative management (n = 7)		100% (7)		14% (7)	14% (7)					100% (1)	57% (7)	100% (1)	80% (5)	80% (5)
Organization change (n = 7)	29% (7)	43% (7)	43% (7)	43% (7)	100% (7)	29% (7)	14% (7)	71% (7)	43% (7)	50% (2)	100% (4)	100% (2)	67% (3)	50% (6)

Numbers in parentheses indicate the base number of studies on which the percentage is based, i.e. the denominator.

The percentages represent those studies which reported no negative, mixed, or zero-change findings for the dependent variable in that column.

ment the work experiments by showing that a particular action lever is associated consistently with a specific criterion variable over a wide range of studies. A convergence in the two types of studies would provide a sound empirical base for generating specific action alternatives.

Approximately 500 correlational studies were reviewed. Many of the studies involved factors which were clearly not action levers, since they would be difficult if not impossible to manipulate in an organizational context, for example age or marital status. Concentrating on those variables which appeared to be organizationally manipulable, the correlational studies indicated a large number of variables to be related to attitudes, fewer to performance, and the fewest to withdrawal behaviour. Two kinds of manipulable variables were found to have the greatest number of relationships with these criteria: (i) the nature of supervision; and (ii) work itself. Democratic and supportive supervisory styles were positively related to attitudes and performance and negatively associated with withdrawal behaviour; task autonomy and challenge showed similar relationships with the criterion variables. These findings were supportive of the results from the experimental studies. Autonomy especially seemed to underlie many variables, e.g. autonomy regarding work task, democratic supervisory styles, organizational climate, which were found to be related to the criterion variables.

In summary, the field experiments indicate that certain action levers, most notably autonomy, task variety, and feedback, produce improvements in work life quality. The findings from the review of correlational studies on variables such as supervisory style and the work itself support the impact of the above action levers. A caution, however, is that the internal validity of individual studies is low.

Contingencies

The effective manipulation of any action lever requires knowledge of those factors upon which valid changes are contingent. Most work experiments provide anecdotal data about such factors, but whether or not these contingencies actually operate is rarely tested. Nevertheless, our review of experimental studies revealed some agreement on important contingencies. These were: worker engagement in the change process (discussed further under Processes of Change, below); support for the changes by top management and first-level supervisors; and workers' possession of higher-order needs, such as the need for independence.

The correlational studies, on the other hand, often investigated empirically those contingencies that affect a particular relationship. Contingencies are empirically derivable from correlational studies in two ways: (i) individual studies using multivariate analyses determine which variables affect the strength of a relationship between two variables; for example, the strength of the positive relationship between supervisor supportiveness and work satisfaction varied inversely with workers' independence needs; and (ii) comparison of studies investigating the same relationship reveals under what contextual conditions the relationship holds. The latter technique could also be used with work experiments if there were more variance in the results, that is, if there were more of them reporting zero or negative results. Most of the contingencies identified by the correlational studies reviewed were concerned with some characteristic of the worker. Authoritarianism, needs for independence, job involvement, and level of job were some of the contingencies that were found to moderate a particular relationship. A few reflected the work context—pay system, considerate leader behaviour. Overall, the correlational studies and subjective reports in the field experiments lead to the conclusion that contingency variables are numerous and powerful in the area of work change, reflecting a rich complexity for decision-makers.

Processes of change

Now that we have identified relevant action levers and those conditions upon which positive outcomes are contingent, it is imperative that we have some knowledge about how to carry out organizational change effectively. Since correlational studies do not manipulate variables, they are not useful for understanding processes of change. The work experiments provided a wide array of anecdotal data concerning organizational changes, though the change process was not a direct focus of experimental study. Each study used a method of change that was unique to its organizational context. There were many similarities, however, that make it possible to outline the steps taken in a typical change process: (i) gaining organizational support: higher-level management sanction was a prerequisite for all of the experiments; (ii) choosing an experimental site: experimental work units were often chosen based on the commitment and interest of first-level supervisors and workers; (iii) analysing and generating change proposals: data were collected from the experimental unit to determine the changes that were needed; (iv) implementing changes: action levers were manipulated under relatively protected conditions; and (v) evaluating results: the results of the changes were evaluated under normal working conditions.

The work experiments differed among themselves in two ways that are significant for understanding organizational change. The first difference concerns the level of change. One set of experiments was directed at individual jobs, another at work groups, and still another concentrated on organization-wide changes. As the level of change moved from individual jobs to organization-wide change, the scale of change became progressively larger. The time-scale of change was longer, the amount of disruption in organizational functioning increased, and the probability of the separate changes interacting in unpredictable ways became higher. Larger-scale changes also were more difficult to contain, and the effects often amplified beyond the experimental unit. In summary: the higher the level of organizational change, the more uncertain and disruptive the change process, and the greater the need for support from higher organizational levels.

The second way in which the work experiments differed among themselves was in regard to whether or not workers participated directly in the change process. Those experiments that restructured individual jobs did not have worker participation, while those that made group and organization-wide changes involved workers in the change process. In part, this difference can be attributed to the necessity of including workers in those changes involving interpersonal and group processes. Since individual job restructuring did not manipulate this action lever, while group and organization-wide studies did, it is likely that a change in interpersonal and group processes requires direct participation by workers if it is to be successfully manipulated.

Overall, research reports of experimental studies provide valuable subjective information on change processes, but the effects of different change processes have not been empirically investigated.

Implications

Developing strategies in individual organizations

The research discussed above provides much of the information needed on the effectiveness of action levers, but less of the equally necessary information on contingency factors and change processes. The lack of sufficient information in the latter two areas, combined with the solid indications from available research that contingencies and change processes are crucial, indicates that the strategy maker in a particular organizational context must acquire additional knowledge on-site. Therefore, two issues must be considered: (i) how knowledge from available research can be utilized, and (ii) how the remaining knowledge can be gained on-site.

Regarding the first issue, the findings of the review provide knowledge in terms of a list of action levers which research indicates to have impacts on job satisfaction. From these, innovators may choose factors which have favourable effects in contexts similar to their own. If contingency effects are not met by the context itself, then the contingency variables must be manipulated. That is, innovators on-site may have to manipulate more factors than simply those which are thought to be the actual action levers. Somehow, the innovator must then search the literature, a difficult process, to determine what change processes are appropriate for the action levers chosen.

A better approach is to start with one of the conceptually-based change orientations found in the review of field experimental studies. Each of the four change orientations was found to be effective in producing desirable changes in quality of work life variables. The innovator should choose the change orientation which is most consistent with his context, remembering that the higher the level at which change is to occur, the greater the uncertainties. The advantages of using a conceptual approach tested and modified in previous studies are: first, the conceptual base enables the innovator to make predictions of the effects of his manipulating certain action levers; second, the approach indicates that several specified action levers are to be manipulated together; third, the field experiments performed using a particular change orientation provide data on how the lever can be manipulated, what problems are likely to arise, and what factors the approach is contingent upon. Findings from correlational studies can provide a valuable supplement to such an approach by providing further information on contingencies. Only if the innovator cannot find a change orientation which matches his organization's context and its policies does it seem preferable to choose action levers unguided by one of the change orientations.

Let us now consider the issue of gaining knowledge on-site. The complexity of quality of work life suggested by the available evidence on contingencies and change processes makes it clear that developing and implementing any strategy requires much innovation *in situ*. The innovator must therefore collect valid information on-site to guide his efforts. Chiefly, this information concerns whether expected results occur in the short run and indicates whether unexpected contingencies have arisen and whether the change processes require modification. Valid information is also needed in order to know whether the desired effects of the innovation are occurring and whether the effects observed are due to the innovation or to some confounding factor. Without such knowledge the innovator has no valid ground for recommending the continuation of his innovation or its application to new sites. Past field experimental research and recent improvements in quasi-experimental methodologies provide a technology by which the innovator can acquire such information (Campbell and Stanley, 1963). The requirements for valid knowledge are not difficult to attain in almost any organizational context; they include alternatives such as the use of control groups, time-series data, unobtrusive measures (Webb *et al.*, 1966), and involving workers in the change process in order to obtain feedback from them. Using these requires planning before the innovation is put into effect, so knowledge-gathering must be built into the innovator's strategy.

If the gathering of valid information is so vital to both strategic and short-run decision-making, why is it so rare? Why have so few field experimental studies in the review been well designed? Our contacts with innovators suggest that most managers responsible for work change projects perceive them as pilot projects which must demonstrate to top management that the innovation will be successful. To those responsible for the innovation, the value of accurate assessment is thereby minimized. One solution is to separate the evaluating and innovating roles in the organization, but this solution would make it less likely that the innovator would put the required effort into collecting data useful for his short-run decisions. A more basic solution is to remove the innovator from his 'trapped' position (Campbell, 1969) and make him concerned with attaining the objective stated by the policy rather than demonstrating the efficacy of a particular solution. Accurate feedback would then become crucial, not only for providing information indicating when the strategy required modification,

40

but also for indicating when the entire strategy did not appear fruitful and another should be tried.

Societal improvements in quality of work life strategies

The poor design of most of the individual field experimental studies in the review suggests a strong need for rigorously designed evaluation studies. In addition to its value to the immediate on-site innovator, gaining of knowledge from a well-designed study has great value to other innovators. It can guide future on-site innovation in terms of choosing overall change strategy, learning how to manipulate various action levers, anticipating what problems will arise, and estimating how long it will take before positive effects occur. It is certain that a much larger number of field innovations have taken place than have ever been reported (Cummings, 1973). A recent workshop drawing upon innovators in the relatively small area of north-eastern Ohio produced over 10 field innovations, only one of which had ever been published. Compare this with the 57 published studies covered in the entire review. The knowledge that many more innovations are attempted than are ever reported, combined with the very positive nature of the results in the reported studies, leads to the suspicion that studies finding zero or negative results are severely under-reported. Reporting of such negative results would provide invaluable information to innovators on contingencies and on what change processes have been un-successful and should therefore be avoided.

To encourage the reporting of field innovations and their results, especially negative results, new incentives for innovators and their organizations are required. These incentives can be created by area-wide or nation-wide organizations—unions, manufacturers' associations, governmental agencies, foundations—which can facilitate the designing of research for individual organizations, pool results from a large number of similar innovations, and provide the information to the innovators involved and to organizations at large.

By performing such activities, national organizations can encourage the two processes discussed here as essential to widespread development of effective quality of work life strategies: (i) utilizing knowledge already available from research, and (ii) developing knowledge on-site. Unless knowledge on action levers, contingencies, and change processes is developed and utilized, improvements in work life quality will depend solely on intuition and chance.

Acknowledgement

The research on which this paper is based was supported by National Science Foundation Grant GI-39455, Research Applied to National Needs Division. The research was conducted in collaboration with John Bigelow, Rupert Chisholm, Roy Glen, Susan Manring, Edward Molloy, William Notz, Suresh Srivastva, and Jim Waters.

References

Campbell, D. T. (1969). Reforms as experiments. *American Psychologist*, **24**, 409–429.
Campbell, D. T. and Stanley, J. C. (1963). *Experimental and Quasi-Experimental Designs for Research*. Rand McNally.
Cummings, T. G. (1973). *Companies are Publicity-Shy*. An interview which appeared in Special Report No. 661, *American Machinist*, 12 November.
Srivastva, S., *et al.* (1974). *Productivity, Industrial Organization and Job Satisfaction: Policy Development and Implementation*. Unpublished report to the National Science Foundation, Case Western Reserve University.
Webb, E. J., Campbell, D. T., Schwartz, R. D., and Sechrest, L. (1966). *Unobtrusive Measures: Nonreactive Research in the Social Sciences*. Rand McNally.

4

Work Structuring

Friso J. den Hertog
Philips Gloeilampenfabrieken, Eindhoven, Holland

A Copernican Revolution

The demand for alternatives for our mechanistic production systems becomes more urgent every year. It is not only the behavioural scientist who foresees the 'coming crisis of production management', as Davis (1971a) has called it. 'Quality of working life' and 'organizational renewal' have become common expressions in the language of journalists, politicians, managers and trade-unionists.

For decade after decade we have been trying to adapt the human being to the job he is doing. 'Put the right man in the right place in a social climate in which he feels at ease'. That was the message of social science. As Davis indicates in Chapter 5, technology and the jobs that resulted from it have long been accepted as facts of life by organizational sociologists and psychologists. Nowadays, however, it is becoming clear that blueprints for organizational design which look so sophisticated on paper are no longer functioning very well in actual practice. Thus we hear that 'the human element no longer fits into our mechanistic and bureaucratic systems'.

For many people there has been a kind of Copernican revolution: the employee no longer revolves around a fixed job, but rather the job revolves round him. So the revolution in our way of thinking is almost dialectic in character.

Organizational philosophy

The early work of Karl Marx, especially the 'Paris Manuscripts' (Marx, 1966), has been a very important stimulus in recent discussions on the alienating tendencies in modern mass industry. Behavioural science was not so much inspired by his later economic and political reviews as by his early humanistic analysis of the development from craft to manufacture and mass production (Blauner, 1964, p. 1,4). Marx established that this development is characterized by progressive mechanization, specialization, division of labour, reduction of skills and task content, verticalization and isolation of the individual (Marx, 1966, 1867). For him the effects on the human being were clear: (a) alienation from the product and fellow workers, (b) self-estrangement, (c) the breaking of organic ties, (d) one-sided use and development of skills and capacities, and (e) deterioration of the worker's values.

The early Marx might be called the 'first anti-Taylorist before Taylorism existed'. He hit hard at the most popular pushball of industrial behavioural scientists today: the organizational philosophy of Frederic Winslow Taylor. Taylor assumed that the sole motivation for people to perform well is financial and that the best way to optimize a production organization is to create maximum specialization and repetitiveness and to reduce variety and training time (Clark, 1972).

In the last 15 years a number of writers have questioned this technocratic view in which the problems on 'the human side of enterprise' were taken for granted. In doing so they picked up a lot of ideas from the early Marx. Blauner (1964) pointed out that the attitudes of workers were related to technology: in mass-production industry, reduction of freedom goes hand-in-hand with alienation. Psychologists like Herzberg (1966) and Likert (1967) show how talents are wasted, money is squandered and people frustrated.

The social-technical system theorists (e.g., Emery, 1972) show us the process of technological suboptimalization and its consequences for the system as a whole: a diminishing capacity of groups and individuals to learn and adapt to the environment. Elton Mayo's studies on the primary groups in industry stress the importance of workers' social ties (Roethlisberger and Dickson, 1939). Burns and Stalker (1961) in their studies propagate a development from the mechanistic closed system to the organic system.

The industrial relations platform

Industrial relations are the second platform on which the Copernican Revolution becomes manifest. Only a few years ago our industrial engineers held the opinion that $1\frac{1}{2}$ minutes was the natural limit for work cycles in a long line production system. 'Create longer cycles and it will cost you money. Besides, people are not capable of doing more complicated work so fast and they won't even like it'. That was their philosophy: $1\frac{1}{2}$ minutes as a maximum.

In 1973 the $1\frac{1}{2}$-minute cycle was the subject of trade union action in Germany, the 'IG Metall', one of Germany's biggest unions, including it in their package of claims during the collective bargaining in that year. Their demands for a 'better quality of working life' were pressed home by several strikes. So the $1\frac{1}{2}$-minute cycle made its reappearance, but this time as a minimum! The maximum had become a minimum. Talk of dialectic change!

Organizational practice

The most important processes are perhaps those that have started in organizational practice itself. In the academic world changes in traditional theoretical views often lead to weighty intellectual discussions. In organizational life a radical change of view is often of a far more dramatic character: it is not just an intellectual idea that is at stake, but also the roles and positions of workers in a social system.

In companies such as Volvo, Saab, IBM, ITT, ATT, Texas Instruments, Polaroid and Philips the search for alternatives has been going on for many years. Although most reports on these efforts are optimistic in tone, reality proves that the processes of change require a lot of energy and progress very laboriously.

Signals for Change

The feeling that new approaches are needed is widespread, but what facts are compelling industrial practice to be reconsidered?

It is proposed to illustrate here the need for change by considering studies which have been done in and outside Philips. The Philips organization offers work to 400,000 employees in approximately 60 countries. In Holland it has over 50 establishments with a total of 90,000 employees. Philips produces a wide range of manufactured goods from light bulbs, integrated circuits, radio, television and 'white goods' to professional equipment such as computers, X-ray tubes and cyclotrons.

Labour turnover

The analysis of labour turnover data collected by Philips' Department of Industrial Psychology has played an important part in the history of work structuring.

Figure 4.1, overleaf, shows the distribution of the job levels we offer in four of our mass production plants in relation to the distribution of capacities of people working on those jobs as measured by a selection test for unskilled and semi-skilled labour (Arends, 1965).

The levels of the test correspond to three job categories: simple (S), medium-level (M), and more complex semi-skilled types of work (C). The need for workers meant that even the least capable candidates on the labour market had to be taken on (L). We see that in three out of four cases workers' capacities

46

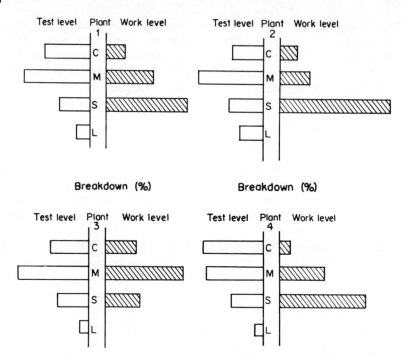

Figure 4.1. The capacities of actual staff at four factories compared with the level of jobs they do

do not match the jobs we offer them. They are too good; their capacities are greater than those needed. So we spoil talent, but that is not the whole story: at the same time we are creating alienation and stimulating labour turnover.

Porter and Steers (1973) emphasize the importance of the use of moderator variables in analysing the relationships between job characteristics and labour turnover. In our research the level of capacities frequently proves to be an excellent tool. An example is given in Table 4.1 (Arends, 1973). The table shows the percentage of labour turnover of a group of newcomers for each capacity level (high or low test scores) in relation to the relative difficulty of the work they perform.

It is clearly seen that:

(i) High capacity is related to high turnover (43%), but those placed on simple work had a significantly higher turnover (57%) than those engaged on more complicated types of work.
(ii) The same applies to workers with lower capacities, but the percentage turnover figures are lower throughout.

The population in this investigation consisted of newly-recruited foreign workers in a German television factory (N = 197). The belief that foreign workers would more easily accept the routinized and monotonous jobs proved false: they react in the same way as their native-born colleagues: they leave.

Table 4.1. The relation between % turnover, work and test level

Test level	Total	Simple work	More complicated work
High	43%	57%	21%
Low	21%	27%	12%

Labour turnover is a costly problem, which in many companies occurs among newly recruited staff. This is illustrated by the 'survival curve' in Figure 4.2.

The labour turnover figures are not always as bad as in this factory (Arends, 1967), but the same tendency was found in 20 factories inside and outside Europe. The turnover problem is caused by newcomers who, most of them voluntarily, leave the company during, or soon after, the introduction period because they are dissatisfied and frustrated. This type of labour turnover is costly indeed; money spent on recruitment and training is not recovered because the worker drops out before he becomes productive. The continuous stream of newcomers leaving spoils the working climate for those who stay, while the image of the company as an employer is harmed on the labour market.

Absenteeism

Absenteeism is a complicated phenomenon. It is very difficult to study its direct causes (Porter and Steers, 1973), and it would seem that the character of the problem is determined by a complex of factors. Fried, Weitman and Davis (1972) were, however, able to isolate one relationship between task variables and absenteeism in their study of a paper mill. Their investigation among 230 male workers over a period of 6000 man-weeks revealed that of the 40 job

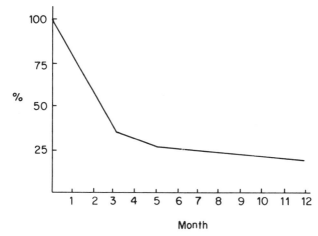

Figure 4.2. The survival curve: % of 'stay-ons' in the course of months after their entry to the factory

stations studied, those where conditions were such that employees could set and/or adjust their own machine had less absenteeism associated with them (p. 428).

Stress

Cools (1963) analysed the complaints of stress in a Philips population of women workers. At that time 50% of the sample ($N = 180$) expressed the feeling that they were being rushed and made nervous in the job. The complaints were most frequent among women who were very dissatisfied with the organizational arrangements. It was remarkable that no other factor in the questionnaire was correlated with a feeling of stress. Cools concludes that the lack of autonomy and of scope for individual discretion is one of the most important causes of stress in industry.

The quality and quantity of the work done is largely conditioned by the ponderous industrial system in which people work. Van Beek (1964a) used a questionnaire to compare job attitudes in three production systems: a long assembly line without buffer stocks ($N = 75$), an assembly line with buffer stocks ($N = 105$) and a short line ($N = 25$). Stress was significantly related to the worker's lack of control over his own pace. Van Beek pleads for small work units in which each member is able to control the quality and quantity of his own production.

Inflexibility of the production system

In a period when television was becoming popular in Holland and sales were increasing very rapidly, a lot of trouble with delivery dates was experienced in the television assembly department. This formed a direct inducement to study the problems of the assembly line organization, namely its poor morale and its quality and output problems. The continuous assembly line, where each worker passes a panel on to his neighbour every 2 minutes at the command of a light signal, was studied from three points of view: output, quality and morale. An experiment was started in which the assembly line of 104 workers was divided into five groups with buffer stocks between adjacent groups.

The racks which were placed between the groups could contain a maximum of 30 units, about 1-hour's production. The inspectors, who were formerly stationed at the end of the line, were now placed at the end of the group to ensure quicker feedback of the results. The introduction of buffer stocks reduced waiting time due to lack of materials by 55%. Waiting times, however, are caused not only by external factors such as irregular supply of material. They also result from the fact that workers never finish operations at the same moment. A lot of time is wasted by variations in average speed between workers (balancing losses) and variations in the speed of the individual worker (system losses).

Van Beek (1964a) concluded that 'the problem of balancing the line, well known from practice, is not in the first place the division of tasks on the basis of official standard times, but rather the adaptation of these tasks to the speeds of the workers' (p. 164). These problems tend to be greater in long lines without buffer stocks. The quicker feedback raised quality remarkably. This experiment illustrates the limits of human adaptation to a mechanistic system. The long continuous assembly line is not such an ideally efficient system as industrial engineers believed for many years.

Changes in values

In our society we are nowadays confronted with rapid changes in values. These changes mean '. . . that the use of individuals to satisfy the economic goals of an organization is no longer a viable social value. People will not let themselves be used' (Davis, 1971b, p. 30). A growing need for more influence and information among the workers themselves can also be noticed. Van der Bruggen's survey (1972) of a big Philips factory showed very clearly the widespread need for delegation of responsibilities and for more information about management policies at all levels.

The rising level of education is perhaps the most dramatic threat to the production systems of today. In our labour market in Holland we find hardly any young workers who have not had at least 3 years of secondary education. The supply of skilled workers is outgrowing the number of unskilled workers available. Yet we have a vast number of jobs that only require 2 to 6 weeks' training. An investigation among 115 workers between the ages of 15 and 23 years at a Dutch Philips plant (Wester, 1973) showed that over 75% of them were convinced they could do more complicated work than they were being offered. In particular, leavers from lower technical colleges who are placed in lowly skilled jobs feel this underload most keenly.

Davis (1971b) gives a very striking example of the consequences of raising the school-leaving age in Norway. In the past about 80% of boys were willing to work in the maritime industry. Only a few years later this proportion had declined to 15%. A better education had created higher expectations regarding working life and changes in values.

Conclusion

In the relation between the workers and the organization it was always the former who had to adapt to the latter. Step-by-step we have come to realize that it is time we adapted the organizational design to the people to whom it offers work. Technological optimization has taken place at the cost of the social system. The consequences have become clear in the flexibility and output of the system and in the workers' reactions.

The Development of Work Structuring Within Philips

Some history

Earlier in the 60's top management became aware of the problem of attracting and holding staff (van der Graaf, 1965). The Philips concern was expanding rapidly about that time and the question of whether the production force could keep up with increasing sales was becoming more urgent every year.

Impressed by research into labour turnover, job satisfaction and workers' reasons for leaving, the top management set up a study group. After 2-years' investigation the committee came to the conclusion (Koolhaas, 1963) that: 'the monotonous short-cycle job does not fit into a time characterized by growing ambitions for social recognition and functional responsibility' (p. 1). The group advocated adoption of a new approach to organizational design. This was described in the publication *Work Structuring* (1968) as: 'To organize the work, the work situation and the conditions of labour in such a way that, while maintaining or improving efficiency, job content accords as closely as possible with the capacities and ambitions of the individual employee' (p. 4). The development of the new approach was encouraged by the management of the staff department and by local management and resulted in a number of seminars and in a few dozen experiments being started.

In 1968 a 'balance sheet' was drawn up (van der Does de Willebois, 1968). The development of work structuring was seen as taking place in three phases:

(i) *The work environment phase* ('flowerbox' phase). The original report of the study group contained many recommendations for changes in the working environment.

(ii) *The actual work phase.* The second phase in these activities is mainly concerned with the employee's job: job enrichment, job enlargement and job rotation.

(iii) *The departmental structure phase.* Delegation of responsibilities to people and groups at the bottom of the organization chart leads to a redistribution of job elements. As a result the line can often be shortened, both in the production departments and in the ancillary departments.

In 1970 the Board of Management formally committed itself by writing a letter to all plant managers encouraging them to initiate new experiments. Special budgets, it said, would be available to compensate for initial production losses. Two members of our Board assumed formal responsibility for promoting a widespread implementation of the new approach. Figure 4.3 shows the number of projects started annually in a 10-year period.

The philosophy

In the same year in which our Board sent out its letter of intent, an interdisciplinary staff group was formed to do research, develop training

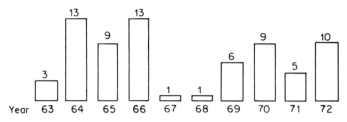

Figure 4.3. The number of projects started

programmes and start pilot studies in new areas. This group described work structuring in the following terms: 'Work structuring is a form of organizational renewal and development to optimize the functioning of the system as a whole. It starts with the acknowledgement of the fundamental equivalence of the social and technical economical factors'.

This work structuring philosophy is closely connected with the ideas developed by the Tavistock socio-technical system school (Emery, 1972, Thorsrud, 1972). Central to those ideas is the conception of the organization as an open system in which individuals and groups interact in a continuous exchange with the environment. The organization is characterized (Davis, 1971c, p. 187) by 'joint optimization', which means that 'when achievement of an objective depends on independent but correlated systems such as a technological system and social system, it is impossible to optimize for overall performance without seeking to optimize these correlative systems jointly'. The socio-technical system approach refers to the process of organizational development (Thorsrud, 1972) focused on the enlargement of the system's capacity to learn from its own experiences and to renew itself.

Elements of work structuring

In every concrete project we find a combination of a number of elements, which together constitute work structuring. Work structuring always refers to an integration of changes in a department as a whole. The most important elements are sketched below.

1. *Job enlargement* (horizontal load). The work cycle is enlarged by adding more tasks of the same level. The work becomes a module, with a certain identity. The number of people working in a group can be reduced.

2. *Job enrichment* (vertical load). Job enrichment refers to the qualitative change in the job. Work formerly done by the foreman and by people from other staff and auxiliary departments is brought to the shop floor.

3. *Job rotation*. Group members take over each other's jobs for a certain period of time. They learn more tasks and rotate in accordance with a roster or by mutual arrangement.

4. *Feedback on quality and output*. Inspection of their own work and short feedback loops create conditions in which workers learn. The workers are given an opportunity to see the process as a whole and to take decisions.

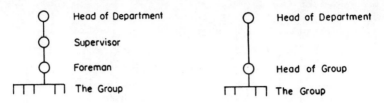

Figure 4.4. Deverticalization

5. *Small product groups.* Production is organized in small stable groups, each making a product that is complete in itself.

6. *Job consultation.* Job consultation is a very central element of work structuring. Once every 2 or 3 weeks the workers and their supervisors meet in groups to discuss the problems of the last period and possibilities for improvement.

7. *Deverticalization.* The shortening of the organizational hierarchy makes it possible to delegate responsibility to the production workers. The most usual deverticalization is illustrated in Figure 4.4. The head of a group has a supporting rather than a controlling function.

Work Structuring in Practice: Four Cases

The following four cases will give some idea of work structuring in practice. They have been chosen at random to illustrate various aspects of change in job design.

Individual assembly of channel selectors

The old shift line. Originally the channel selector for television sets was assembled in shift lines with 20 work stations. The job at each work station involved three operations with average work cycles of 1 minute. Only one panel could be stored between any work places. Individual work pace depended greatly on that of fellow workers. Every 3 minutes a light signal indicated that the panels were to be passed to the next position.

Problems. The problems of this classical production system showed a strong resemblance to those of the long television line, previously discussed:

  (i) System and balancing losses.
  (ii) Breakdowns and waiting times.
  (iii) Poor feedback of quality.
  (iv) Low flexibility due to continual load problems.
  (v) High turnover and absenteeism.
  (vi) Complaints about nervous strain.
  (vii) Low task commitment.

Individual assembly. The new system had to be more flexible and had to give more personal freedom of work pace and movement. In the new set-up the work cycle varies between 10 and 17 minutes. Each individual worker assembles a complete module of the channel selector. The group prepares its lot for transfer and receives the quality figures immediately. Previously the selector was trimmed in a special group. Now the trimming is done in the assembly group itself. The workers register their own output and hours of work. The position of supervisor and foreman were combined into one, namely the head of assembly. The workers can now move around the department and vary their pace without disturbing the entire line (Buitendam, 1966).

Economic results. It became very clear from experience with the first experimental line that the workers were more committed to the job. They felt themselves more responsible for the quality of the product. Their willingness to accept correction increased. The new system was far more flexible than the old one and people could replace each other very easily. Waiting time was reduced considerably.

Social effects. The 20 workers in the test group (13 women, 7 men) were interviewed a year after the switch. They were asked: 'Would you prefer to return to the line? Why, or why not?' The answers can be found in Table 4.2.

Conclusion. This experiment illustrates firstly, that division of labour and the line itself are not essential for efficiency. Secondly, the project makes it clear that job enlargement can be an adequate approach to the problem of work pace and the lack of freedom at the work place. It enlarges not only the horizontal work load but also the margin of freedom for variation in individual behaviour (Ulich, 1974).

The new system has released workers from the tyranny of the light signal. So we do not agree with writers, such as Ford (1969), who stress only the importance of the vertical load of the work. Job enlargement can help to change the entire work system.

Table 4.2. Question: "Would you prefer to return to the line?" ($N = 20$)

	Frequency
Prefer go to back	—
Don't know	2
Prefer to stay	18
Question: "Why not?"	
You can work at your own pace, independently of others	14
You are not pushed any more, you can take it easy for a while	11
Better relationships	3
The workers cannot harm each other's production any more	3
You can move outside the department	1

Autonomous groups in a television factory

Autonomous groups. 1969 is a very important year in the history of work structuring. A department head was anxious to know how far it was possible to go on changing the structure of work. He started to experiment. 'What is the optimum number of workers in a group and what is an optimum work cycle?' Those were his basic questions.

Together with a friend in the personnel department he began to develop a plan for a new alternative: the autonomous group. Many work structuring elements were integrated in the final plan, which is shown in Table 4.3. In the same year management approved a budget for the start of a first group. The project required an entirely new layout.

In 1970 a second group started. Two years later the first evaluation was carried out, the short black-and-white line ($N = 24$) and a long colour line serving as reference groups.

Economic results. After 2 years of experimentation the wage and cost component of the factory delivery price was reduced by 10%. The Efficiency Department concludes (Van Broekhoven, 1973) that 'autonomous groups offer a good alternative to the conventional line and do not by definition raise the level of costs' (p. 9).

These positive results are ascribed to the following factors:

(a) Lower absenteeism.
(b) Less waiting time.
(c) Better coordination.
(d) Reduced training costs.
(e) Deverticalization.

The prices of new machines, the cost per square metre of floorspace, wages and the cost of consultation hours, however, have all risen.

Table 4.3. Comparison of the old and new systems

Work structuring elements	Short line	Autonomous group
Job enlargement (work cycle)	3 to 4 minutes	20 minutes
Rotation	Sporadic	Regular
Job enrichment (delegated tasks)	—	Quality control, ordering of material, distribution of work etc.
Smaller groups	25 to 30	7
Job consultation	—	1½ h once every 2 weeks
Deverticalization	Supervisor/foreman	Head of assembly
Feedback	Long loop	Short loop

Figure 4.5. A television line 13 years ago

Social effects. Attitudes and job behaviour were measured by three methods: questionnaire, interview and observation (den Hertog and Kerkhoff, 1973). The comparative investigation yielded the following conclusions:

(i) Job satisfaction is much higher in the autonomous groups than on assembly lines. No one really wanted to leave the group, while on the assembly line many workers (especially young men) would have preferred to leave. Job satisfaction was higher, but the same applies to expectations; the members of the new groups feel the need to proceed further along the new paths that have been decided upon.

(ii) In the interviews with the 14 members of the experimental groups and 24 workers of a short line making the same product, the workers were asked two important questions in connection with a broad range of job aspects: (a) 'How often are you able to influence matters?' and (b) 'How often do you want to exercise an influence?' Although they believe they have more influence than previously, they still want much more. The retrospective part of the interview indicates that this difference between work situations is not just due to sampling errors. The workers stated how they had changed in the process: they had learned to see the assembly work as a whole, they had learned to see their own mistakes and those of others and they wanted to correct them.

56

A commitment towards the other members had grown such as they had never experienced in other working situations.

(iii) Observation of the short line revealed the existence of small homogeneous subgroups. Relations with these subgroups were excellent, but the relations and coordination between the groups repeatedly gave rise to problems.

Conclusion. One of the most important things that we learned from the experiment with autonomous groups is that work structuring itself is a learning process in which people learn to control their own work situation, to see the system as a whole and to exercise influence in a functional way. They become difficult to handle, but in a positive way: they act as quality control for management!

The project cannot claim to offer irrefutable scientific proof that the new system is the best. The samples are too small, no measurement had been done previously and the interventions were too complex. The real merit of the project lies in the changes it brought in the surroundings: people who were educated and brought up in the dogmas of classical organization theory discovered that the 'other way' worked as well or even better. This they discovered not from reading books on modern management but by experiencing the changes in their own lives.

Figure 4.6. Television assembly in autonomous groups

Job integration: operators and setters

Operators and setters. Until now we have focused our attention on the problems of the assembly line. Many work structuring projects, however, were initiated in order to change the character of the machine operator's job. The following case is illustrative of this kind of job design (van Beek, 1964b).

The experiment was carried out in a department of a metal parts factory where automatic presses were operated by 20 men. The operators fed in metal strips and the presses stamped or pierced components in large numbers. The operator's task was to watch the machine, take samples of the product and and supervise the input to the press. He had to take particular care of the dies, which are very expensive. Every operator was in charge of one press.

Once in 24 hours the dies were changed by semi-skilled workers called setters. These were recruited from the best operators and learned their job by going round with an experienced setter. The status of the setter's job was apparently higher than that of the production workers or operators.

Problems. The flexibility of the department was low because of its highly specialized jobs. Multiple Moment Analysis showed that much time was lost by poor coordination among the operators, setters, quality-controller, foreman and supervisor. Operators often had to wait for a long time before the setter could change the die. Management also wondered who would be willing to do this simple work in the future. Enrichment of the operator's job could make it more attractive.

Integration of functions. The operator's job was finally enriched by integrating it with the setter's. For this purpose almost all the operators attended a full-time training course that lasted 6 weeks. At the outset the management had grave doubts about the success of the project. The risk of damage to machines was high and it was not certain that every operator was fit for the new job.

Economic effects. Waiting times were reduced very considerably. Most employees were now operating more than one machine without difficulty. Less time was spent on coordination. The quality level remained the same.

Social effects. Six months after the start of the experiment all the people involved were interviewed (van Beek, 1964b). The interviews showed that the men now saw their work as more interesting, challenging and meaningful. They enjoyed much more freedom to talk and move about. Their work had acquired more importance and had more responsibility connected with it. Some results from the interviews are presented in Table 4.4, overleaf.

The course created a team spirit. Wages are the only negative aspects, although prospects of an upgrading were held out: 'We are still not being paid for the job we do'.

58

Table 4.4. Question: 'What do you think of your new job in comparison with the old one?'

MORE INTERESTING

'Before, it was often difficult to keep your eyes open; now you can keep going'. 'The work has become much more interesting. What a bore it was in the old days; you checked the drawing a dozen times, simply to have something to do'.

MORE FREEDOM

'We often say to each other: how things have changed! Before you could not leave your press; now you can change the die without asking anybody for permission'.

MORE MEANINGFUL

'You are learning something; you know the background'.

RESPONSIBILITY

'I know I'm more useful than before'. 'You are responsible; you know how to set the machine and you are able to correct the faults yourself'.

RELATIONSHIPS

'We understand each other much better'.

Conclusion. Management is often afraid to delegate maintenance and repair work to unskilled workers for fear that something might happen to expensive machines. This experiment shows that when conditions are created in which people can learn and understand more of the process, they will become involved and be able to cope with much more complicated situations. People must be free to make mistakes before they can learn from mistakes. The enthusiastic attitude of the workers was partly due to the sharp contrast with the old situation, and in his report of the change van Beek (1964b) expected that subsequent newcomers would react less exuberantly.

Autonomous groups in bulb assembly

'Special miniatures' are small bulbs made for special purposes (dashboards, telephone, etc.) in fairly small batches. The production process is partly automated, but the finishing process is done manually by female workers. The final assembly part of the process used to be carried out on short production lines, with 12 to 14 women working at two or three tables situated one behind the other.

Everybody had one task, often with a cycle of less than 1 minute. One of the women was given more responsibility: she acted as a kind of assistant foreman and 'utility woman' at the same time.

Problems. The department had a lot of problems. The theoretical production norms were not being achieved. The proportion of rejected products was very high. The production process as a whole was very hard to supervise. The women showed very little interest in the work itself and in the results of their units. They lacked proper knowledge of quality and of production demands. In addition, absenteeism was high. The lines consisted of two or three small informal groups (3 to 4 women) who kept blaming each other for bad results and low quality.

The autonomous group. In developing an alternative system the starting point was the need of the women to work in small groups whose composition they themselves selected. The new alternative grew in continuous consultation with the workers themselves. The main changes are listed below:

   (i) Formation of small groups (of four people).
  (ii) Every woman performs four operations instead of one.
 (iii) Job rotation.
 (iv) Short line: no foreman or 'assistant (woman) foreman'.
  (v) Delegation of the foreman's duties.
 (vi) Group consultation.
(vii) Quick feedback.

After an experimental period of 6 months with one group the project was extended to three more groups.

Economic results. The change to autonomous groups had a very positive effect on the production costs, which would have been 20% higher if the change had not been made. Reduction of the number of final rejects (from 9% to 5%) and a remarkable increase of output accounted for this economic improvement.

Social effects. A before-and-after study was carried out by means of a questionnaire. The women in the whole department were twice asked to respond to 25 items on a five-point scale. They were asked two questions: (a) 'How satisfied are you with this aspect of your work?' and (b) 'How important is this aspect for you?' The reference group comprised the rest of the female personnel in the department, 30 of whom were working on the short lines.
    Analysis of the data revealed that all the subgroups in the department replied more positively to the general question: 'Do you like your work?' The experimental groups, however, were less satisfied about specific items such as wages, possibilities of promotion, their influence in the department and information from management. At the same time the importance ratings of most factors increased.
    The interviews also revealed very clearly that the old situation is no longer an acceptable alternative. The women would quit if they had to return to the lines. Working in the autonomous groups is preferred because of the following factors:

   (i) Better relationships and cooperation.

(ii) More autonomy.
(iii) Less monotony.
(iv) Possibility of talking about problems in the group.
(v) Influence on process control.
(vi) More knowledge.
(vii) No assistant foreman on your back.

Conclusion. There are a lot of people in the work structuring field who are very sure about the categories of employees who have to be omitted from work structuring projects. Married female workers and foreign workers belong to these 'minority groups'. This project showed how easily we become prejudiced. Once again it showed that we have to try to find out the truth.

At the start of the project the women were hardly interested in the so-called 'intrinsic factors'. They volunteered because they found some aspects of the situation, namely the social aspects, attractive. Before the experiment they were quite satisfied with their old jobs. After working a year in the autonomous groups, however, they changed their opinion about their previous job: it was monotonous, automaton-like and so on. Also, peoples' expectations and values change when they enter a learning situation. That is the problem with interpreting before-and-after questionnaire data. Workers are asked to rate their satisfaction, but after a year their norms as to what is satisfying or not have changed. The shift in importance ratings can be seen as an indication of the change in values. Our first aim must be to try to find a connection with some manifest needs. Our second aim is to avoid removing the positive elements of the old situation (Turner and Lawrence, 1965).

Recent trends

A new field for work structuring has been found in mechanical workshops. The need for greater influence on the work situation and job enrichment is perhaps most clearly shown among craftsmen in these workshops. Three projects have been started in this sector.

At the moment the layout of a whole factory is being changed to introduce a product line involving 300 workers. The management is proposing to develop a 'cell structure' of small interconnected product groups in which most of the specializations are brought together. Another programme of change throughout a plant has been brought into operation in the television factory at Bruges. The collar assembly lines have been divided into groups of 3 to 5 workers. Each group makes one module of the set.

Work structuring is developing more and more into an international approach within the Philips organization. Projects can be found in many countries: Denmark, Sweden, Belgium, the United Kingdom, France, South Africa and so on.

The last trend to be mentioned is the job consultation project. Local Dutch personnel and organization workers are involved in a system-wide implementation of job consultation. Job consultation was described above as one of the central elements of work structuring. It is our hope that organizational renewal will receive an impetus from this process.

Work Structuring: Reappraisal and Final Conclusions

Reappraisal

Our Workers' Council issued a report in 1973 with the title: 'What has Philips done in the work structuring field in Holland: a view from the shop floor'.

The report summarizes the work structuring projects that have taken place over the years within the Dutch Philips organization. The count stopped at 54. After an analysis of the quality of the projects and the numbers of people concerned the Council nevertheless came to the conclusion that work structuring as a broad organizational renewal had not been achieved to any real extent in the Philips concern. Only 3% of the workers in Holland have been involved. Many of the projects lacked quality and were implemented without the participation of the people involved. One of the biggest problems, according to the Council, is the lack of professional support in the strategy of change; the experiments often do not expand into their immediate environment.

We are very conscious of the fact that work structuring is now in a very important and difficult phase. We no longer need the success of small well-designed experiments. Our experience proves that work structuring offers a good alternative to our present production systems. It is the strategy for systemwide change that has to be developed. The main question is no longer: 'What are the direct effects of an experimental manipulation on job satisfaction, absenteeism, quality and so on?' The new central question is concerned with the learning process which is taking place: 'Has the experiment been a adequate intervention in the process of self renewal?' As our next step work structuring has to become an integrated part of policy in the management of local production and engineering departments. As van Beinum (1973) has commented in discussion: 'Self renewal means learning, and learning hurts'.

Evaluation research

Many evaluative studies in the field of job design have an experimental character. Input and output variables are operationalized as precisely as possible, groups are manipulated and effects are checked by reference to control groups (see, for instance, Ford, 1969, and van Beinum, 1964). They follow the 'billiards' model in explaining the dynamics of social change: 'Push your cue in the right direction, give the right siding and you make a cannon'.

Work structuring and job design projects however, are changes with broad aims and often develop via successions of unstructured interventions. Experimental design is limited in its ability to study complex changes. The agent of

62

change is not a doctor carrying out experiments on his patient (Schein, 1969), the patient has to cure himself. This means that the scientifically controlled experiment often does not fit into the optimal strategy for change.

Besides, the questions themselves are changing: they are concerned primarily with the function of an experiment and only in the second place with its direct effects. There is a need for research into the dynamics of the change process: evaluation of strategy and interventions; analysis of the forces for and against, etc. Weiss and Rein (1970) advocate an alternative methodology, characterized by '(a) process-oriented qualitative research, (b) historical research, or (c) case study or comparative research' (p. 105). From a methodological point of view, experimental design remains superior in situations in which aims can be clearly recognized and intervention is simple. These situations are however uncommon in day-to-day reality.

Self-fulfilling prophecies

Many publications exist in which the need for job design, work structuring, job enrichment etc. is questioned. They show how job values are related to occupational class (Friedlander, 1965) and to individual differences (Hulin and Blood, 1968; Wild and Kempner, 1972). The unskilled worker is not interested in the 'intrinsic factors'; his values are predominantly of instrumental origin. Money, security and leisure time have been found to be far more important than the 'work itself' (e.g., Goldthorpe *et al.*, 1968).

It is not the present aim to question the data. It is the conclusion which has to be tackled. The authors are not aware that they are raising the *status quo* to a norm. 'They opt for the *status quo* when they decide to take presently existing states of affairs as the ones they would support' (Argyris, 1972, p. 115). Supporting the *status quo* means strengthening a self-fulfilling prophecy, strengthening a vicious circle of the kind illustrated in Figure 4.7.

The work structuring projects show that values change when a man is placed in new situations where he finds a possibility of learning and exercising influence on the direct work environment and where quality and output can be controlled by himself. The old job has become 'automaton-like' for the ladies in Terneuzen.

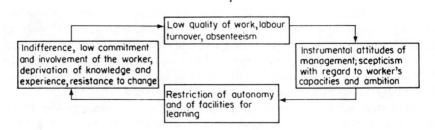

Figure 4.7. The vicious circle

One year ago they were quite satisfied (den Hertog and Vossen, 1974). Man adapts to the situation in which he is living.

The Hawthorne effect

In every seminar or lecture on work structuring, job enrichment, etc., the first question after the lecture is always the same. Someone is sure to get up and say: 'That was a fine talk, but what about the Hawthorne Effect?' In work structuring lectures we have a standard answer to this standard question: 'Well, what about it?'

In fact we admit that the Hawthorne effect plays a part in our projects. But at the same time we ask ourselves: 'Why don't we use it?' (Thorsrud, 1972, Doyle, 1971). The systematic and conscious use of the effect can make a very functional contribution to the proces of change. Experimental groups often start work under great stress. The expectations of the people affected are high and unforeseen problems arise. Reinforcement from these affected can compensate for some of the starting problems. Besides, nobody has ever mentioned the 'Anti-Hawthorne Effect'. Yet it exists. Some changes in production systems threaten the people affected. They corrode existing power relations between all kinds of line and staff departments. This Anti-Hawthorne Effect gives at least as much trouble as the original effect, but both are inevitable if changes are to be achieved which matter to the people involved.

Changing the process of system design

The change of our production system by the implementation of relatively small experiments costs a lot of time and energy. For a long time experiments were needed to prove our philosophies. They are still needed because we are asking ourselves different questions every time. For the process of system-wide change, however, different strategies are needed. One of these strategies has to grow from the social scientists' input to the process of technological design. Within the Philips organization the first steps have been taken: a few social scientists are involved at a very early stage of product and system design in order to advise their technical colleagues about the social consequences of their technical design.

We agree with Davis (1971c) that behavioural scientists have to be in at a very early stage. Prevention is better than cure.

References

Arends, G. (1965). Internal research note, Philips, Eindhoven.
Arends, G. (1967). Internal research note, Philips, Eindhoven.
Arends, G. (1973). Internal research note, Philips, Eindhoven.
Argyris, C. (1972). *The Applicability of Organizational Sociology*, Cambridge University Press.
Beek, H. G. van (1964a). The influence of assembly line organization on output, quality, and morale, *Occupational Psychology*, **38**, 161–172.

64

Beek, H. G. van (1964b). *Werkstrukturering bij automatische persen*, Philips, Eindhoven.
Beinum, H. J. J. van (1964). A field experiment on stabilization of work groups, redistribution of authority and communication, *Proceedings of the Fifteenth International Congress of Applied Psychology*.
Blauner, R. (1964). *Alienation and Freedom*, University of Chicago Press.
Broekhoven, R. van (1973). *Experiment in work structuring at the television receiver factory Eindhoven*. Part I. Economic evaluation, Philips, Eindhoven.
Bruggen, A. L. A. van der (1972). *Evaluatie-onderzoek afdelings-kommunikatiegroepen Philips Nijmegen*. Internal research report, Philips, Eindhoven.
Buitendam, A. (1966). *Kanalenkiezers*, Internal research report, Philips, Eindhoven.
Burns, T. and Stalker, G. M. (1961). *The Management of Innovation*, Tavistock.
Clark, P. A. (1972). *Organizational Design: Theory and Practice*, Tavistock.
Cools, E. (1963). *Waarom is het ongeschoolde werk zenuwachtig en gejaagd?* Philips, Eindhoven.
Davis, L. E. (1971a). The coming crisis for production management: technology and organization, *International Journal of Production Research*, **9**, 65–82.
Davis, L. E. (1971b). Readying the unready: Post-industrial jobs. *California Management Review*, **13**, 27–36.
Davis, L. E. (1971c). Job satisfaction research: The post-industrial view, *Industrial Relations*, **10**, 176–193.
Does de Willebois, J. L. van der (1968). *Werkstrukturering als organisatievernieuwing*, Philips, Eindhoven.
Doyle, F. F. (1971). Job enrichment plus OD, a two-pronged approach at Western Union. In J. R. Maher (ed.), *New Perspectives in Job Enrichment*, Van Nostrand Reinhold.
Emery, F. (1972). Characteristics of socio-technical systems. In L. E. Davis, and J. C. Taylor (eds.), *Design of Jobs*, Penguin.
Ford, R. N. (1969). *Motivation through the Work Itself*, American Management Association.
Fried, J., Weitman, M. and Davis, M. K. (1972). Man-machine interaction and absenteeism. *Journal of Applied Psychology*, **56**, 428–429.
Friedlander, F. (1965). Comparative work value systems, *Personnel Psychology*, **18**, 1–20.
Goldthorpe, J. H., Lockwood, D., Bechhofer, F., and Platt, J. (1968). *The Affluent Worker*, Cambridge University Press.
Graaf, M. H. K. van der (1965). *Attracting and holding staff*, Philips, Eindhoven.
Hertog, J. F. den and Kerkhoff, W. H. C. (1973). *Experiment in work structuring at the television receiver factory Eindhoven*. Part II, Evaluation of the social psychological effects of autonomous task-oriented groups, Philips, Eindhoven.
Hertog, J. F. den and Vossen, H. P. (1974). *Organisatievernieuwing Speciale Miniatuur Terneuzen*, Philips, Eindhoven.
Herzberg, F. (1966). *Work and the Nature of Man*, World Publishing.
Hulin, C. L. and Blood, M. R. (1968). Job enlargement, individual differences and worker responses. *Psychological Bulletin*, **69**, 41–55.
Koolhaas, L. S. (1963). *Rapport commissie werkstrukturering ongeschoolden*, Philips, Eindhoven.
Likert, R. (1967). *The Human Organization: Its Management and Value*, McGraw-Hill.
Marx, K. (1867). *Das Kapital, Kritik der Politischen Oekonomie*, Hamburg.
Marx, K. (1966). *Texte zu Methode und Praxis, II. Pariser Manuskripte 1844*, Rowohlts.
Porter, L. W. and Steers, R. M. (1973). Organizational, work and personal factors in employee turnover and absenteeism. *Psychological Bulletin*, **80**, 151–176.
Roethlisberger, F. J. and Dickson, W. J. (1939). *Management and the Worker*, Harvard University Press.
Schein, E. H. (1969). *Process Consultation*, Addison Wesley.

Thorsrud, E. (1972). Job design in a wider context. In L. E. Davis and J. C. Taylor (eds.), *The Design of Jobs*, Penguin.

Turner, A. N. and Lawrence, P. R. (1965). *Industrial Jobs and the Worker*, Harvard University Press.

Ulich, E. (1974). Die erweiterung des handlungsspielraumes in der betreiblichen praxis. *Industrial Organization*, **43**, 6–8.

Weiss, R. S. and Rein, M. (1970). The evaluation of broad-aim programs: Experimental design, its difficulties, and an alternative. *Administrative Science Quarterly*, **15**, 97–109.

Wester, P. (1973). *Uitslag enquête jongeren-commissie Volt*, Philips, Eindhoven.

Wild, R. and Kempner, T. (1972). Influence of community and plant characteristics on job attitudes of manual workers, *Journal of Applied Psychology*, **56**, 106–113.

Work Structuring. A summary of experiments at Philips, 1963 to 1968 (1968). Philips, Eindhoven.

5
Developments in Job Design

Louis E. Davis
University of California at Los Angeles, USA

Introduction

This is at once a good and bad time to review developments in job design, for we have arrived at a turning point conceptually and are caught in a dilemma in terms of application. The dilemma is in no small part a consequence of the phenomenon of culture lag—the very slow diffusion of ideas and of theory. It has been 20 years since I originated the term and the concept of *job design*. Now, in the midst of growing acceptance and application of the concept, albeit in a variety of modes, I find the concept no longer very stimulating for further research, and the forms of application far too limiting.

Three sets of developments have caused me to revise my view that jobs, as an organizational unit, are a conceptually appropriate basis for analysis, design or redesign of work systems, or that they are a practically appropriate unit for making changes in organizations to enhance organizational effectiveness and improve the quality of working life. Before reviewing the technical, social, and research developments leading to this position, the focus of concern must be indicated since jobs have served as a useful concept to a large group of persons ranging from psychologists and sociologists through union officials and personnel officers to government census takers. Moreover, those concerned with studying the consequences for the individual of his participation in modern

68

business, industrial or governmental organizations also find jobs the appropriate unit of study.

My research and practical interests, however, reach beyond—to the structure
of work organizations and to the content of the relationship between men and
organizations, called jobs. There are two concerns: (i) the design and development of viable organizations that can maintain themselves in ways that support
and enhance the societies of which they are a part; and (ii) the design and
development of roles for the organizations' members that promote and support
them as healthy, whole, responsive human beings. By viability we mean
organizations that can develop the capacity continuously to meet the rapidly
changing and growing demands from their economic, social, and technological
environments as well as such demands from their members who increasingly
question the very basis of their relationship to the organization. In the United
States, the situation is further complicated by a fundamental reordering—slow
and uncertain though it is—of society to make it open to all by providing
equality of opportunity, to begin facing the limits of growth, and to
accommodate the changing values of youth, our future population of organization members.

In the United States this is a disappointing period: the position of researchers
and policy-makers who are largely trapped in the concepts and values of the
industrial era have been reinforced by the current popular view of jobs and
work. In that view jobs *are* the organization, for they are the visible link between
men and how the work of society and its organizations is accomplished. Of
course they are the most visible aspect of the organization: they are named in
union contracts, in job titles, and are the focus of considerable conflict. Jobs
are what men and women prepare themselves to do, are alienated from, and
become obsolete in their abilities to perform. Behind the popular focus is the
not so invisible reality that in technologically advanced societies and organizations, jobs are man-made inventions designed to suit a number of technical
and social system needs and are constantly changing. Jobs are inventions
coming out of the designs of larger organizational and technical systems:
therefore good strategy suggests examination of these larger systems to make
available significant opportunities for change and for fundamental research
and development studies into the processes of design.

Failure to engage with the larger systems traps, on the margins of an
organizations' central problems, those who seek to modify it and its
derivative jobs. Researchers are also trapped once they accept the form of the
organization and its technology as given. Such entrapment has led to study
after study of relations between different role holders totally devoid of any
reference to organizational environments and technology. It has also produced
numerous studies of the individual, his characteristics and motivations, quite
disconnected from futures, environmental forces, the demands of organizational
structure and technology. Needless to say, the contribution of such studies to
the knowledge needed for design or redesign of effective jobs has been minimal
(Davis, 1971a). We are treated to the spectacle of seeing jobs being designed in

the 1970's almost universally according to the precepts of scientific management as if we were back in the 1910's—the heyday of F. W. Taylor. Of course, we also see large numbers of psychologists and various specialists in organization development, job enrichment, etc., busily modifying the designs to attenuate the disastrous consequences of the present approach for men, managers, and organizations. The trap is that research has proceeded from these attempts and that what has been learned may be of doubtful value in understanding how people function in well-designed organizations. It is analogous to developing an understanding of people by concentrating research on abnormal behaviour.

It is appropriate at this point to refer to the original definition of job design and recall that it is a statement which defines domain and objectives, and that it is not, as is so often mistakenly assumed, a statement of technique or programme. Davis and Canter (1955) defined the concept of job design as a process: 'It is the organization of a job to satisfy the technical-organizational requirements of the work to be accomplished and the human requirements of the person performing the work'. From this definition it can be seen that neither technique nor programme are specified for reaching the objectives. This contrasts with job enrichment, job enlargement, job rotation, etc., all of which are specific predetermined prescriptions forecast to be useful.

The search for the means of satisfying the goals of job design over the last 20 years has led to the present state of development. When the concept was originated, job design had, in common with the above techniques and programmes, an acceptance of a central organizational precept of scientific management—that the man and his job constitute the fundamental building block of organizations. Organizational network relationships and the dependencies in the technology were unwittingly overlooked. F. W. Taylor in his scientific management system partially understood and provided for them in an organizational superstructure deliberately separated from the work place. Taylor's main concern was how to use men, those necessary but very peculiar machines. He could concentrate on jobs partially because of the simpler deterministic technologies that dominated his era and his comforting reliance on the organizational superstructure for integration. His intellectual and practical descendants continue in the same mould.

The consequences for almost all present work organizations are structures and practices that are coercive, rigid, and depend on behaviour regulation for achievement of objectives. At the workplace, all work and informational activities are narrowly fractionated and methods and tools are so completely specified as to always require preplanning. Task fractionation not only reduces skills and eliminates learning; it permits an ever higher level of coercion and behaviour regulation. These structures and practices have been with us so long that they are mistakenly viewed as essential requirements of industrial-era organization, about which little or nothing can be done. They have become institutionalized in agreements among managements and unions which largely concentrate on mitigating their effects and sharing the gains rather than eliminating the causes.

Technological Determinism

More pernicious and enduring than the fractionation process in organization and job structures is the effect of technological determinism, which enters through the design of technical systems and their accompanying artifacts— machines, tools, computers, programmes and so on. The present view of the relationship of technology to organization and job structure, carefully nurtured for the past 150 years, is the dangerously simplistic perspective of technological determinism. This holds that technology evolves according to its own inherent logic and needs, regardless of social environment and culture. Further, it holds that to use technology effectively and thus gain its benefits for society, technological development and application must be uninhibited by any considerations other than those thought relevant by its developers, engineers or technologists.

Technological determinism has generally been invoked to support the organizational and institutional *status quo* of the industrial era. For example, the claim is made that organization structure and behaviour are predetermined by technology and unalterably locked into its needs. Doomsayers predict the impending collapse of society as we know it given the negative consequences of a substantial number of technical developments. While it has been shown that there are some correlations between technology and organization structure and organizational process, there are possible choices based on social system values and assumptions. Additionally, it is part of our new learning that the determination of technological form and its unalterable application is both misleading and defeatist. It is well known that many technological alternatives are considered by technical system planners, of which only one form is put forward. The new view alerts us to look at the design process of production technology itself to see which social system planning and psycho-social assumptions were considered in the design of various technical system alternatives. Further, we have learned that we need to have made explicit what economic and social as well as technical factors were included in the decision process of choosing a technological form.

In the design and development of technology, we are dealing with the application of science to invent a technique and its supportive artifacts (machines) to accomplish transformations of objects (materials, information, people) in support of certain objectives. The invention of a technique may be engineering to an overwhelming extent, but in part is also social system design. If, then, we look at work, we can see two sets of antecedent determinants that constrain the choices available for design of tasks and job structure. First, there are the social choices already contained within the technological design; second, there are the social choices contained within the organization design undertaken to use the technology. Our present appreciation is that one rarely finds technological determinism in the pure sense of technological or scientific variables exclusively determining the design or configuration of a technical system. On the contrary, technical system designs most frequently incorporate social system choices, made intentionally or included accidentally either casually or as the result of some omission in planning. In this sense, engineers or technologists can be called social-system engineers, and they are crucial to evolving new organizational forms and job structures.

In a paper in which he castigates engineers for making poor social-system choices in their technical-system designs, Williamson (1972) calls on engineers to accept their obligations as social system engineers.

Davis, Cherns and associates (1975) in a review of the effects of technology attack technological determinism on two grounds. In the first place the shape of technology is not predetermined by its own developmental 'laws' but in substantial part by the psycho-social assumptions which its designers have planned into it. Once its requirements were planned in and then regarded as a given, behaviour followed the only path available, amply fulfilling the prophecy implied in the design. Secondly, technological design incorporates assumptions about human behaviour, the relative value of man and machine and the nature of organizational design. Organizations thus betray in their organizational design values dominant in society at the time their technology evolved.

The increasingly rapid changes in technology, social values, demographic factors, economic factors, and developments in organizational research are now limiting the applicability and continuation of industrial-era values, technological determinism and notions of organizational effectiveness. The total impact of these changes for advanced industrial countries has moved the issues involving man and his relation to work into the political arena. On the part of individual employees the movement is from expectations to *entitlement* to rights; on the part of managers the movement is to seek governmental assistance. One of the indications of this profound change in the United States can be seen in the creation of the National Commission on Productivity, the first such agency in peace time. The inclusion of productivity in national policy based on congressional debate is supported by widespread concern over it among managements and some unions. The questions now being asked are: why are people not as interested in work as they were before, and why has the 'work ethic' declined? The question not being asked is: what does productivity now mean to the individual in the workplace? However there are traps for many managers and for researchers who continue to see relationships between organizations and their members entirely in internal and personal terms; and for unions, responding to the majority of their members who are over 30 years of age, who continue to see the relationship largely in terms of sharing the rewards, protecting health, and curbing management—not seeing that the relationships themselves are being questioned by their younger members, the future majority of the labour force.

Technological Changes

Changes in technology have to be seen on two levels: the actual one in terms of the fundamental transformation processes, and the intellectual one in the acceptance of advanced technology as the cognitive model for relations between man and production processes. Additionally, the effectiveness of technology in satisfying material needs has shifted employment in the United States from the production of goods to the creation of services; the vast majority of our workforce is now engaged in the latter. The widespread native expectation in the United States that the shift to white-collar work would bring with it a high quality of working life is now regarded as an unfounded assumption, since white-collar work is increasingly being organized on the principles of production technology.

Technology as developed during the industrial era has had a powerful impact on the organization of work. This trend began about 1790 with a number of technical inventions and social developments in England. It led to the factory system and the coordination of man and machines, stimulating the movement to rationalize or streamline the utilization of labour, and the modern concept of division of labour for economic purposes. The latter was made possible by the deterministic character of industrial-era technology; what was to be done, how it was to be done, and when it was to be done were all factors which were specifiable.

Organizations which evolved during the industrial era have reflected both this deterministic technology and the values and beliefs of Western society. A new kind of specialization of labour emerged in which jobs were deliberately fractionated so that unskilled people could perform them. Moreover, man's role as an energy supplier in production technology was gradually eliminated, while his other role as a guider of tools is increasingly being transferred to machines as part of the continuing process of mechanization.

The most striking characteristic of the new, sophisticated, automated technology is that it absorbs routine activities into machines rather than leaving them for people, creating a new relationship between a technology and its embedded social system. Workers in automated systems become interdependent and are required to respond to stochastic, not deterministic, conditions; they operate in an environment where the important events occur randomly and are unpredictable, raising needs for commitment and wide competence. Man's third traditional role is the only one that remains in advanced technology or in automated work processes: he is the controller or regulator of the working situation or system and the diagnoser and adjuster of difficulties. Similar changes are taking place in service industries based on information technology.

Thus the new sophisticated stochastic technology requires skills related to regulation, skills in monitoring and diagnosing, skills in the adjustment of processes. In organizations utilizing conventional technology such skills are lodged in the superstructure of supervisors and middle managers. These skills can be related more to group efforts and tasks than to individual jobs and assignments. In turn, such group activities can have an impact on organizational structure. However, designers of technology with their implicit assumptions about individuals and social systems mediate between the new stochastic technologies and their behavioural, job, or organizational effects. Unfortunately, there are numerous instances of organizations and job structures designed in response to stochastic technologies as if they were deterministic, with resulting dysfunctional consequences. Most prominent are those in large scale services using computer systems, in effect white-collar assembly-line organizations.

Societal Changes

General features of changes in society have been reviewed by Cherns in Chapter 1 and Vansina in Chapter 6. It is intended here to deal with those changes in values and beliefs in the United States that bear directly on the relationship between man and work. As may be expected, new values are emerging and the relative importance of earlier ones are changing, much more so among American youth than among the older segments of the population. Additionally the society is witness to an ever-increasing rate of change in organizations, institutions, and technology. The latter contribute to changes in values by stimulating the rising level of expectations about satisfying material, social, and personal needs. The changes in technology also provide the wealth to support continuously rising levels of education, which, in turn, are changing the attitudes, aspirations, and expectations of major segments of society. The seeming ease with which advanced technology has satisfied material wants, coupled in the United States with the provision of subsistence-level support for its citizens, has stimulated a growing concern on the part of groups and individuals about their relationship to work, its meaningfulness and value: a concern for the quality of life at the work place.

There are three important aspects to these changes in values and beliefs. The first is the sheer growth of negative assessment of the quality of the relationship between man and work. The second is the growth of a quite different ordering of priorities between older and younger workers which amounts to a redefinition by the younger people of the work ethic and the meaning of success (Yankelovich, 1974a). Growing numbers are challenging the price and meaning of success if it involves sacrifice or unpleasantness. There is a trend away from postponing self-gratification for success, accompanied by growing emphasis on self and the realization of one's own potential, growth, and actualization. Questions are raised such as 'what is being done to me'; 'what do I have to give up for success?' New responses have introduced a shift in priorities in which 'what happens to me?' ranks above 'how much will you pay me to work here?' and have increased the frequency of the cry that 'I am a thinking person, not a machine element'.

Accompanying these has been the growth of the 'psychology of entitlement', of a new agenda of social and individual rights on which former desires are becoming rights to health, to education, to retirement, to determine where I am going and what is happening to me. These developments have challenged the cult of efficiency and have raised opposition to the implacable unfolding of rationalization, to bureaucratization, to growth for its own sake, and to people becoming the roles they play in carrying out the functions of society.

The third aspect of the changes in values and beliefs centres on differences between college and non-college youth. Although by 1973, the values of college youth have almost all been accepted by non-college youth, some differences pointing to future difficulties are the strengthening of the work ethic among college youth and its weakening among non-college youth, as well as the quiescence of college youth and the growing discontent and dissatisfaction among working class youth (Yankelovich, 1974b). Working youth are exhibiting new attitudes toward work, stressing the quality of life criteria which are remarkably similar to those of college youth. Working youth no longer want just satisfactory pay or job security; they also want the opportunity to do self-rewarding and interesting work. The future concern for society, therefore, lies with the difference in opportunities between college youth who know they 'have it made'—can get into the system and into better jobs—and the majority of non-college youth who face the threat of alienation in the work place though being locked into meaningless jobs.

The growing participation of women in the work force inadvertently poses a threat to non-college workers by undermining the social contract between man and society, which is based on making sacrifices of self for family by bearing the frustrations and emptiness of the work place. A breakdown in this fragile bargain threatens the entire social order, for it binds the social structure together in important ways (see Chapter 1).

Two other trends must also be considered as being of central importance: the decline in population growth to a zero level, and the growth in women's liberation movement. These trends combine to increase both participation of women in the work force and their seeking work for purposes of self-fulfillment. Non-college women have few opportunities to find satisfying fulfilling work, and jobs tend to be the means for making ends meet. These developments may inadvertently threaten the social contract of men whose jobs are just jobs.

Theoretical Changes: From 'Job' to 'Role'

Another influence on current thinking comes from the developments in organization research which instruct us to view organizations as systems, particularly as open socio-technical systems, and jobs as system components (Emery, 1969; Emery and Trist, 1960; Katz and Kahn, 1966). The systems view becomes crucial in complex technical settings, whether the product is goods or services. If access to design of technology is to take place, then the systems position is mandatory; otherwise we are constrained to accept the technology and organization structure as given, thus limiting ourselves to marginal opportunities for design or redesign of jobs. The developments in socio-technical theory have become particularly helpful in analysing the technical systems that underlie work processes of organizations; they have provided the means for joint social and technical systems design. The latter frequently reveal fundamentally different structures of organizational units and jobs.

The consequences of conducting research and design in a systems context are engagements with larger organizational entities, dealing with greater complexity, increasingly dealing with roles of members in the functioning of the organization (or new definition of jobs), and viewing existing (and classic) job designs as comprising only some of the 'tasks' or activities carried out by an organizational member. Both research and practical application to improve the quality of life at the work place create the need to consider role design rather than job design.

Similarly, study or design of larger systems changes the relationship with the organization, inexorably moving toward action research (Davis, Cherns *et al.*, 1975). The slow but growing development of knowledge through action research is helping to support the engagement with organizations for design purposes while adding to our knowledge through research. The methods of action research permit us to relate to an organization as a totality and to its members as real people, confronting the needs of both. In so doing, all issues of who is to participate, how organizations are to learn, how developments are diffused or kept from encapsulation, become prominent. New research and application approaches are needed, particularly in the United States where the current situation is dangerous in the almost complete exclusion of unions from the arena of job and organization design.

Current State of Research

There is an ever-widening gap between what is being learned by direct engage- ment with organizations through action research and the knowledge generated by research in the various academic disciplines. Much of the knowledge gained from action research seems to invert the knowledge acquired from discipline- based research, with its implicit values and arms-length approach to existing situations that lead to the acceptance of technology and organization structures as given. This is not the place to debate the central question of the appropriate methods of research for studying and accumulating reliable knowledge about work organizations and workers. However, it remains a central issue that must be faced, and the sooner the better since so much of the research is done by academicians who are forced into split loyalties—to the subject of their interest, organizations and workers on one hand, and to the academy on the other.

We are at present in a peculiar position: most of our learning is coming from action research and from case studies of changes made in organizations and in jobs. The utility, difficulties, and limitations of these methods of acquiring knowledge have been explored at some length by Davis, Cherns and associates (1975) and by Clark (1975). What is very much needed is to extend as well as refine and strengthen these methods so as to increase the rate at which reliable knowledge can be accumulated. At the same time, action research studies are providing leads that need to be pursued by discipline-based researchers who should become better acquainted with those studies.

The focus on an action research mode of direct engagement with organizations to create new forms of working—providing enhanced relationships between man and work—derives from two central facts about life in the work place. Both of these points do the disservice of adding complication and casting doubt on what we already have accepted as reliable knowledge. The first is that in advanced industrial societies, most if not all organizations, processes and jobs are inventions under constant modification; they are man-made, based on an existing world view or culture (assumptions about what will be successful and about the perceived environment). Any research that treats organizations and jobs as natural entities will tend to provide misleading results. The second fact is that what we are studying or measuring are often the consequences of 'the iron law of adaptation' or the self-fulfilling prophecy. This is particularly clear in studies of job satisfaction. The law of adaptation states that people act out the roles required of them and to a large extent adapt, accommodate or adjust to these circumstances invented by others in which they find themselves. People make the best of the situation, particularly when it does yield material rewards, and other alternatives are either not available or not attainable. Having made the bargain and accepted the various costs to self and family, the situation becomes 'normal' or is expected by those affected. The widespread resigned acceptance in advanced industrial societies of the belief that one must endure a poor quality of life at the work place as a cost of acquiring its material rewards is one example.

The question arises: what do we expect to learn from such situations? If we wish to learn all about adaptation and its costs, we should study existing organizations, technology, and jobs. If, however, we wish to learn how organizations can effectively meet the needs of society and the needs of their members, how human aspirations and potential may be fulfilled, how innovation takes place, how social responsibility evolves, then we must avoid the trap of the iron law of adaptation. And this sets another task for the researcher, moving him into action research; he must first develop organizational structures, technology, and jobs that are based on different concepts and have joint goals of effectiveness and high quality of working life.

To increase the present rate of learning, more organizational experiments must be developed dealing with new forms, roles, relationships and jobs. The many experiments with alternative ways of working that are being conducted in Sweden, in response to the movement for 'industrial democracy', are a noteworthy effort. In this regard, the situation in the United States and United Kingdom is improving because the political and social demands for enhancing the quality of working life have stimulated the growth of a number of demonstration experiments which should aid our opportunities to learn.

If we are to be realistic about man's relation to work, we must recognize that we are dealing with systems consisting of men, technical processes and their machine artifacts, having multiple objectives, satisfying multiple needs, and being embedded in changing environments. This recognition clearly requires us to proceed in research on a systemic basis, focusing on work systems that seek to respond to the environmental forces impinging on the organization.

Thus we must adhere to the higher order 'rule of compatibility or consistency' of all aspects of the work system and environment. Inversely we cannot predict what we will learn nor how valid will be the learning if we proceed by piece-meal examination of favourite relationships, such as man–machine, motivation, enriched or enlarged tasks, autonomy, rewards, shared power, and so forth.

Job design, therefore, has to be viewed as being at the end of the chain, or the ultimate consequence, of a series of choices relating man to the work to be done by an organization in a society. In exploring new ways of working, job content and organization structures have recently been emphasized; this has provided a distorted picture of the reality of life at the work place. At the level of what the worker is asked to do, our examination has to include such factors as meaningfulness, identity, relatedness, wholeness, feedback and closure of the tasks or activities performed. At the level of the relationship between man and organization, our examination has to include maintenance of technical processes and equipment, of organization and individual. And our examination also has to include factors reflected by the response of individuals and groups involving income and equity of income, security of employment, physical working conditions and safety, future careers and opportunities for learning, satisfaction of individual and social needs, individual differences and individuality at the work place, resolution of conflict, organizational goal development, autonomy, power, authority, influence, coercion, political arrangements between worker, union, and management.

The design of new organizations and follow-up developments have taught us the absolute necessity of a systems approach and applying the 'rule of compatibility or consistency' in relation to the above factors. These efforts involve not only the design of jobs, groups, and organization structures, but also the design of the supportive organizational environment. Such compatible support systems have to be designed as pay and reward systems, discipline, entry and advancement rules, authority, responsibility and power distribution, career systems, learning, etc. Failure to do so ultimately leads to distortion of job and group designs.

Another crucial lesson learned from both field studies and new design undertakings at the level of systems is that the job as the 'unit of organization' is not particularly useful for analysis or design. The time has come to abandon the term and the concept of job design, although it is clear-cut and simple, and replace both with 'work system design'. This appreciation came to full flower through a series of attempts to redesign jobs in order to enhance their quality in relation to the many factors noted above. In field experiments, I was very quickly confronted with the proposition that jobs may simply be the prescribed part of the total relationship between man and organization and that each individual undertakes a variety of additional tasks and activities in fulfilling a number of roles necessary for the functioning and maintenance of the organization and its members (Davis and Trist, 1974). Thus in attempting to enhance the quality of life at the work place, there are opportunities for useful change in the content and the structure of roles. Treating the non-job content and structure as 'informal' and the job as 'formal' has proved to be dysfunctional both for the needs of the organization and the individual, and not least for developing an understanding of the organization's functioning. Unremittingly, I have been led to the conclusion that for analysis and design, the appropriate boundary around the individual or group in work organizations includes the full and extended role comprising the full set of tasks and activities performed, be they prescribed, operational, informational, maintenance, improvement, regulatory, or other. However, for both research and design needs, the issue remains how to locate the boundary, that is, how to choose the appropriate 'unit of analysis', so as to identify the comprehensive set of roles undertaken by the individual or group. Experiences of designing new organizations are increasingly providing more complete insight into the factors and systems that affect the choice of boundary.

Still other pieces of learning derived from field experiments begin to approach the specification of the objectives of organization and job design. It is clear that many new designs and organizational experiments that provide effective organizational performance and a high quality of life at the work place seek to satisfy a number of goals. Given social values and the state of technological development, these goals seek to achieve: (a) a self-maintaining social system, that is, one that functions and will continue to function without various forms of external coercion; (b) control of boundary conditions; members of the organizational unit are the regulators and controllers of the work process that produces the planned outcomes, and the role of protecting the boundary between the unit and its environment is undertaken by management; (c) self-developed commitment to goals which appears to grow out of the member's or group's autonomy, self-regulation and control, self-evaluation and feedback, and growth and development; (d) viable futures for the organization's members based on security, knowledge, learning, and paths of movement in the organization; (e) challenge and meaningfulness in the activities to be undertaken; (f) responsible autonomy on the part of members or groups, which includes localized authority(work authority), localized planning, control and regulation; and (g) the means by which members maintain their adaptability and the organization's adaptability to external demands.

A number of dilemmas and requirements are thus posed. Responsible autonomy, self-regulation, localized control and so on all act to shift the boundary of roles to encompass the next higher managerial levels. If one man's job enrichment is not to become another man's job impoverishment, we must include supervision and management within the unit of analysis. Self-regulation and control also shift the role of the supervisor and manager to that of comanaging, that is, providing for development of requisite competence internally and protecting the boundary of the organizational unit by intervening to regulate disturbances in the external environment. Therefore, we cannot concentrate on the design or redesign of workers' jobs without including supervisors' and managers' jobs. The goal of self-maintaining social systems focuses our attention on the need for reducing bureaucracy, on the removal of coercive processes and instruments. This presents a continuing dilemma for continued experimentation in what are still largely autocratic organizations.

Lastly, self-organization and self-development remind us of the universally prevalent phenomenon in large organizations, namely, over-design or over-specification. In accord with the principles of scientific management that organizations are like clockworks and will only operate if they are completely specified, and coupled with bureaucratic practices which seek to specify all relationships, we find that organizational practices and job activities for individuals or groups are almost always completely detailed. To provide such machine perfection, professional groups such as industrial engineers and organizational analysts have evolved to provide the necessary detailed specifications. Unfortunately, some research and application developments directed at forms of organization that support enhanced quality of working life have fallen into the trap of specifying details of tasks and relationships. Such endeavours, though well intended, are coming to be called the 'new Taylorism'. An important research need in support of design of organizations and roles is to study and develop the concept of minimum critical specifications of organization to strengthen self-organization and local adaptation.

Advanced technology alters in radical ways the relationships between man and work and the meaning of work itself as conventionally defined. Recent experiences, not yet reported, in the design of new science-based organizations have shown me that advanced technology provides new opportunities for designing organizations and roles free of the constraints and concepts of scientific management and bureaucracy. Also, advanced technology is much more flexible in providing alternatives for appropriate socio-technical designs. Some of the requirements have been reviewed by Davis (1971b) and Davis and Taylor (1972). Experiments around advanced socio-technical systems are needed to provide new opportunities for learning about organizations, jobs and roles.

Conclusion

The focus of this review has been on recent developments as well as changes in my own thinking about job design, or, more accurately, role design and work systems design. Some of these have derived from field experiments involving redesign and others from the design of new organizations including their technology. A general review of the research findings on jobs, tasks and assignments, which may be found in the literature, is not included. In this sense this paper is a report of the state of the art. To continue learning and remain relevant in face of the needs being voiced in western societies, we must urgently develop more demonstration-experiments of different ways of working. That will require more researchers who engage in action research models, procedures, information exchange, and common and acceptable methods of measurement. Such experiments will provide the means for studying worker behaviour in settings free of the constraints and dogma of industrial-era organizations. This paper has indicated that we are suffering from the unintentionally misleading outcomes of research that has focused only on the work process and its tasks assigned as jobs. The concept that should be the focus of our inquiries is role development and work system development, rather than job design. Future studies will have to include technology design together with organization design as parts of joint socio-technical systems.

References

Clark, A. W. (1975). *Experience in Action Research*, Jossey Bass.

Davis, L. E. (1971a). Job satisfaction research: the post-industrial view, *Industrial Relations*, **10**, 176–193.

Davis, L. E. (1971b). The coming crisis for production management: technology and organization, *International Journal of Production Research*, **9**, 65–82.

Davis, L. E. and Canter, R. R. (1955). Job design, *Journal of Industrial Engineering*, **6** (1), 6.

Davis, L. E., Cherns, A. B. and associates (1975). *Quality of Working Life: Cases and Commentary*, The Free Press.

Davis, L. E. and Taylor, J. C. (eds.) (1972). *Design of Jobs*, Penguin.

Davis, L. E. and Trist, E. L. (1974). Improving the quality of work life: sociotechnical case studies. In J. O'Toole (ed.), *Work and the Quality of Life*, Massachusetts Institute of Technology Press.

Emery, F. E. (ed.) (1969). *Systems Thinking*, Penguin.

Emery, F. E. and Trist, E. L. (1960). Socio-technical systems. In C. W. Churchman and E. L. Trist (eds.), *Management Science Models and Techniques*, volume 2, Pergamon Press.

Katz, D. and Kahn, R. L. (1966). *Social Psychology of Organizations*, Wiley.

Williamson, D. T. N. (1972). The anachronistic factory, *Proceedings of the Royal Society*, A331, 139–160.

Yankelovich, D. (1974a). The meaning of work. In J. M. Rosow (ed.), *The Worker and the Job*, Prentice-Hall.

Yankelovich, D. (1974b). *Changing Youth Values in the 70's*, McGraw-Hill.

6
Beyond Organization Development?

Leopold S. Vansina
International Institute for Organizational and Social Development, Kessel-Lo, Belgium

To most of us, social scientists, practitioners or interested laymen, organization development (OD) is a very ambiguous concept, referring to a variety of activities and social science interventions in organizations. This was clearly communicated in the excellent American review by Friedlander and Brown (1974), which examines publications bearing on the various techno-structural and human processual approaches to the improvement of task accomplishment and human fulfilment in organizations. It is not my intention to do the same work over again, nor to add to their study those European works which have not been published in English. Instead the field of organization development will be approached from a discussion of the organization and its environment, and then through a description of some essential aspects and strategies relevant to organization development.

This approach has been carefully considered. Firstly, my socio-cultural background and biases will come, inevitably, to the surface in the course of this chapter. But they will appear in relation to a concrete field and not as an abstract or academic subject. Thereby, one can avoid making the invalid assumption that there are homogeneous groups of social scientists living in clear-cut geographical areas in the Western world and one can circumvent sterile, ethnocentric discussions or arguments between European and American scientists. The selected approach provides, however, sufficient ground for exploration of the impact and relevance of society upon the orientation and work of the social scientist.

Secondly, a discussion of the organization in relation to its environment provides a frame of reference necessary to distinguish anachronistic or senti-mental values (e.g., blind obedience) from those that presently arise 'as a human response to persisting areas of relevant uncertainty' (Emery and Trist, 1972, p. 68) and become effective guides to behaviour. Furthermore, a deeper understanding of the organization in relation to its environment enables us to work with parts of the organization, as sub-systems which must be kept open to their internal and external environments. And, indeed, the social scientist is mostly working with sub-systems, since the whole organization can seldom be approached in its totality, for sheer reasons of size, and for the overwhelming uncertainties and anxieties (turbulence) that such an approach would create.

Finally, it is hoped that this approach will sharpen our awareness that organizations cannot just be conceived as open systems struggling for survival in a hostile or turbulent environment, but as purposeful institutions in society.

The Organization and Its Environment

Approaches which refer to adaptations or (sometimes) changes in organizations in relation to their environments are of several kinds. Examples are participation and industrial democracy, techno-structural interventions, job structuring and design, work organization; and human processual interventions, such as team building and intergroup relations development. They appear to be necessary—but not always conscious—adaptations or changes to increase the chances of organizational survival in a turbulent environment.

Many social scientists have emphasized, described, or analysed the rate and nature of these changes within the organization itself and in the environment (Bennis, 1966; Lawrence and Lorsch, 1967; Schon, 1971; Touraine, 1969; Burns and Stalker, 1961; Emery and Trist, 1965, 1972), to an extent that it almost becomes redundant to review their major conclusions. Nevertheless it is often surprising how many social scientists and academics still seem to be operating with a narrow frame of reference or 'appreciative system' as Vickers (1968) calls it. The widespread appreciative system is one which is more open to new OD technologies and superficial research projects than to the complex realities of organizations, their environment and society at large. Consequently, it is still relevant to summarize the major developments and influences affecting our existence.

The turbulent environment

The dominant characteristic of our society is the complexity of the environment. The dynamic properties arise not only from the interactions between organizations, but from the environment itself. The complexity is so high and the dynamic processes so unpredictable that authors like Emery and Trist (1972) wonder whether 'individual systems can, by their own efforts, successfully

83

adapt to them' (p. 53). Nevertheless some kind of adaptation to the environment is a *conditio sine qua non* for survival for any living (biological or social) system. Four trends have been identified by Emery and Trist as contributing influences to this turbulence: (a) the growth of organizations and their interrelatedness; (b) the increasing interdependency between economic and other facets of society; (c) the reliance upon scientific research and development; and (d) the tremendous increase in the speed, scope and capacity of communication.

Some expressions of turbulence and rapid changes

Under the title 'Theory deserts the forecasters', *Business Week* (1974, June 29) discussed inaccuracies and difficulties of present economic forecasts based on 200-years' economic thinking. According to this review, leading social scientists are aware that the economic foundations upon which their forecasting is based are too narrow and insubstantial and that they need to draw on political science, sociology, and psychology as well as on economics' own tradition. Only then will we be able to explain the present frightening world of inflation, shortages and international repercussions.

The economic lifetime of products becomes smaller and smaller. The time required for the diffusion of major technological innovations is shrinking from 150 to 200 years in the case of the steam engine to about 15 years for the transistor. Individuals are consequently forced to adapt themselves—consciously or unconsciously—several times during their lives to these technological developments and their requirements (Schon, 1971).

Besides this economic and technological turbulence, people are confronted with socio-political unrest, often expressed in divergent attitudes towards business, work and organizational membership. Although these socio-political changes in mentality and attitude are most visible among younger people, they are not at all restricted to the younger generation. Their parents as well as older colleagues are increasingly being affected by their thoughts and concerns. The socio-political unrest is thereby diffused into society where it is reaching centres of influence and decision taking.

This younger generation has been raised in a climate of relative political, social and economic security but faces now a world with a frightening and, most of all, with an unpredictable future. Three features of their attitudes may be highlighted.

Attitudes towards business. The younger generation is not a homogeneous group. Nevertheless, the traditional lifegoals, like progress, social advancement, wealth, are no longer unanimously accepted as they once were. Business corporations are criticized for pursuing huge profits, for their attitude towards minority groups and developing countries, and for a lack of respect for the sovereignty of nations. Yet youth is not so much interested in more prosperity as in fairness, well-being and prosperity for more people (Athos, 1970).

Attitudes towards work. Different trends can be identified in the attitude towards work. A first trend is most clearly expressed by the spokesmen of the 'Internationale Situationniste' in France, but it is equally present in other parts of Europe and the United States. These spokesmen are no longer searching for organizational structures that stimulate or allow their members to grow and to realize themselves. Certainly the existing power structure must be destroyed, but most of all *the value* of productive work must be questioned. The technological civilization has pushed the value of work to the extreme of being something sacred, something that eventually would liberate mankind. In contrast with Marxism, which believes in the constructive value of work but fights against the exploitation of it, they oppose the values that underlie work. Productive work according to them should be devalued, should be reduced to the strict minimum in order to enable people to become free and involved in a new type of free and creative activities (*'des activités ludiques'*) (Gombin, 1971).

A second group of people basically accepts the economic and social values of work, but tries to create organizational structures that allow people to develop themselves on the job or at least lead to the improvement of the quality of working life.

Finally, there is a third category of people that for a variety of reasons passively accepts the present situation with the entailing benefits and costs. The benefits are a relatively high income, freedom from responsibility through the close specification of jobs and work methods, the bureaucracy of organizations, the power struggles between unions and managements, the social security laws and the practice of the medical profession. On the other hand the costs are alienation of work, of oneself and of society.

Attitudes towards membership. The quality of organizational membership is changing. This becomes evident in the high rate of turnover or of so-called 'sickness' absences. Organizations seem to lose their power of providing a desirable identity and meaning to their employees. There is a growing number of individuals who are willing to work for an organization but on their terms and without becoming a committed member. Their psychological contract is quite clear. They are willing to work even with devotion for so many hours a day, but nothing more; they do not accept the values or the final objectives of the organization at all. This kind of qualitative marginal membership allows them to be at the same time, for example, a manager of a profit centre and a communist.

Maladaptations of social systems to turbulent environments

On the level of social system, Emery and Trist (1972), following Angyal (1941), describe three passive adaptations or maladaptations to the overwhelming complexity of the environment.

1. *Superficiality* which is achieved by denying the deeper roots of common humanity and individual alienation from oneself. This can be observed from the

way someone deals with issues of developing countries, social classes, ethnic groups etc., and from the desire to take part repeatedly in a variety of temporary closed systems, in which the individual through pseudo-psychological or pseudo-religious means, or drugs, can escape from his deeper psychological roots and concerns into a Nirvana. The latter aspect comes clearly to the surface in books like *Turning On*, by Rasa Gustaitis (1969), and in the variety of brochures announcing the latest sensitizing, energizing and mystifying programmes.

2. *Segmentation* of the parts of social systems, through which the parts are enabled to pursue their own ends without respect to the total system. The reaction of the European Common Market to the recent 'oil crisis', may be a good example of segmentation into individual nations as an escape from the complexity of the different bilateral relations with the Arab countries and diverse national interests. One may wonder to what extent the so-called polarization of trade unions is not another example of segmentation, where unions become more exclusively engaged in social claims without economic consideration (Touraine, 1969).

3. *Dissociation* is more an individual response to complexity, whereby the individual human being withdraws from his fellow human beings to escape the growing unpredictability of what might follow or what might be expected from him if he relates to them. 'Stay away!', 'Don't get involved!', 'Be yourself and don't let yourself be influenced by others!' are suggestions which one hears more and more. The willingness to develop relationships, in which there is a continuous but also changing pattern of 'give and take', of coordinating behaviour, appears to be in steady decline, while qualitative marginal membership is spreading.

Purposeful adaptations of organizations

Emery, Trist, Ackoff and others distinguish passive from active adaptations. The former type denotes changes in the organization to perform more efficiently in a changing environment, while the latter type refers to organizational adaptations directed to change its environment 'so that its own present or future behaviour is more efficient' (Ackoff, 1970, p. 18). Since both types of adaptations are often combined, I prefer to talk about constructive adaptations. These are adaptations, consciously or unconsciously directed to increase the chances of survival of the organization in a complex, changing environment.

I wish now to analyse and review the basic properties and activities that organizations need to develop in order to survive, so that adaptive approaches such as job design and organization development can be better integrated in the crucial overall problem of vital and meaningful transactions between organizations and their environment. It will become evident that the present state of knowledge in this field is still rather limited. Furthermore, that the developments of the 'desired' organizational properties or activities meet, in practice, a lot of obstacles because they often run counter to systemic maladaptations and socio-political developments.

Increasing the scope of reaction and action possibilities. In order to deal with the uncertainty and unpredictability of the environment, Ackoff has advocated responsiveness planning for organizations. 'Such planning is directed towards designing an organization and a system for managing it that can quickly detect deviations from the expected and respond to them effectively. Hence responsiveness planning consists of building responsiveness and flexibility into an organization' (Ackoff 1970, p. 17). It is no longer sufficient to develop this type of responsiveness to deviations or to new information (Schon, 1971) in only one part or sub-system of the organization. Indeed, each sub-system interprets its internal and external environment and processes in its own systemic way. Consequently, no sub-system is able to fulfill this function for the total system, especially when the system operates in an overwhelmingly complex and changing environment. In practice this means that all sub-systems (members in a variety of organizational positions, but especially those who hold boundary positions) should take responsibility for detection of deviations and of new information, and for reacting in appropriate ways.

The best, or at least the most acceptable way in our Western culture to build in responsiveness is by increasing redundancy of functions of the individual parts, ideally within each member of the organization (Emery and Trist, 1972; van Beinum, 1972). Herbst's (1970) new design philosophy gives some idea how this can be achieved. He has suggested that the structuring and functioning of organizations should not be based on total specification design but on minimal critical specification design. On the individual level this means that only the essential aspects of the job are defined. The individual is thereby granted time and possibilities to explore and specify further his role and responsibilities and to develop his abilities even if these may not be of use in the present situation or foreseeable future.

Flexibility in allocation of resources. If one succeeds in a developing a rich repertoire of reaction and action possibilities, the organization needs to acquire the appropriate flexibility in structure and resource allocation to make optimal use of this increased responsiveness. Some organizations have spontaneously created 'task-forces', 'project teams' or 'matrix organizations' to improve and to speed up the allocation of resources. Schon (1971) has suggested various types of networks that through the interconnectedness of the parts with one another (rather than through a centre) enhance organizational responsiveness and the emergence of required resources. One question stands out however: how much flexibility can a social system tolerate before it faces disintegration? More precisely, how often can one leave and enter temporary systems, and how much uncertainty can a human being cope with?

The search for commitment and shared values. The two previous organizational properties lose most, if not all, of their effectiveness if the organization does not succeed simultaneously in obtaining commitment from the parts and the individual members. But commitment is a gift, which is made when the objectives and modes of behaviour of the organization match a member's own goals and values (Trist, 1970). Since objectives (personal and organizational), values and opinions about what is meaningful, fair and right, change (even within the lifetime of an individual), the search for shared values, for a reasonable balance between individual and organization, requires a continual managerial effort. And as the maintenance of the conditions upon which commitment rests is an ongoing process, so is the search for commitment.

The creation and management of learning systems. Many social scientists have drawn attention to continual learning as a primary requirement for human and social systems to survive in a turbulent or rapidly changing environment. It appears that this continual learning should take place on at least two levels.

(i) On the individual level, members should be able to learn about their own functioning, their own management or other practices, as well as about the reasons for this functioning or practices.
(ii) On the sub-system and system level, it should be possible to gain understanding of the internal and external processes and how the boundary conditions are managed, as well as understanding the reasons for existence of the sub-systems and the total system in their environment.

Learning at both levels can, however, no longer rely exclusively on the rational/experimental model. As Schon has put it: '... we are largely unable to "know" in situations of social change, if the criteria of knowledge are those of the rational/experimental model' (1971, p. 201). Learning under these conditions seems to be based on understanding the present situation, which means identifying (a) the relevant forces or parts operating in a social field, (b) their interrelatedness, and (c) the relations between the relations of these forces or parts.

While these forces are multiple and most often in flux, one has to rely more and more on the experience of the situation in the here-and-now, and the understanding of this experience. The latter implies that the here-and-now includes its historical development, which reveals at the same time its developmental trends. Without this time dimension, the attribution of meaning is made impossible.

This type of learning through understanding, on which one comes to rely in conditions of high complexity and rapid social change, does not allow accurate predictions of future developments or generalizations to other social fields. 'The learning agent must be willing and able to make the leaps required in existential knowledge. These are the leaps from informational overload to the first formulation of the problem, from an absence of theory to convergence on a design for public action, and from the experience of one situation to its use as a projective model in the next instance' (Schon, 1971, p. 235).

Since organizations have objectives and activities which are different from those of learning systems, they must have different systemic properties. Consequently, the organization has to design ways and means to move in and out of the learning system into the work system. A first enabling condition is the development of a learning mentality characterized by an interest in learning from experience and in the understanding of the experience, and a broad frame of reference including a socio-technical view on organizations, their environment and society at large. Secondly, one must have gained competence in managing the transition from a 'work system' into a 'learning system', in both time and space. Timing is important. If one moves into a learning system too late one is tempted to become involved in too much retrospective analysis, with a likely reduction of attention to the experience in the here-and-now and with an entailing loss of relevance for the future. If one moves in too fast, before the situation has fully presented itself, one is likely to miss the relevant data and most of all the process.

The importance of space has been described previously by the present author (Vansina, 1974) and others (e.g., Zand, 1974). Briefly, the relevant parts (sub-systems, persons in roles) must be present or represented and the subsequent explorations or confrontations must take place in a 'collegium' where everyone can contribute from his organizational position and background, where one can analyse and reflect without jumping into decision taking, and without the interference of formal authority and power, proper to the work system.

Thirdly, one must be able to make appropriate use of existing management practices and techniques. This often presupposes an adjustment of these techniques to generate information that is as well suited for learning as for controlling. Planning, for example, provides an ideal situation for understanding how the system is functioning in relation to its environment. It is, in my understanding, exactly this that Ackoff underlined while writing: '... the principal value of planning does not lie in the plans that it produces but in the process of producing them' (Ackoff 1970, p. 15).

So far we have described four organizational properties or activities that have arisen as constructive adaptations to survive in a turbulent environment. From this it may appear that organizational survival is the ultimate goal that justifies all types of actions and the mobilization of all efforts. I do not believe this and have already indicated that learning for improvement through simple feedback on the functioning of the parts or the total system is no longer sufficient. Learning should as well include understanding the reasons for existence of the parts and of the total system. Survival of an organization cannot, therefore, simply be recommended without an evaluation of its possible costs and benefits for society, even for the world at large. In other words, the survival of organizations must be studied in a framework of social planning and ecology, and organizational death or discontinuity, however painful, cannot be excluded as alternatives (Barrel, 1973).

Certainly, many social scientists will argue and find evidence that an appropriate concern for corporate social responsibility is a sign of good management and an aid to survival (Bowman, 1974). Others will continue to advocate that task accomplishment (or productivity) and human values can be integrated if you adopt this or another leadership or management style or that these divergent goals can be made compatible through OD-technologies. All this appears to be, however, a response to a simplified social field, a passive defence against its complexity. The pretended integration of productivity and social responsibility, concern for production and concern for people, performance and human satisfaction does not press for choice in a particular culture of politics and protestant ethics. It fosters avoidance, instead of pressing for conscious choices and responsible optimalizations between economic progress and social responsibility, between productivity and human or social values, between performance and satisfaction.

It is clear that the role of organizations, private and public, is in the process of redefinition. New linkages between private and public organizations and their environment need to be activated, leading to increased interdependencies and changes in priorities and values. But the understanding and the technology for the development of these constructive linkages, and the necessary change in organizational priorities and values has yet to be acquired and implemented. Up till then, we are only entitled to talk about organizational adaptations and not about institutional change.

Organization Development

The preceding discussions made it clear that my views on organization development have been modified over time. Organization development is a learning strategy, including interventions from a variety of disciplines, aiming at developing the necessary organizational properties and activities to enable the organization to become a purposeful institution which can responsibly perceive, react and act, learn and choose. The learning strategy can, at least initially, be directed towards parts (for instance an individual in role, an aggregate or a sub-system) but always in relation to its social field. Eventually, however, a genuinely effective and responsible learning strategy must deal with the total system, or the organization in relation to its environment and society.

Before discussing some fundamental characteristics of this strategy, it may be useful to look at the requirements and conflicts that such a conception of organization development raises for any person involved in this field, be he internal or external consultant, manager or non-manager.

Conflicts and fields of tension of the social scientist

In our present society the social scientist or any person active in the field can no longer remain neutral in the face of the social, economic and political developments. This is not only because science loses its neutrality in its application. Indeed, it becomes political, in so far as it is always being applied with some implicit or explicit objectives in mind. But more so, because neutrality of the social scientist means alienation from society, and it is difficult to conceive how an alienated person can help others, individuals or organizations, to deal with their alienation, and how he can contribute to developing organizational properties, enabling learning and conscious choice. Even the so-called 'neutral' social scientist is political, in the sense that he rides along with the prevailing sets of priorities. Would it be far astray to say that the predominant sets of priorities in our Western culture make us interpret national and international developments, with their social, economic and ideological implications, in predominantly economic terms?

The social scientist must have come to some understanding and choice *vis à vis* these developments, but he cannot impose his understanding, choices and values on his client. Certainly, in situations of unstability and overcomplexity, where one is confronted with the limits of knowledge, one is tempted to revert to power-play or ideology. Power-play becomes the substitute for inquiry. 'It makes the political dimension of inquiry the exclusive one and treats inquiry itself as a cover or rationale for the resolutions achieved through dominance' (Schon, 1971, p. 228). This approach is, for example, clearly analysed by Pettigrew (1975), and without question it is often practiced. Or one appeals to ideology, a closed theory that is 'held as right, inherently and once-and-for-all' (Schon, 1971, p. 228). These ideologies may be marxistic, capitalistic liberal or technocratic, they provide the priorities and the answers, and thereby certainty where there is none.

> The social scientist has to live and to work with the internal conflict between his personal values and priorities and his respect for the values and priorities of the client.*

In my work in the field, I have encountered another conflict, between planning change or organizational flexibility on the one hand, and the search for stability on the other hand. Apathy, loss of identity and a recoil to rigid individualism are well known individual reactions to too frequent changes. Nevertheless, the social system is often required to respond to changes or variance in the technical system. Sudden changes in market demands, price controls, or price speculation on basic materials are absorbed by moving people from one workgroup or setting to another. Often these changes are necessary for survival, but one has to search for ways and means to maintain minimal stability for the health of the individual members and to protect the integration of the total system. Curiously enough, the search for stability often meets as much resistance as the planning of change. Unfortunately, however, not much attention is yet given to the search

---

* 'Client' is used here to denote the person, the sub-system or total system towards which the learning strategy is directed. It does not refer at all to the legal client, the sponsor, the person or group who gives the assignment to an internal or external consultant.

for stability within the organization and within the environment, as has been indicated earlier.

The social scientist, or any person active in this field, must be able to optimize consciously the divergent requests for change and flexibility and for stability and continuity.

The development of the learning strategy is more often than not initiated because the client, or someone in charge, has identified some difficulty or conflict that endangers the functioning of a part or a sub-system, or the survival of the organization. Usually, the client or the sponsor has not only some idea about the nature of the issue, but also about the kind of desired solution, or ways of improvements. The social scientist may, however, have a different opinion about the nature, scope and depth of the problem, as well as about what kind of approach or action seems to be most appropriate, or how the organization can or should be developed. He may even arrive at the conclusion that the client's view about the nature of the issue or about the desired action is itself an essential part of the overall problem. Nevertheless, he has to work from where the client is, while exploring at the same time the validity of his own views and assumptions. The discrepancy between these two levels, reflecting two states of being, must not be too great or collaboration becomes impossible. And this may indeed be a reality he has to face.

The social scientist must be able to operate simultaneously on two levels, and in an entailed field of tension, stemming from the client's state of being and his own professional state.

These three intra-personal conflicts are part and parcel of any person active in this field of work in organizations. They need to be understood, and one has to learn to handle and to live with them.

Essential characteristics of the learning strategy

The reader may have been surprised that the three major conflicts or fields of tension of the consultant have been described as internal realities and not as conflicts between the social scientist and the client whose outcome is determined by the existing power constellation. Without denying the existence of power, I do believe that too often these internal conflicts or fields of tension are externalized, or projected into the interaction between consultant and client. They consequently come to distort and muddle unduly the relationship between client and social scientist. Only when these conflicts are recognized as internal can they be properly handled, leaving the social scientist more free to develop a consultative relationship. In this section three main features of such a learning process will be examined.

(1) *The learning strategy is designed in a consultative (collaborative) relation-*

ship between the client and the consultant. This type of relationship is 'one of joint effort, where there is mutual determination of goals, and in which each party (client and consultant) has equal opportunity to influence the other' (Clark, 1972, p. 79).

It is a relationship in which competences and expectations can be checked, in which the relevance and consequences of various approaches and actions can be explored. But most of all, it is relationship in which one can search for shared values and joint responsibility for learning and outcomes.

The consultative model differs markedly from the interventions of traditional management and organizational consultants. For instance, it differs from the 'Engineering model' discussed by Gouldner (1961). In this model, the consultant accepts the client's definition of the issue or assignment, and collects and analyses the requested lacking information (as an engineer would design, purchase or build the required machinery). The consultant typically presents a report to the client which includes the compiled information, his conclusions and recommendations. The definition of the issues, the objectives of the intervention are not jointly defined, nor are the facts and data worked through with the client. Consequently, the reports usually end up on a forgotten shelf.

The consultative model also differs from the 'Peritus model' proposed by O'Connell (1968) and described by Clark (1972) as a relationship in which the consultant initially diagnoses the organization, supervises a number of pilot tests, and later uses his authority of expertise and 'the power of facts and rational argument to gain commitment to change' (p. 82).

The Engineering and Peritus models are neither designed for learning, nor for planning change, but for planned change and *ad hoc* problem solving. Some social scientists, for instance Harrison, claim that the consultative relationship is a cover developed by the consultant behind which he really operates either according to a Resistance-oriented model or a Client-oriented model. Therefore the consultant should reject the consultant model and declare himself to be working with one or the other. In the Resistance-oriented model, the consultant really decides on the appropriate goals of the intervention and not the client. However, the consultant attempts to gain acceptance for his goals from the client, through a variety of means like coercion, manipulation, persuasion and charisma. In the Client-oriented model the consultant searches to discover what the goals of the client are, and where his 'free energy' is available to work with. It is the client who decides what the objectives of the intervention are and not the consultant.

Such a rejection of the consultative model is based upon misunderstanding of the power relationship and the essence of a relationship itself. Power relations in this field, as in most other fields nowadays, are characterized by reciprocity and hence also possibilities for negotiation or even voluntary decision not to use power at all. The consultative relationship does not imply equal power for both consultant and client at all times, but a relationship in which power can be made visible. One of the characteristics of power is that it is most often invisible. Although both parties have the responsibility to make the power structure visible, it is most often the social scientist who, through his professional education and role responsibilities, takes the initiative. But making power visible is in itself an act of power. This power stems from the clarification of the process (relationship), the interpretation of reality, leading to a reduction of uncertainty (Laing, 1967). The problem lies not in taking or in submitting to power, but in the internal personal strength to clarify openly the power situation. Such a clarification is essential, both for the further development of a collaborative relationship and for understanding the system. It is a necessary condition to obtain commitment for a joint effort and to take joint responsibility for the determination of the goals and means of the intervention.

The consultative relationship, like any other relationship, is something to be achieved. In the process of developing collaboration one partner may at one point in time have more influence than the other. For example, the client may have a clear idea of what issue he wishes to work on with the consultant. The latter, however, may genuinely see the issue to be a different one, and therefore feel responsible to explore with the client for what reasons, rational or irrational, conscious or unconscious, he has defined the issue and the means of intervening in that particular way. The entailing discussion then becomes a mutual search for· understanding of the functional value of the resistances of client and consultant, and how the respective internal conflicts are handled, so that both are able to make conscious decisions.

The fact that the realization of a consultative relationship is difficult does not mean that it should be rejected. The two other alternatives, Resistance-oriented and Client-oriented models, are dichotomies of a relationship in which one of the parties, consultant or client, accepts that he will be manipulated by the other.

The importance of the consultative relationship, however difficult to achieve, cannot be underestimated. Firstly, it ensures that the organization development process moves forward organically and not mechanically, with understanding and respect for existing opinions and values related to work and organizational life. It ensures that these are not repressed, nor overruled by manipulation or sheer coercive power. It is exactly in this area that many projects of job-structuring and design and work organization have failed. Changes have been imposed because it was felt that they were good for the employee or the organization without appropriate consultation and preparation of the people whose work, interests, habits and identity were affected.

Secondly, the consultative relationship allows the various parties involved (consultant, management, unions and employees) to explore and define areas of activities where their divergent objectives and interests (organizational flexibility, economic progress, social responsibility, performance, satisfaction and so on) are compatible and where there is room for joint optimization.

Thirdly, it guarantees that organization development maintains its link with the actual organization and its environment, including society, which together form the dynamic field of action within which the learning strategy is to be realized. Models for an ideal organization or an ideal society have their value as goals, but they can not be imposed.

In the consultative relationship a psychological contract is worked out between client and consultant after mutual expectations, competences and tolerance for uncertainty and stress have been explored. This contract should include, according to Argyris (1972):

(a) the right and the possibility to collect valid and relevant information which,
(b) must enable the client or client system to make free but considerate choices, and
(c) to obtain internal commitment to implement decisions resulting from joint effort.

Furthermore, the psychological contract should include the mutually achieved determination of (a) the goals of the learning strategy, (b) the nature and the depth of the intervention, (c) the commitment to interpret and learn from the data, and (d) some basis for continuity in efforts and learning. Such a contract is neither static, nor completely defined at the outset of the intervention. It needs inevitably to be completed, adjusted or even terminated within the consultative relationship.

2. *The learning strategy is an integration or at least a combination of various disciplines.* Reviewing the definition of organization development of the leading American social scientists (Beckhard, 1969; Bennis, 1969; Lippitt, 1969; Hornstein, Bunker and Burke, 1971) and their European pupils, it is tempting to conclude that they aim exclusively at the improvement of the social system (interpersonal, group and inter-group relations) based on experiential learning and the social sciences (the human processual approach). They seem to conceive the organization as a social system in which technology and economics are to be taken as fixed and unchangeable factors. The progress of technology being inexorable, the human factor in organizations is seen as almost the only one that can be influenced.

Those other American and European social scientists, such as Davis (1957), Emery and Thorsrud (1969), and Thorsrud (1972) who have been largely influenced by the pioneering work of the Tavistock Institute, take technological and task characteristics into account; they do not talk about organization development, but about job design, the organization of work, industrial democracy, etc. Both sets of approaches, the techno-structural and the human processual approach, appear to complement one another conceptually. In practice however one approach is, for one reason or another, preferred over another, or they are used in random sequence. This can leave great holes in the development of the organization, and confusion and frustration in the people concerned.

Leavitt's (1964) suggestion that organizational change can be approached through any of the interrelated factors of Task (including objectives and priorities), Structure, Technology and People has not had the expected impact, partly because it is always an abstract and simplified model of reality. Leavitt rightly underlines the interrelatedness of these factors, but interrelatedness does not mean that a change in one factor leads automatically to modifications in the other factors. Only the social system is able to make conscious choices to adapt or to change itself and/or the other set of factors, Task, Technology and Structure. The extent to which the social system has power or control over the other sets of factors varies from one situation to another. For example, in a packaging department the people working with the concrete objectives (number of products to be packed per day), the packing equipment, the set structure of the work force and the work are influenced by all these factors over which they themselves have no control. The objectives may be set by production and marketing; the technological specifications are made by the engineering department or by an outside machine manufacturing company. The people concerned may change the structural aspects (e.g., develop teams), resulting in a mismatch of structure and technology. In other words, if the controlling influence is unequally distributed amongst the set of factors in a concrete sub-system, tension will be building up within that sub-system, eventually leading to a reestablishment of the old *status quo* or a disintegration of the system.

It is evident in this example that the unit of intervention cannot be the packaging department, but must include those persons who have a controlling influence over the other variables. Otherwise any intervention in that subsystem is bound to focus only on the people, with the results described above. The inclusion of all persons who together have a controlling influence over the four sets of factors in the unit of intervention does not lead to an automatic change in the factors and their influence pattern either, but it does lead to conscious choices. The importance of conscious choice or optimalization is not highlighted in Leavitt's work, but in the work of the Tavistock Institute through the concept of an open socio-technical system (Trist *et al.*, 1963).

In the integrated approach, whether one uses the improved model of Leavitt, or the open socio-technical system model, all sets of factors and their interactions are studied and are part of the social scientist's frame of reference. Without this frame of reference, the social scientist runs the risk of seeing opposition or hesitations in the social sub-system as 'resistance to change' while being actually confronted with the shadow of the technical sub-system. Indeed, the technical sub-system cannot talk directly, but its influence on the social sub-system is indirectly expressed by the persons in it. If the social scientist does not understand this, he is likely to chase the shadow of the rabbit, but not the rabbit. In other words, his intervention is focussing on the wrong sets of factors, and his relationship with the client becomes defence-analytic rather than one of understanding.

A specific intervention may however focus on one or more sets of factors, or more on the technical or on the social sub-system. The amount of weight given a particular set of factors depends on:

(a) the assessment of its respective influence on the actual difficulties, or inappropriate state of optimization;

(b) the assessment of the interaction pattern of the variables; and

(c) the need to give additional weight through the intervention to one or more sets of factors to reach a level of more appropriate optimization.

The social scientist who uses the integrated approach is working by preference with internal resources from various disciplines, in a kind of project team. The function of this project team, often called a working party, is two-fold, firstly to provide a group in which different disciplinary approaches, interests and values can be recognized and worked through so that a kind of integration, based on shared values, can be achieved; and secondly to lay a basis for continuity of the work when the social scientist is not available or has terminated that particular assignment.

The question often raised in this respect is what and how much the social scientist needs to know about the various disciplines, in terms of technology, economics, socio-political sciences. In my opinion, the social scientist has to know the implications of technological, economic and socio-political requirements for the social system in terms of constraints and possibilities. This does not mean that he needs to be a multidisciplinarian, but that he has sufficient education (a) to raise questions about the overall process of interacting sets of variables under normal conditions and in possible critical circumstances, and (b) to understand the sub-objectives, concerns and cognitive maps of the various disciplines, to be able to mediate between these various cultures and search for their integration.

3. *The learning strategy focuses on understanding and planning change and not so much on planned change.* Organization development has been strongly linked to, if not identified with planned change. Requests for assistance or so-called 'OD projects' are most often motivated by experienced or anticipated difficulties in introducing planned change. The over-emphasis on planned change has led to *ad hoc* interventions, disconnectedness of efforts, without much success and learning. Disconnected changes can be as much a defence against the overwhelming complexity of reality as bureauracy can be in our present environment—a defence around which client and consultant often collude. The first maintains his management-by-crisis culture and the latter can make a living on superficial, 'instant relief' interventions.

The question is not simply 'change or no change?', but a search for an answer to a set of interrelated questions like:

(a) Change for what *purposes*?

(b) Change for *whose* purposes?

(c) Change with which *means*? and

(d) What are the *costs* and *consequences* of these intended changes?

These questions can only be answered when one has gained an understanding of the structure, the function and the functioning of a particular system in its environment. Without satisfactory answers, the social scientist makes himself vulnerable to political manipulations whereby he becomes the agent to maintain the *status quo* within superficial adaptation processes. But the answers confront the consultant with his professional values and press for choice: to take or not to take the assignment under those conditions?

Not much seems to be known about planning change as a continual effort. From professional experience, I can mention a few points:

(a) Understanding and planning change are interdependent processes. Without understanding the complexity of the present situation, the planning of change is meaningless and without direction.

(b) Planning change should be linked to the search for stability, the search for shared values within and outside the organization, and the search for continuity, so that change can acquire developmental or growth characteristics.

(c) Planning change includes the development and revision of two strategies: a strategy for the development of internal competences and shared values, and a strategy for continuity in the process and diffusion of competences and shared values.

(d) It includes counselling work with members of the organization. The turbulence in the external world seems to reactivate unconscious processes within groups and individuals with disturbing consequences. The continual learning and the search for shared values confronts the individual with the changing relevance of his work, skills and competences, or even his profession, and he has internal conflicts between principles, values and behaviour.

Much more needs to be learned about planning change. At present, we know more about the destructiveness of disconnected planned change efforts, by which the social system is led to believe that after this one change there will be stability.

In search of strategies for organizational work

Organization development cannot be conceived as a series of unconnected OD projects, but as a continual effort to understand and learn from the dynamic interactions between systems and their environment. Since this requires a long term commitment from the organization, various strategies or models are being developed to guide the introduction and diffusion of organization development within a specific social system.

Van Dongen (1971) has described three strategies based on three different models of organizations.

1. *The classic American model.* This model has been advocated by Beckhard (1969), when he defined organization development as a planned effort to improve the effectiveness and the health of the organization that is guided from the top. The 'top-down' strategy, is congruent with the more traditional conception of organizations. Indeed, structuralists place the responsibility

for controlling and directing the organization at the top of the hierarchy. This strategy, which coincides with the classic distribution of power still prevailing in many organizations, appears to be the most effective, according to the American research data, reviewed by Friedlander and Brown (1974). It is also the dominant strategy for most job enrichment projects, in which the power is not allowed to be questioned.

2. *The social action model.* This model is most often used in industrial democracy, work structuring and projects aiming at the improvement of the quality of working life. The interventions focus on the bottom of the hierarchy. The roles and responsibilities of the next higher level are modified on the basis of the understanding gained at the lowest level. Proposals for change are usually submitted for approval to a steering committee with representatives of several hierarchical levels, often with representatives of the unions.

To my knowledge, this model has, up till now, only been adopted with the formal agreement of top management. There are, however, indications in certain countries that the works council will acquire the right not only to decide on consultancy issues and organizational changes, but also to appoint consultants.

The advantage of this model is that the understanding of what happens at the lowest level can be included in the decision making higher up in the organization. Furthermore its practice announces a new conception of organization, in which the various sub-systems and their interconnectedness gain importance. As such it places emphasis on the process of organizing more than on structure.

3. *The aggregate or community model.* It is difficult to describe this model. In organizations one has aggregates which are not part of any clearly defined sub-systems; they are spread over a variety of sub-systems. Consequently, they are not represented in the formal, nor in the informal organization; they are often invisible. Nevertheless, they are part of the total system and as such they exert influence. But their influence, as well as their values are difficult to identify, simply because they appear in a diffuse and unorganized form. Examples of these aggregates are the older employees, the female employees, the foreign assignees, the accident prone, the clients of the company's medical centre, etc. The strategy consists in bringing an aggregate together to understand the interaction between them and the various parts of the organization. It may even consist in making the aggregate a group.

4. *The organizational understanding model.* The disadvantage of each of these three strategies rests in the fact that they can be perceived by the system as power strategies, while they are not necessarily designed for that purpose. The first two strategies can be conceived as an alignment of the consultant with respectively management or the workers. The aggregate strategy may, but not necessarily, include an effort to unite what has been divided.

Although all three have their benefits, most of us will recognize that they have no general applicability. Therefore one has to search for models and strategies which are less likely to be labelled as power strategies, while generating sufficient understanding and cooperation of the system and its power structure. Although, it has been said that one mostly learns about a system while attempting to change it, this does not justify a pure trial and error approach to organizational work. Therefore, it is important to develop strategies whose primary characteristic is to allow the organization (or a part of it) and the social scientist to understand its present state of operating.

Structuration either through division of labour, through the technology or professionalization, the segmentation of the parts, the physical and geographical lay out, and the mere size of organizations make it difficult to understand: (a) the internal processes of the various parts and the whole in relation to their specific environments; (b) their respective external processes; and (c) how the boundary conditions and adaptive processes are being managed. The strategy, then, consists essentially in temporarily removing the structuration and segmentation, so that the internal and external processes, the management of the boundary conditions and values become visible, so that the state of operating can be understood. This implies the study of the conscious and unconscious processes, organizational and personal, that maintain the structuring and segmentation of the system and the data and thereby prevent understanding.

The strategy does not call for the introduction of new values, except those related to continual learning and understanding, but for a joint diagnosis and interpretation of the data that has come to the surface, either from the formal or informal systems or from aggregates. The aim is to develop through understanding and direct experience more appropriate appreciative systems and cognitive maps which can form the basis for further development and conscious choice.

Organizational Understanding

How this broad strategy will be applied in practice seems to depend on two factors, the social scientist and the nature of the initial assignment.

The social scientist

A major influence is how and to what extent the social scientist has earned the right and credibility to intervene as a consultant. Social scientists who for various reasons, such as age, opportunities, professional competence and so on, have not been able to earn the right and the credibility to be a consultant through their own work in organizations tend to borrow credit from others or from the formal organization. In the first case, they may 'hitch-hike' on the achievement of other professionals, with an overemphasis on big names and on the minor modifications which they add to the classic approaches of their masters.

100

Consequently, their ability to listen, and to adapt their approach or 'technique' to the specific dynamics of the situation is largely reduced. In the second case, they may press the organization for recognition and for a formal position that allows them to operate. Inevitably, that entails an increased dependence of the internal or external consultant on the formal institution to which he belongs, its values, frame of reference and techniques.

A second feature is the internal strength of the social scientist which allows him to clarify the power structure or explore with the client delicate issues and cope with the inevitable internal fields of tension. The internal strength is largely psychological, and to some extent derived from personal achievements and from some economic security. They provide him the necessary internal security to be on the frontier. Without this internal security it is difficult to listen attentively to what is being said, distinguishing and recognizing the personal views from the organizational positions which the persons occupy, identifying the trans-situational subjects and objects which the client uses to talk about his real concerns, expectations and frustrations. This posture of the social scientist is quite different from working solely with what he himself experiences and thinks in a given situation. It does not exclude awareness of personal feelings, but they are more a subjective indicator of what the client or system is doing to him (requiring further exploration) than a directing or action-initiating part.

A third influence is the social scientist's particular frame of reference which guides, but not directs, his explorations. The consultant with an integrated approach to work in organizations searches for answers to the following set of questions before committing himself to a particular strategy.

(a) What is the 'ground' that produces the 'figure'; or what is the organization in relation to its environment that produces this assigment?
(b) What is the complete work cycle of the total system or a particular sub-system in terms of input, throughput, and output characteristics?
(c) To what extent is the assignment or problem determined by the following?
    — the nature of the work itself, for example, degree of uncertainty, variance.
    — the objectives set or pursued.
    — the social sub-system, or the way it is organized to meet the objectives and to adapt to outside and inside influences, for example, values, habits, unions.
    — the way the work is organized, for example, technology, job design and work-structural characteristics.

How and the degree to which all these questions will be explored depends largely on the nature of the assignment, the second major feature which has been identified as influencing the operation of the organizational understanding model.

The nature of the initial assignment

The entrance to an organization or part of it, for the external as well as for the internal consultant, is usually a 'problem' or a request for assistance in designing a new plant or jobs, or in introducing new technologies. Although 'problem solving' assignments have characteristics which distinguish them from 'assistance' assignments, they have been grouped together in this discussion.

In Table 6.1, the nature of the initial assignment is defined in terms of specificity and scope. The result is a four-field square with the dominant developmental characteristics of the strategy.

Field one. The assignment is not specified, or only described in general terms (because the problems at hand and the alternative solutions are still vague), and covers the total or a large part of the organization. Illustrative presentations are: 'we must bring our organization in line with the developments!', 'We want to become a truly multinational organization!', the introduction of industrial democracy or participative management, or the design of a new plant. With this type of assignment, the organization and the social scientist are at the conception stage of the strategy, and a number of options are still open.

The initial efforts are therefore directed towards understanding the total organization in relation to its environment, towards the identification of the 'ground' which at the same time produced the assignment and upon which the assignment has to be realized. One useful method, besides the study of the traditional, existing qualitative and quantitative assessments of the organization, is the diagonal diagnosis. This method consists of interviews with 'persons in roles' at various hierarchical levels and in different positions in the organization. The aim is to discover 'the ground', and to understand roughly the organization in terms of (a) the various sub-systems, (b) their interrelatedness, (c) their respective internal and external environments, and (d) the long and short term objectives. The social scientist can then discuss and explore his understanding of the situation in a face-to-face setting, with the aggregate of persons interviewed. The temporary removal of the traditional structural

Table 6.1. Nature of assignment and strategy characteristics

Specificity	Scope	
	Sub-system	Total system
Clear and detailed	*Field 4* Appreciation of relevance	*Field 2* Selection of sub-system
Unclear and general	*Field 3* Study of boundaries	*Field 1* Overall diagnosis

segmentation enables at least an aggregate of the organization to share in the organizational diagnosis. Under certain conditions, however, the social scientist may decide not to have this confrontation in a group setting, namely, when he feels that too much turbulence will be created which cannot be controlled. In these instances, individual discussions on the overall organizational diagnosis are to be preferred. This more intimate setting facilitates further exploration and working through.

This information base enables the social scientist to carry out two kinds of search. On the one hand he can explore the relevance of the assignment for the organization, its objectives or desired state, leading to a clearer specification of the project and the expected gains and costs. On the other hand, it allows him to search for the most appropriate sub-system to work with initially. Indeed, the 'grand design' approach to the total organization often ends in failure. More turbulence is created within the system than one can cope with. The social scientist in turn loses credibility and eventually control over the processes he himself helped to trigger off. Therefore, it appears desirable to specify the assignment and to focus initially on a thoughtfully selected sub-system. In other words, the assignment is moved into field two in Table 6.1.

Field two. The assignment is clearly specified (either because the problem has already been defined, or one has decided on a particular solution) and covers the total or a large part of the organization. Examples are the introduction of computer technology, management by objectives, participative management as Likert conceived it, and so on. If the assignment has been specified by the client alone, the social scientist will attempt to explore the wider context in which it presents itself, before venturing into the selection of a particular sub-system, based either on the classic American, the social action or the aggregate model. In other words, the social scientist will take the client back to field one, to gain understanding or to review the client's understanding of the total organization and the 'ground'. The acceptance of this type of assignment presupposes a wide understanding of the organization acquired through considerable study or a long-lasting relationship. Without this basic understanding, it becomes very difficult to appreciate the relevance of the assignment, and to identify the relevant sub-systems and their linkages to the whole. Consequently, the social scientist is tempted to work at random with isolated parts on *ad hoc* assignments.

A few criteria can be suggested to facilitate the selection of a sub-system to start working with, in order to produce a regulated snowball effect.

(a) The extent to which a particular sub-system is internally motivated and to which, through its linkages to the whole, it may positively stimulate the organization or diffuse the developments.
(b) The extent to which the project can be realized in a particular sub-system without too many disturbing or conflicting influences from its internal or external environment.

(c) The extent to which a particular sub-system can decide and regulate the speed of its development. It may become evident that any kind of work in a particular sub-system requires further exploration of specific aggregates. In these instances, the selection of aggregates precedes the selection of sub-systems.

With the selection of the sub-system, the assignment is moved to field four. This does not mean that the assignment becomes restricted to one or usually a set of sub-systems, but that in that setting the work is to be started.

Field three. The assignment is not clearly specified (either because the problem or the alternative solutions are not specified) and focusses on a particular sub-system; for example, 'Our department is falling behind!', the introduction of work structuring or socio-technical system work.

The social scientist in this type of assignment will explore with the client either the relevance of a particular solution for the operating state of that sub-system, or the nature of the problem itself. Such an exploration will focus on the boundary conditions of the sub-system, its relevant internal and external environment and the position and function of that particular sub-system in the total organization. In other words, the assignment will sequentially be studied in its characteristics of field three, field two and field one before it can be moved back from field one to field two and eventually four. During each step, one is confronted with the evaluation and decision about the meaning and feasibility of the assignment. But at the same time, one has the opportunity to develop preparatory actions to deal with interfering influences or constraints, taking into account the function of that particular sub-system and its relation to the whole.

Field four. The assignment in field four in Table 6.1 is clearly specified in terms of content and scope, for example in cases of job enrichment or team building. The dominant characteristic here is the appreciation of the relevance of the assignment. The explorations inevitably include the study of the relevance of the content of the project for that particular sub-system; the investigation of its boundary conditions and relations with its internal and external environment, and the function of the sub-system in the whole. Again it appears that the social scientist in his attempts to understand the assignment, moves the project back to fields three, two and one, before it can be brought to field four.

It must be said, however, that specific assignments of specific scope are the most tempting. They appear neat and clear from the start, but the dangers lay ahead. Illustrations are the development of closed or isolated sub-systems through team building, and job enrichment or work structuring at the shop floor which do not anticipate the consequences for higher management levels. However tempting it may be, one cannot work with one sub-system without the total organization in mind.

A careful analysis of the nature of the initial assignment, with its systematic movements back and forth from one field to another, enables client and

104

consultant to understand where they are in relation to the overall organization, to the particular sub-system, and most of all to the assignment concerned. The role and implications of the client and in particular of the sponsor in the 'problem solving' or 'assistance' assignment can thereby be brought to the surface.

The ensuing tactical and strategic plan to start working with a particular sub-system or aggregate and relevant connecting sub-systems needs, however, to be revised and reconsidered regularly as one goes along. This is achieved through a repetition of the same systematic explorations of sub-systems, their boundaries, their interrelatedness with the total organization, and vice versa. The organizational understanding model suggests an approach to strategy development which has basic characteristics of open systems planning.

Conclusion

Organization development, or even better work in organizations, cannot be defined solely on the basis of felt needs within the system. It presupposes an analysis of the organization in relation to its environment and to society at large.

Organization development requires an integrated approach based upon a consultative relationship with the client and its internal resources. A simplified approach, exclusively based on social psychology cannot but be, in most cases, an 'instant relief', a temporary superficial adaptation.

The social scientist in this field of work is confronted with a variety of internal and external pressures. The necessary internal strength and security, the broad frame of reference can hardly be acquired from adherence to a set of OD techniques or participation in encounter groups. It is something to be achieved through a continual analysis of oneself in society and learning derived from understanding the complexity of men, work, organizations and society.

References

Ackoff, R. L. (1970). *A Concept of Corporate Planning*, Wiley.
Angyal, A. (1941). *Foundations for a Science of Personality*, Harvard University Press.
Argyris, C. (1970). *Intervention Theory and Method: a Behavioral Science View*, Addison-Wesley.
Athos, A. G. (1970). Is the corporation next to fall? *Harvard Business Review*, **48**, 49–61.
Barrel, Y. (1973). *La reproduction sociale: systemes vivants, invariance et changement*, Anthropos.
Beckhard, R. (1969). *Organization Development Strategies and Models*, Addison-Wesley.
Bennis, W. G. (1966). *Changing Organizations*, McGraw-Hill.
Bennis, W. G. (1969). *Organization Development: Its Nature, Origins and Prospects*, Addison-Wesley.
Bowman, E. H. (1974). Some research on corporate social responsibility. European Institute for Advanced Studies in Management, working paper number 29.
Burns, T. and Stalker, G. (1961). *The Management of Innovation*, Tavistock.
Clark, P. A. (1972). *Action Research and Organizational Change*, Harper and Row.
Davis, L. E. (1957). Toward a theory of job design, *Journal of Industrial Engineering*, **5**, 19–23.

Emery, F. E. and Thorsrud, E. (1969). *Form and Content in Industrial Democracy*, Tavistock.

Emery, F. E. and Trist, E. L. (1965). The causal texture of organizational environments. *Human Relations*, **18**, 21–32.

Emery, F. E. and Trist, E. L. (1972). *Towards a Social Ecology: Contextual Appreciations of the Future in the Present*, Plenum Press.

Friedlander, F. and Brown, L. D. (1974). Organization development, *Annual Review of Psychology*, **25**, 313–341.

Gombin, R. (1971). *Les Origines du Gauchisme*, du Seuil.

Gouldner, A. W. (1961). Engineering and clinical approaches to consulting. In W. Bennis, K. Benne and R. Chin (eds.), *The Planning of Change*, Holt, Rinehart and Winston.

Gustaitis, R. (1969). *Turning On*, Lowe and Brydone.

Herbst, P. G. (1970). *Socio-technical design, strategies in multi-disciplinary research*, Report of the Work Research Institute, Oslo.

Hornstein, H. A., Bunker, B. B. and Burke, W. W. (1971). *Social Intervention: A Behavioral Science Approach*, The Free Press.

Laing, R. D. (1967). *The Politics of Experience*, Penguin.

Lawrence, P. R. and Lorsch, J. W. (1967). *Organization and Environment*, Harvard Business School.

Leavitt, H. J. (1964). Applied organization research in industry: structural, technical and human approaches. In J. G. March (ed.), *Handbook of Organizations*, Rand McNally.

Lippitt, G. L. (1969). *Organizational Renewal*, McGraw-Hill.

O'Connell, J. J. (1968). *Managing Organizational Innovation*, Irwin.

Pettigrew, A. M. (1975). Towards a political theory of organizational intervention, *Human Relations*, **28**, 191–208.

Schon, D. A. (1971). *Beyond the Stable State*, Random House.

Thorsrud, E. (1972). Job design in the wider context. In L. E. Davis and J. C. Taylor (eds.), *Design of Jobs*, Penguin.

Touraine, A. (1969). *La societe post-industrielle*, Editions Denoël.

Trist, E. (1970). A socio-technical critique of scientific management. Paper presented to the Edinburgh Conference on the Impact of Science and Technology, Edinburgh University.

Trist, E. L., Higgin, G. W., Murray, H. and Pollock, A. B. (1963). *Organizational Choice: Capabilities of Groups at the Coal Face under Changing Technologies*, Tavistock.

Van Beinum, H. J. J. (1972). Some aspects of present-day environmental changes and their implications for organizational behaviour. Paper presented at the International Conference of Reinsurance, Monte Carlo.

Van Dongen, H. (1971). Over hanteren van gedragswetenschappelijke methoden in hiërarchische organisaties. Unpublished paper.

Vansina, L. S. (1974). Improving international relations and effectiveness within multinational organizations. In J. D. Adams (ed.) *Theory and Method in Organization Development: An Evolutionary Process*, Institute for Applied Behavioral Science.

Vickers, G. (1968). *Value Systems and Social Processes*, Basic Books.

Zand, D. E. (1974). Collateral organization: a new change strategy, *Journal of Applied Social Science*, **10**, 63–89.

7

Ethical Issues
in Organizational Change

John Rowan
Consultant social psychologist, London

I am angry at what I see happening in the factories and offices which I go into. I am angry at the way we keep having to rediscover the importance of democracy and participation. I am angry at the way we keep slipping back into the old ways which we know do not work, and which insult human beings. I am angry with myself for being so slow and ineffectual in bringing about any change.

It is not enough to be angry; but that is where this chapter starts. We have to understand why we keep failing and making nonsense of everything we say we believe in.

As a social psychologist I have given up the pretence that I am a value-free scientist, with no beliefs of my own. But as soon as I say what I believe in, someone will stand up and say, 'Those are *your* beliefs, and why should I change to please you?' This somehow paralyses me or starts an argument in which I am on one side and the other person is on the other, and nobody wins or changes. The intention here is to take a big step back from all that, and look at the belief systems which are actually available, so that we can take a cool look at them and see what might be involved in taking up any one of them. Instead of trying to argue one ethical position against another, let us try to look at what it means to be ethical at all.

It is possible to do this in a very basic and practical way because of the work of Lawrence Kohlberg (1969a, 1969b, 1973; Kohlberg and Kramer, 1969; Kohlberg and Turiel, 1973), who has made a study, over many years now, of the moral judgements people actually make, as distinct from what they talk about at conferences, seminars and dinners.

He finds he can reduce the answers to only six different levels. We might think, without having considered it very much, that there were many ways—perhaps thousands—of looking at the world from a moral point of view, but in practice it seems that this is not so. In practice people only use six of them. (Those who may find this hard to accept are invited to look at the paper by Kurtines and Greif (1974) which strongly criticizes almost everything about Kohlberg except this. This is all the more impressive since they clearly come from a social-learning orientation which is hostile to everything which Kohlberg stands for.)

At the first level, we obey the rules to avoid punishment. This is the kind of 'morality' which Somerset Maugham once defined as 'Do what you like, with one eye on the policeman on the corner'. The rules are just there, and we do not question them. But we also have our own impulses, and act on them if we can. If we are caught, we give in as gracefully as possible, even though reluctantly. This is the morality of cheating on the income tax, or the parking meter, or the bus, and paying up cheerfully in the unlikely event of the axe falling. The rules are nothing to do with us—they are someone else's rules—it just so happens that they belong to so neone powerful who can punish us if we disobey them. At this level there tends to be a strong belief in fate and luck—somehow all the real power is somewhere else, outside us. Thinking is extremely short-term, and goals have to be personal, proximate and precise. Sexual and aggressive feelings are near the surface, and tend to be acted on.

At the second level, we adopt a horse-trading approach to life. We are still basically only thinking of our own advantage, but now we are not taking rules as in any way final. We will give up something in order to get something else—an exchange or profit-and-loss orientation. It is a competitive and opportunistic way of looking at the world, which makes us wary of other people. We try to exploit and manipulate them before they can exploit and manipulate us—because that is all there is, if we are realistic. Our advantage is their disadvantage, and *vice versa*. In the language of game theory, this is a zero-sum approach. There is a lot of skill at this stage, and a great interest in developing social skills, so that we can negotiate better to get what we want. But it is difficult, because at this stage our thinking is very rigid and stereotyped, and so the skills we learn always come out rather stiff and unconvincing, like a human impersonator. We refuse to take responsibility for anything except success; anything else is blamed on outside forces, which are seen as basically fearful and threatening.

The third level which Kohlberg found in his research he called Personal Concordance. At this level, our main desire is to be liked. We will do anything which will get us a lot of social approval. We need to know what the majority view is, so that we can go along with it. We want to belong and to fit in. We may show this by wearing badges, ties, blazers, a visible uniform of some kind. We may show it in our conversation, by talking about the right things, having the right sort of opinions, and praising each other for doing it. 'Yes, I think he's basically a sound chap. He's a regular guy, he's all right, he's one of us'. At this level we may seem very nice, but in fact it is not niceness but fear. And if we are told that something very nasty is the in thing, the done thing, the expected thing, then we will do that nasty thing without any real resistance. But it is not obedience, more a liking to be liked, and a great fear of disapproval and dislike. To be an outsider is the worst fate of all, but it is all right to be like the Vicar of Bray in the British folk tune, who changed from Protestant to Catholic and back again in order to survive in the Civil War.

Now already at this third level we come across one of the crucial things which Kohlberg says. He says that people cannot understand the level which is two stages above them—they have to distort and misrepresent it. They may actually like it (Rest *et al.*, 1969; Rest, 1973), but they cannot understand or use it. This is partly because each stage is more logically complex than the preceding one. So already, at level 3, we are at a level which those who are operating most of the time at level 1 cannot understand or fully appreciate.

The fourth level is what Kohlberg calls a Law-and-Order orientation. Here there is still a great desire for conformity and a great fear of the group, but now it is couched in the form of a principle—that the important thing is to find one's duty and do it. There is a great emphasis on legitimacy: what is the correct thing to do? There is much more emphasis on guilt: one is not just in danger of going against the group, one is in danger of incurring legitimate censure from an actually ordained authority. There is a strong need for structures, so that it will be clear to everyone what the correct action would be in any circumstances. Also at this level there is great rigidity, and still a lot of stereotyped thinking. This is the stage where we are most likely to find what Merton has called 'trained incapacity', where the rules loom so large that they may make it impossible to carry out the policy for which the rules were designed. If stage 3 is the archetypal conformist, stage 4 is the archetypal bureaucrat. He desperately needs approval, just as much as the conformist, but it must be the legitimate approval of those who are in the correct position and applying the correct objective standards. And he really believes that there are such things as objective standards. He wants an organization which does not in any way rely on personal feelings or personal caprice, and he looks down on the conformists as being loose-thinking, arbitrary and unprincipled. His status is extremely important to him, and symbolizes the whole system of legitimate standards which justifies his superiority to those beneath him. Any threat to authority is a threat to his whole construction of reality. There is not really much difference between levels 3 and 4, they are both wanting to conform, but the level 4 person knows better how to do it.

There is in a sense a bigger gap between levels 4 and 5 than there is between any other two of the levels. It is at stage 5 that we can start talking about making the law, rather than just simply obeying the law. There is a lot more self-respect at this stage, which does not depend so much on the approval of other people. It is possible to question rules in the light of their consequences, and their implications for the general welfare. The thinking at this stage is much less stereotyped, and perception is clearer, less defensive. The person is able to think much more flexibly, in the light of long-term goals. There is still a great emphasis on the importance of law and impartial rules, but now they are seen as having a rational basis, in terms of democratic values. We want to have the rules, but we also want to know why they are there, so that they can be changed if necessary. This is called the Social Contract stage by Kohlberg. It brings with it a great interest in research, and in the whole question of the unintended consequences of action. All at once, communication takes on a whole new meaning and is seen as a two-way process, in which the other person is a participant rather than a target.

The sixth level which Kohlberg found he called the stage of Individual Principles. Here it is the person's own autonomous conscience which matters most. We may well have a general orientation to the majority welfare, and to democratically-decided laws, but ethical principles, incorporated into our own selves, take precedence. Self-imposed laws have the greatest value; self-imposed discipline is the best. The person at this level can express his or her own feelings readily, because they are part of his or her own value system, rather than a separate thing. There is the feeling of identity in one's morality, rather than seeing it as imposed in any way. It is hard to draw the line between intellectual judgements and subjective feelings, because one is operating from a centre inside oneself which is itself neither exclusively intellectual nor exclusively emotional.

I feel slightly unhappy about this sixth level, because Kohlberg has never been able to find enough people operating consistently at such a level to really make the description quite convincing. My own feeling is that all the really important philosophical doctrines about ethics only really start to appear at this level, and that it is much more complex than Kohlberg thinks. He has actually speculated in print that there may be a level 7 or even a level 8. It has been argued elsewhere (Rowan 1973a) that four higher levels are necessary if we are to make sense of certain political facts. So these very high levels are not nearly so well described and explored as the first five levels.

But the important thing is that these levels of morality were found by actual research, rather than coming out of someone's head as a logical schema. And what is also clear is that it is only levels 5 and 6 which would count as morality or ethics at all.

Since the time of Kant, an important distinction has been made in philosophy between heteronomous rules, which are imposed from outside the person; and autonomous rules, which come from inside the person. Kant argued, and clarified the whole area of ethics enormously by doing so, that it is only autonomous rules which can even begin to be argued about as ethical or not ethical.

As long as we are in the realm of heteronomous rules, we are treating people, or being treated, as means to an end. But being treated as a means to an end is to be treated like a thing, not like a person. It is only when we treat people as persons that we even begin to act in a way which can plausibly be called ethical.

And we do that by treating them as ends in themselves, rather than as means to our ends; in reverse, we insist on being treated as ends in ourselves, and refuse to be treated as a means to someone else's ends. Maslow (1968) has pointed out that the healthier we are mentally, the more we will resist being treated as a means to someone else's end. From our point of view here, however, the important thing is that it is only with autonomy that any real choice becomes possible. And it is interesting that when Milgram (1974) was trying to reduce his experimental subjects to a sub-ethical level of behaviour, one of the phrases he used was—'You have no choice—you must go on with the experiment'.

So the step from the first four levels to level 5 or 6 is a momentous step. It is the step from a set of sub-ethical levels to a world in which ethical discussion and action becomes possible. As Wright (1974) says, 'The transition between (these) levels marks a significant watershed in terms of the *nature* of the possible bases of social order ... (After it) people can consciously and intentionally construct and maintain a social order of their own choice'.

It must be emphasized that what we are looking at here is an empirical matter. We are not making theoretical pronouncements about what might be the case, or what ought to be the case, but simply describing what is there, and what can be shown to be there. Each of these stages builds on, incorporates, and transmutes the previous one. Each stage is qualitatively different and represents a structured whole that is hierarchically synthesized with the preceding stages. Kohlberg found that in our culture, about half of the adults are stuck at level 4, with 3 and 5 as rather poor runners-up, representing about one-fifth of the population each. It has been remarked elsewhere (Rowan 1973b) that this needs some explanation; children mature naturally through the stages until they reach level 4, but instead of moving straight through to level 5, there seems to be a gap or barrier placed there somehow. Instead of arriving at the higher levels which it looks as though children are tending to rise towards, adults appear to function mostly at the lower levels. And there is much evidence to show that this barrier is placed there by the family, the school, the work situation, the leisure situation, the political situation, the mass media. In all these areas, people are systematically narrowed and reduced to less than what they are capable of being. Some evidence for this in the family and the school is given in the reference just cited, and also in Simpson (1971). We shall be considering work in the later sections of this chapter.

What we are saying is that normal development moves us up the Kohlberg levels, as part of the maturational process. And this movement is a movement towards what Maslow (1973) calls 'full humanness'. It is a movement towards being an autonomous person, who originates action rather than merely reacting or being acted on. But there is also such a thing as being stuck, or even moving back down the scale. And this regression down the scale is a movement towards the opposite end of the scale.

But if, as we have seen, the lower end of the scale is less adequate, more rigid, less logically complex, less integrated, more compartmentalized, then this movement is essentially a destructive one. It is a movement towards alienation.

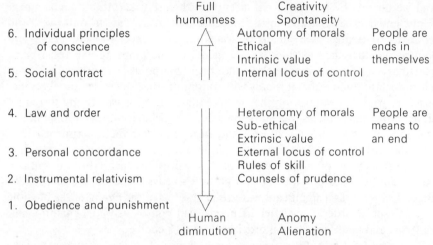

6. Individual principles
   of conscience

5. Social contract

4. Law and order

3. Personal concordance

2. Instrumental relativism

1. Obedience and punishment

Full humanness

Creativity
Spontaneity
Autonomy of morals
Ethical
Intrinsic value
Internal locus of control

People are ends in themselves

Heteronomy of morals
Sub-ethical
Extrinsic value
External locus of control
Rules of skill
Counsels of prudence

People are means to an end

Human diminution

Anomy
Alienation

Figure 7.1. Characteristics of Kohlberg's levels

It is a movement towards the state of being a pawn. Figure 7.1 sums up the point which we have now reached.

It can be seen in this figure that the phrases 'internal locus of control' and 'external locus of control' have been added. These refer to some research work carried out by Rotter (1966), who found that in external control the effects of a person's action are 'typically perceived as the result of luck, chance, fate, as under the control of powerful others, or as unpredictable because of the greater complexity of the forces surrounding him'. In cases of internal control, on the other hand, the person perceives that 'the event is contingent upon his own behaviour or his own relatively permanent characteristics'. This has to do with the question of responsibility for one's actions, and clearly the higher up the scale a person is, the more responsible he or she will be for his or her actions. In the lower parts of the scale, people will feel less and less responsible for their actions the further down the scale they are.

It is interesting that, in his research, Kohlberg found that people could talk quite convincingly about the level one above their own—although being quite unable, as we saw earlier, to appreciate the level two above their own. So what we seem to have here is a situation where the vast majority of the population have got blocked or stuck at level 4 or below, even though many of them can talk quite convincingly about level 5. Now this is very curious, because children develop naturally up the levels quite predictably to level 4, as we have seen, and if they can actually understand and like level 5, it seems all the more curious that they cannot actually move up to it. Why should this be?

The Ego and the Self

For some hints towards an answer, let us look at some quite different research carried out by Jane Loevinger (1966, 1969, Loevinger *et al.*, 1970), on ego development. She worked on different populations with different measuring instruments (rather more sophisticated from a technical point of view), and also found six levels on which people could operate. And again, as with Kohlberg, each one seems to include, and to rise above, the previous one. These are her levels:

1. *Pre-social or Symbiotic.* This represents a stage before the child has any sense of ego at all.

2. *Impulsive.* A very concrete stage, easily dominated by one perceptual stimulus. There is little holding back or reflection. The person sometimes seems to be acting 'at random'.

Delta. A stage between 2 and 3, dominated by the need for self-protection. All the person's efforts seem dominated by the theme of holding things stable. This may take the form of imposing very strict rules, or behaving in a very repetitious and stereotyped way. Mastery and control are very important.

3. *Conformist.* Going along with the crowd. Liking to be liked. Sociable, but basically quite anxious about rejection. Ready to reject others who do not conform.

4. *Conscientious.* Bound by self-imposed rules, which are much more derived from personal experience. But often a split between what is believed to be right and actual ability to carry it out. Much more feeling of being a real person. Dependence upon others is becoming much less heavy.

5. *Autonomous.* Greater ability to relate to other people as an individual. Greater ability to recognise different aspects of oneself as real. Ability to live with oneself. A good level of self-esteem. Some feeling of achievement of potential.

6. *Integrated.* Full selfhood. Flexible and creative. Humorous in unexpected ways. No need to be loved and appreciated by everyone. No need to be thoroughly competent and adequate. No unrealistic fears about possible catastrophes. Ability to face internal conflicts and the external world.

And again, what she found was that people were somehow blocked from reaching the higher levels. Most of her subjects were operating at her level 3, which is more or less equivalent to Kohlberg's levels 3 and 4 taken together.

This seems an amazing coincidence, but it is much more than that. It is like one of those discoveries that often happen in science, where a theory seems to hang in the air until the time is ripe, and then to drop, like fruit, into everyone's back garden at the same time. For not only do Kohlberg's levels correspond with Loevinger's, but both of them, if we adopt a suggestion put forward by David Wright (1972, 1973, 1974), correspond with Maslow's (1970) levels. What Wright did was to add one more to Maslow's list of basic needs, which he calls 'effectance'. Effectance motivation has been written about at length by Robert White (1959, 1960, 1963). He points out that we all have a need, particularly strong at certain stages in our growth, just simply to master the environment or certain skills, and we work on this in quite an obsessive way until we have it sorted out. And we all have this need just to do something well—it may be something important or quite trivial—just for the sake of the pleasure it gives us in

Maslow	Kohlberg	Loevinger
Self-actualization	*Individual principles*	*Autonomous integrated*
Being that self which I truly am Being all that I have it in me to be A fully-functioning person	True personal conscience Universal principles fully internalized Genuinely autonomous Selfishness B	Flexible and creative Internal conflicts are faced and recognised
Self-esteem 2	*Social contract*	*Conscientious*
Goals founded on self-evaluated standards Self-confidence Self-respect	Utilitarian law-making Principles of general welfare Long-term goals	Bound by self-imposed rules Differentiated thinking Self-aware

The Great Gap

Maslow	Kohlberg	Loevinger
Self-esteem 1	*Law and order*	*Conformist 2*
Respect from others Social status Recognition	Authority maintenance Fixed social rules Find duty and do it	Seeking general rules of social conformity Justifying conformity
Love and belongingness	*Personal concordance*	*Conformist 1*
Wish for affection, for a place in the group, tenderness, etc.	Good-boy morality Seeking social approval Liking to be liked Majority is right	Going along with the crowd Anxiety about rejection Need for support
Effectance	*Instrumental hedonism*	*Self-protective manipulative*
Mastery Personal power Control Blame and retaliation	Naive egocentrism Horse-trading approach Profit-and-loss calculation Selfishness A	Wary, exploitative People are means to ends Competitive stance
Safety	*Obedience/punishment*	*Impulsive*
Defence against danger Fight or flight Fear World is scary	Deference to superior power Rules and external impositions	Domination by immediate cue, body feelings No reflection Retaliation fears

After David L. Wright. Omitting lowest level of Maslow (physiological) and of Loevinger (pre-social, symbiotic).

Figure 7.2. A summary of levels

being able to do it. This need has to do with the actual and perceived competence we have in dealing with the environment. This is effectance motivation, and it does not seem to be reducible to any other of Maslow's needs; it really does seem to belong where David Wright has put it.

Now, if we can accept that these three theories line up in the way laid out in Figure 7.2, if only for the sake of argument, what does it all mean?

If it is true that movement up this common scale is not only a normal movement (as all the research has shown) but also a healthy movement, as Kohlberg (1971) has certainly argued, then the implication is that anything which helps people up the levels is to be positively valued. People who have experienced the higher levels invariably judge them to be more adequate and more defensible than the lower levels; and only they have tried both. And the obverse of this statement is that everything which moves a person back down the levels, or prevents a person from continuing to grow upwards, is human diminution. By calling it human diminution, Maslow (1973, p. 32) says:

'... it puts on the same continuum all the standard psychiatric categories, all the stuntings, cripplings and inhibitions that come from poverty, exploitation, maleducation, enslavement, etc., and also the newer value pathologies, existential disorders, character disorders that come to the economically privileged. It handles the diminutions that result from drug addiction, psychopathy, authoritarianism, criminality and other categories that cannot be called "illness" ...'

So at the top of the chart we have what Maslow calls full humanness, and at the bottom we have, if we are talking about adults, human diminution.

And this way of looking at the matter seems to fit the other two approaches as well. They both seem to imply that the person who is emerging on the upper side of the gap is approximating to the 'fully functioning person' of Carl Rogers (1961), a person who refuses to be crippled by the structures of an insane society, someone who at present is rather rare, and consequently has only a precarious social base from which to work, and is to that extent prevented from exerting that influence which might be his or her best contribution to social change.

The question which arises now is this: What effect do our organizations have on this growth process?

The Double Helix

The answer seems so obvious that we do not need to spend much time examining it. Most organizations, most of the time, push people into fixed roles which are clearly going to socialize them (by a process which David Wright has called 'indoctrinated control') into level 4. And it is often much worse than that. Harvey (1967, Harvey et al., 1961, 1966, 1968) has done a good deal of research using a conceptual system and a method which agree with the other three only at the bottom of the scale. His 'System 1' thinking is characterized by 'high superstition, high religiosity, high absolutism and closedness of beliefs, high evaluativeness, high positive ties with, and dependence on, representatives of institutional authority—especially those of more nearly unimpeachable validity, such as God and religion', as well as high rigidity and intolerance. In one piece of research, Harvey and his coworkers found that out of 67 teachers, 75% were operating at the level of System 1, more or less equivalent to Kohlberg's first and second levels. And this approach on the part of the teacher had a negative relationship with the children's achievement, as well as with a number of more important variables. Schools are probably worse than most of our other organizations, but they are by no means unique.

If we want to get something done, it is very tempting to turn another person into a thing in order to achieve it. He or she becomes an instrument of our will, or the will of the organization. He gives up something, we give up something, he does not trust us, we do not trust him. That is normal in our organizations, God help us! But we can easily see now that this is level 2 behaviour. It pushes the other person right down the scale, to a stage which most children begin to come out of at about the age of eleven.

Maybe then we go on to human relations training, and take into account that perhaps people might like each other, and want to fit in with each other's norms and expectations. So we might actually allow them to rise up to level 3.

And if we are very sophisticated, we say that worker satisfaction is not enough—we need task orientation as well. We need real commitment to the organization and its aims. And so we rise to the dizzy heights of level 4.

However, if this is all we are doing, we are not even beginning to cross that gap. If this is as far as we are going, we are cheating human beings of their humanity. We are systematically preventing people from achieving their own growth and their own normal development. And we are certainly stopping people from achieving any real ethical awareness. It could even be suggested that we are often stopping our own ethical awareness. How about you, the reader? What level do you normally operate at? One way of finding out would be to ask the people you interact with most—your wife or husband, your children, your colleagues, your fellow committee members. Another way would be to go to Kohlberg or Loevinger and get yourself tested. But as a quick check, here are some platitudes which I have collected. Do you habitually use any one of them?

> Do as you're told and don't answer back. (1)
> You've got to look after number one. (2)
> You scratch my back, and I'll scratch yours. (2)
> People need people. (3)
> I know which side my bread is buttered. (3)
> Don't rock the boat. (3)
> Each man to his post, and let's get this show on the road. (4)
> People like to know where they stand. (4)

What business are we in? (5)
We need better two-way communication. (5)

The number in brackets refers to the Kohlberg level involved. None has been given for level 6, because it is not certain that there are any platitudes at level 6. If there are any, I do not know what they are.

But if we agree that the answer to the question is that most organizations, most of the time, push people back down the levels rather than lifting them up the levels, the question now arises, what can we do about it? When we look at management theory from our present perspective, it becomes evident almost at once that most of the modern theorists are on the upper side of the gap, and are trying to get people to join them by crossing the gap. People like Argyris, Benne, Harman, Herzberg, Lawrence and Lorsch, Likert, McGregor, Schein and Tannenbaum are all saying, if we read them aright: *You can run an organization successfully without reducing people to sub-ethical levels.*

And this is where we start to get into an unnecessarily disturbed state. We start saying, 'If we are going to be consultants helping people into an ethical world, we have got to be ethically perfect ourselves'. And then it turns out, of course, that we are not ethically perfect. We may be using little bits of manipulation, just like level 2. We may be using little bits of group pressure, just like levels 3 and 4. Yet this does not matter. If we are genuinely bringing people across the gap, they will criticize us soon enough, without our having to torture ourselves. And their criticisms will be part of the lesson we have been trying to teach. And we will fall, laughing, off our pedestals.

This is such an important point that it deserves spelling out in more detail. It may sound as though what is being suggested is that any means is alright, if the end is good enough. This is not it at all. What is being said is that we cannot bring people across the gap by manipulation, and that if little bits of manipulation do creep in, they will soon be seen and rejected by the participants themselves. We cannot bring people across the gap by means of group pressure, and if we do start using bits of group pressure, they will be detected and challenged by those involved.

How then do we bring people across the gap? I would like to suggest that the theory of Charles Hampden-Turner (1971) gives us something useful here. His theory is that what takes us into level 6 is a spiral or helical process. He has ten points on the spiral before the starting point is reached again on a higher level, but here they have been reduced to four in order to make the explanation briefer. A simplification of Hampden-Turner's helix is shown in Figure 7.3.

The starting point on the helix is a person who has achieved some measure of self-esteem and self-awareness (perhaps temporarily, not necessarily permanently)—what we call in everyday language a 'together person'. Such a person can of course be either male or female, but I shall assume her to be female throughout, because we are not nearly conscious enough of the covert sexual assumptions we are making in so much of our writing.

She starts off, then, in a fairly together stage, and Hampden-Turner suggests

118

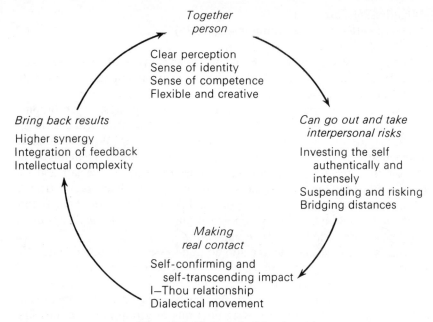

Figure 7.3. The spiral of development

that this includes four basic things—a sense of personal competence, a sense of identity, clear and undistorted perception, and a sense of free and creative existence. At the beginning, these states are not highly developed, but they are present to some degree. Maybe this is just a good day, when she got out of bed on the right side, and the sun shone.

This reasonably happy state enables the second of the four points to be embarked upon. The person can now go out and take some interpersonal risks. She can trust herself to be authentic, and invest herself intensely in her interpersonal environment, without needing so many defences and cover-ups. She can give people the power to get through to her. She can also suspend her cognitive structures in order really to listen to what someone else is saying. She can bridge the distance to another person. This point about bridging distances is very important. Hampden-Turner suggests that one way of measuring how far up the spiral we have got is to assess such things as chauvinism, isolationism, ethnocentrism, etc.

This whole willingness to go out and genuinely meet other people leads to the third of the four points—the ability to make real contact with another person. At this stage the woman we are following here can make a real impact on someone else. Because there is very little holding back, a sense of openness and trust develops between two people. This what Martin Buber has called the 'I–Thou' relationship. At this point two spirals interlock, as it were, and we get a double helix appearing. A dialectic can be set up which then leads to the growth of both parties. And it is important to make a point which has not been clearly enough spelled out by Hampden-Turner, that this involves an essential negative element. The woman at this stage is willing to confront the other person, and say things which may be difficult or hurtful, things which may apparently jeopardize the whole relationship, but which in fact only causes it to grow and develop. Bach and Wyden (1970) explain this whole process very well. To the extent that this dialectical exchange freely takes place, something genuinely new can emerge.

And this leads on to the fourth point on the spiral, an integration of the process so far. The person digests the new information which has emerged, and the changes which have taken place, and makes them part of herself. These changes are not simply added on—like money in the bank—but a real reorganization takes place. And the effect of this is to create a higher state of synergy; the person is better able to use and convert the information she already has available. With this synergy comes a whole higher level of complexity in her intellectual and emotional equipment for facing the world. This means that she is able to meet the world less mystified than she was before, and able to make some sense of what she sees and hears.

And this, of course, leads back to the first point on the spiral: clear perception, a sense of identity, a sense of competence, a sense of free and creative existence. Which enables her to go out again, and so on. This is what is going to take her across the gap, perhaps to Kohlberg's level 5, perhaps even direct to level 6.

If this theory is correct—and it is based on a lot of experience with groups, and a deep analysis of the factors involved (Hampden-Turner, 1966, 1969, 1971)—it suggests that authentic human interaction is the only way in which we learn how to cross the ethical gap. In particular, there seems to be no way in which we can enter level 6 without some personal experience of what it is like to be authentic in a human interaction. It has been shown elsewhere (Rowan, 1975) that certain kinds of group experience, and certain kinds of organizational set-up, can allow authenticity to emerge in people.

But what Hampden-Turner says also is that we can go down the spiral, too. If we have our self-esteem shaken by being put down, our perception gets narrower and more defensive, our sense of identity gets locked in, we are only able to bridge very small distances between us and other people, we cannot make real or open relationships, and so we get very little feedback which we can integrate. In fact, our cognitive structures may get simplified and rigidified. This narrows our perception even further, and so on.

Now what I am saying is that most of our organizations, most of the time, are driving people down the spiral into anomy and alienation, rather than up the spiral into autonomy and moral insight. And often we do this—so sick is the whole situation—with the best of intentions. We actually think it is good for people to be put down, because that way they learn—they learn the task, and they learn to be tough and impervious, and that's necessary in a tough world . . . Well, we can see easily enough now that that is level 2 talk, and helps to create the horror world it purports to deal with. The other way, where we open up to the other person, helps to create, instead, someone who is strong and vulnerable at the same time; and this is a very good description of a level 6 person.

If we know how to drive people down the spiral, and also how to enable people to move up it, this now places the burden of knowledge on us. Again I want to ask you, the reader—what are you doing about it?

Genuine Participation

At this point the talk is not just about ethics, the reader is being asked to think ethically. Where do you come in this? What part do you play? What part would you like to play? What is stopping you?

I am, of course, aware that it is necessary to work on the organization as well as the individual. It is absurd to expect a person to function in a moral way in an organization which is hostile to that. I accept the whole theory of organization development which underlines this point very strongly (Argyris 1970, Lawrence and Lorsch 1969, Fordyce and Weil 1971). But in ethics we always have to look at the individual: here is this person, and what are we going to do about her?

It is this fact which brings up one of the classic dilemmas of the change agent: what do you do about someone who does not want to change? What do you do about someone who does not want to be autonomous, does not want to share power, does not want to communicate with colleagues at the same level, does not want openness and trust, and all the rest of it?

From our present perspective, we can see that this is not an ethical problem at all, but a purely practical one. How do we set up a genuine dialogue with such a person? It may be very difficult, because if the level of distrust is high enough, one party can very effectively refuse to enter into dialogue at all. Or if a person puts on a mask ('I am not speaking for myself, but purely as a representative of Z') and will only speak through the mask, dialogue may be impossible. There is really no substitute for dialogue. Where dialogue is impossible, we cannot bring people across the gap, and we cannot introduce the styles of management which involve participation and democracy. The only honest thing I could do as a consultant would be to resign.

But where dialogue is possible, it seems to be always feasible to arrive at some way of living together in a reasonably honest way, such that opportunities for change are left open, rather than closed off. We are never saying to the person, 'Change to suit me', but rather, 'I know how to help you change if that is what you want'. Some of us go further, and say, 'I genuinely care about you'.

Right at the beginning of this essay, and just now, the word 'democracy' was used. There is a real connection between what happens in organizations and what happens in the political field. If we can encourage people to leap the gap in the organization they work in, we are also encouraging them to take up a moral stance in their lives generally outside the factory or office, school or university, hospital or prison. Carole Pateman (1970) has put together the evidence on this, and has concluded that an individual's politically relevant attitudes 'will depend to a large extent on the authority structure of his work environment'.

If the structure is such as to permit genuine participation, this makes a place for the exercise of level 5 or 6 considerations: each person is treated to some extent as a legislator, rather than merely as a pawn. And this makes a person fit, ready and able to think of political participation in the same way. If we can create an organization of problem solvers, this will help to create a society of problem solvers.

This is why I cannot accept the view which is sometimes put forward that work is necessarily nasty for most people, and the best answer is therefore to pay people more, and concentrate on leisure time for any possible satisfactions. Work is too important a part of people's lives for it not to matter what attitudes are built up there. It is only at the lower levels of rationality that we can believe that compartmentalization of our lives is any kind of answer. It is just giving up the struggle if we adopt any kind of view like this. If we are at all interested in what is and what is not ethical, we must accept that any ethical view worthy of the name must apply to everything.

We can see this clearly enough when it is primitive people who are in question. We hear of this tribe which is extremely honest and punctilious when relating to people within the tribe, but which systematically cheats strangers; we smile and say that we understand perfectly, but what a low level of morality is shown! It should be equally obvious that a 'primitive' level of morality is shown if we say that we want to enable people to rise up the levels to self-actualization in their leisure time, but it is alright to push them down the levels into alienation during all their working hours. No one is ever going to escape from alienation that way.

I want to live in a society which is less oppressive than the present one. I am never going to make it, so long as most people accept oppression and think it is all right. One way of looking at oppression and describing it is to say that an oppressive régime is one which blocks ethical awareness, and prefers people to accept the present state of things. What is being said here is that most of our organizations are oppressive régimes in this sense. Modern management theory, of the type already mentioned, is against this kind of oppression and wants to change it. I believe that this has political implications. Insofar as our general efforts at introducing genuine participation and personal re-education are successful, we are helping to produce people who are going to think ethically about their personal and their political lives too. And insofar as we do that, we are producing people who will be better able, and more willing, to resist oppression.

Now it could be argued that it is hierarchical organization as such which produces an oppressive régime. I do believe that hierarchy as such is harmful, because it diminishes people, and reduces them to a fixed role, so I do want to get rid of hierarchy altogether. But to lay that down as a dogma, that that is all that matters, leaves out a lot. It is better to say that there are four really important things, and leave it to each organization as to how exactly they apply them. This schema is clearer than Pateman's distinctions between genuine participation and the various false forms of participation.

A. Power sharing. Can each person control the decisions which affect him or her? Can each sub-group control the decisions which affect it? This should apply to all four types of decisions: WHAT is to be done; HOW it is to be done; WHO is to do it; and WHEN. And it should apply to all four stages of the decision: assumption of the problem as a problem; production of various possible solutions; selection of a final solution; and the way of carrying out the solution.

B. Lateral communication. Can each person communicate with people who are on the same level, in the sense of having similar functions? Can each sub-group communicate with sub-groups with similar interests, or conflicting interests? Sometimes a barrier to communication is a good thing, but this should be clearly discussed and understood by those most concerned.

C. High synergy. To what extent does the system ensure that what benefits me automatically benefits others too? And that what benefits one sub-group benefits another sub-group too? This may take a lot of skill and ingenuity to get right, but the rewards are tremendous and worth any effort put in. A meeting where people are open and real with one another is one example of a high-synergy system within the organization. Your openness helps me to be more open, and that helps you to be more open again. Your trust helps my trust and so on. Your caring helps me to care.

D. Personal re-education. What opportunities does the organization give for personal growth and personal development? There is nothing automatic about the three previous points, they need to be worked on by people who believe in them. And this means that they have to believe in themselves. But this is difficult, for alienated people. So we have to work on the alienation in ourselves directly, within ourselves, at the same time as we are working on changing the structures so that they are less alienating and hopefully even healing. There is a whole range of ways of working on ourselves to make ourselves more aware, more whole, more creative, more self-actualizing, more able to relate to other people as they really are, and not to some false picture which we need to put up in front of them.

These are large matters, and I have written about them at greater length elsewhere (Rowan 1975), but it seems important to make at least some of those connections here. Insofar as we introduce people to the value of synergy in their working life, we are likely to make them more conscious of the need for synergy in political life. These things are all connected. They form a great circle. Action at any one point has repercussions all round the circle or spiral.

As Philip Herbst (1974) puts it very neatly, in a hierarchical and bureaucratic organization, the structures are constant, and the processes change from time to time. But in the fully participative and democratic organization, there is a figure-ground reversal: it is the processes which are constant, and it is the structures which change. 'The new character of the process is the goal. The structures arrived at are temporary'. This is very illuminating and helpful; all the four points mentioned above are process requirements, and nothing to do with structures.

What is being said is that some ways of organizing are consistent with ethical development, and some are not. And I would like to underline what was said earlier. I am not arguing that most people are sunk at low levels and that we have, by great efforts, somehow to bring them up. I am saying that it is natural to grow, and all we have to do is to find ways of not getting in the way of that growth. At present we *are* getting in the way, and it is this that produces the gap or barrier I have referred to so many times.

And this means that the view which we have been sharing in this essay is not an élitist one. It would be elitist if we said, like Clare Graves (1966), that 'In an organization the probability is that any one employee will be at a certain behavioral level for life'. If we believed that, it would indeed put us in the position of saying, as Hughes and Flowers (1970) do, 'Successfully managing tribalistic employees requires spelling out the work, the pay system, and especially the role of the immediate supervisor'. Clare Graves' most recent research has defined the conditions: 'work groups of about ten people and the boss acting as the total management system, with control over hiring, firing, and pay decisions. Pay techniques must be simple, with an easily understood rationale. Jobs should have short-cycle, rhythmic operations and be free of unfamiliar or frequent changes. To the tribalistic person, his boss is all-important and represents management and personnel programs and policies through his words and actions'. In other words, Graves recommends seeing what level a person is at, and then treating him in such a way as to confirm him in that position. This certainly would be élitist, but I have been saying something very different: it is normal for people to develop up to level 6 (and then of course to whatever may lie beyond level 6), so let us find ways of taking away the barriers which hold people back at level 4 or below.

And this means, of course, that it is not necessary to understand the higher levels before moving up into them. The understanding comes with the growth. Then, of course, there is no problem of imposing one set of values on people with another set; sets of values are not side-by-side in the way that that idea would suggest. And in closing, what I would most like to say is, don't struggle with your problems, just find ways of giving them up. There is no unethical way of helping people up the spiral. If it were unethical it would not work. We just need to do it more, that is all.

Two postscripts, or afterthoughts. The first is just to say that this chapter is intended to be empirical and checkable, not a theoretical exercise. I have been trying to lay out a description of what ethical (and sub-ethical) positions there are, and to spell out some of the implications of the picture which emerges from the research of people like Loevinger and Kohlberg. And it turns out, just like Maslow said, that the facts are not value-free; they powerfully suggest certain 'oughts'. But they still remain facts, checkable like any other facts.

The second is something which happened after this paper had been delivered, all the questions had been asked, and all the points discussed. A shy European scholar came up to me as I was gathering up my papers, and said, 'Throughout your paper you appeared to be adopting an existentialist position, but then at the end, you made the statement about not struggling with your problems and giving them up. Now part of the essence of existentialism is to say that anxiety is not something to be lost, but' (and here he pointed out a quotation from a book he was carrying) 'an ontological characteristic of man, rooted in his very existence as such'. I was rather tired, and a little baffled, and the best I could answer was, 'Well, you see . . . I'm a happy existentialist'.

References

Argyris, C. (1970). *Intervention Theory and Method*, Addison-Wesley.

Bach, G. R. and Wyden, P. (1968). *The Intimate Enemy*, Souvenir Press.

Fordyce, J. K. and Weil, R. (1971). *Managing with People*, Addison-Wesley.

Graves, C. W. (1966). Deterioration of work standards, *Harvard Business Review*, **44**, 117–128.

Hampden-Turner, C. M. (1966). An existential learning theory and the integration of T-group research, *Journal of Applied Behavioral Science*, **2**, 367–386.

Hampden-Turner, C. M. (1969). Black power: A blueprint for psycho-social development? In R. Rosenbloom and R. Maris (eds.), *Social Innovation in the Ghetto*, Harvard University Press.

Hampden-Turner, C. M. (1971). *Radical Man*, Duckworth.

Harvey, O. J. (1967). Conceptual systems and attitude change. In C. W. Sherif and M. Sherif (eds.), *Attitude, Ego-Involvement and Change*, Wiley.

Harvey, O. J., Hunt, D. and Schroder, H. M. (1961). *Conceptual Systems and Personality Organization*, Wiley.

Harvey, O. J., Prather, M., White, B. J. and Hoffmeister, J. K. (1968). Teachers' beliefs, classroom atmosphere and student behavior, *American Educational Research Journal*, **5**, 151–166.

Harvey, O. J., White, B. J., Prather, M. S., Alter, R. D. and Hoffmeister, J. K. (1966). Teachers' belief systems and preschool atmospheres, *Journal of Educational Psychology*, **57**, 373–381.

Herbst, P. (1974). *Some Reflections on the Work Democratization Project 1974*, Work Research Institute, Oslo.

Hughes, C. L. and Flowers, V. S. (1973). Shaping personal strategies to disparate value systems, *Personnel*, **50**, March-April, 8–23.

Kohlberg, L. (1969a). *Stages in the Development of Moral Thought and Action*, Holt, Rinehart and Winston.

Kohlberg, L. (1969b). Stage and sequence: The cognitive-developmental approach to socialization. In D. A. Goslin (ed.), *Handbook of Socialization Theory and Research*, Rand McNally.

Kohlberg, L. (1971). From is to ought: how to commit the naturalistic fallacy and get away with it. In T. Mischel (ed.), *Cognitive Development and Epistemology*, Academic Press.

Kohlberg, L. (1973). Continuities in childhood and adult moral development revisited. In P. B. Baltes and K. Warner Schaie (eds.), *Life-span Developmental Psychology: Personality and Socialization*, Academic Press.

Kohlberg, L. and Kramer, R. (1969). Continuities and discontinuities in childhood and adult moral development, *Human Development*, **12**, 93–120.

Kohlberg, L. and Turiel, E. (eds.) (1973). *Recent Research in Moral Development*, Holt, Rinehart and Winston.

Kurtines, W. and Greif, E. B. (1974). The development of moral thought: review and evaluation of Kohlberg's approach, *Psychological Bulletin*, **81**, 453–470.

Lawrence, P. R. and Lorsch, J. W. (1969). *Developing Organizations: Diagnosis and Action*, Addison-Wesley.

Loevinger, J. (1966). The meaning and measurement of ego development, *American Psychologist*, **21**, 195–206.

Loevinger, J. (1969). Theories of ego development. In L. Breger (ed.), *Clinical-Cognitive Psychology: Models and Integrations*, Prentice-Hall.

Loevinger, J. and Wessler, R. (1970). *Measuring Ego Development*, Jossey-Bass.

Maslow, A. H. (1968). *Towards a Psychology of Being* (2nd edition), Van Nostrand.

Maslow, A. H. (1970). *Motivation and Personality* (2nd edition), Harper and Row.

Maslow, A. H. (1973). *The Farther Reaches of Human Nature*, Penguin.

Milgram, S. (1974). *Obedience to Authority*, Tavistock Publications.

Pateman, C. (1970). *Participation and Democratic Theory*, Cambridge University Press.

Rest, J. (1973), The hierarchical nature of moral judgment: a study of patterns of comprehension and preference of moral stages, *Journal of Personality*, **41**, 86–109.

Rest, J., Turiel, E. and Kohlberg, L. (1969). Level of moral development as a determinant of preference and comprehension of moral judgements made by others, *Journal of Personality*, **37**, 225–252.

Rogers, C. R. (1961). *On Becoming a Person*, Constable.

Rotter, J. B. (1966). Generalized expectancies for internal versus external control of reinforcement, *Psychological Monographs*, **80**, No. 1, 1–28.

Rowan, J. (1973a). Onwards from Maslow, *Self and Society*, **1**, 4–9.

Rowan, J. (1973b). *The Social Individual*, Davis-Poynter.

Rowan, J. (1975). *The Power of the Group*, Davis-Poynter.

Simpson, E. L. (1971). *Democracy's Stepchildren: A Study of Need and Belief*, Jossey-Bass.

Wright, D. L. (1972). Conflict and equilibrium perspectives on social change: roots of a potential synthesis, *Annual Meeting of the American Sociological Association*.

Wright, D. L. (1973). Images of human nature underlying sociological theory: A review and synthesis, *Annual Meeting of the American Sociological Association*.

Wright, D. L. (1974). On the bases of social order: indoctrinated control versus voluntary cooperation, *Annual Meeting of the American Sociological Association*.

White, R. W. (1959). Motivation reconsidered: the concept of competence, *Psychological Review*, **66**, 297–333.

White, R. W. (1960). Competence and the psychosexual stages of development. In M. R. Jones (ed.) *Nebraska Symposium on Motivation*, University of Nebraska Press.

White, R. W. (1963). *Ego and Reality in Psychoanalytic Theory*, International University Press.

8

Professional Ethics and the Quality of Working Life

P. J. van Strien
Gronigen University, Holland

Introduction

In all parts of the world discussions are going on among social scientists about the contribution their work can make, not only towards the happiness of individuals but also towards a more happy and fair world. Among industrial and organizational psychologists the phrase 'quality of working life' has been introduced and, with the aim of improving this quality, projects have been started in different countries under this or a similar name. The theme of this conference has a similar ring, and the inclusion of 'issues of value' in the programme invites an explicit treatment of the moral implications of this aim for the professional attitudes and professional organization of psychologists.

This paper will review the way these discussions, and the wider issues of value, have led in the Netherlands to the formulation of a new ethical code for psychologists. Discussions about professional ethics and social responsibility have of course not been confined to the Netherlands but have been carried on in the United States and in the United Kingdom (see for instance Rapoport, 1970; Bannister, 1973; Warr *et al.*, 1973; Clark, 1974) and no doubt elsewhere. In my opinion, however, these discussions have nowhere been as directly linked with the formulation of ethical rules as in the Netherlands. Probably the Calvinistic spirit, which still gives public life and politics in the Netherlands a somewhat prescriptive stamp, is responsible for the need not only to renew the practice but to formulate new rules of conduct as well.

128

By 1960 the Dutch Psychological Association (N.I.P.) had already adopted an ethical code, but at the end of the 60's it was felt that this code was becoming obsolete, as a consequence of noticeable changes in the practice and the professional attitudes of Dutch psychologists.

In the field of industrial psychology the rapid development of work with groups and organizations, in addition to the established field of personnel selection, led to new ethical problems not covered by the existing code, which dealt mainly with questions of confidentiality and care in working with individuals. Along with these developments in professional practice, a new mentality was arising, especially among younger psychologists. The neutral attitude of the existing practice in which 'service' is the main ideal has begun to be questioned and a more vigorous, partisan position is propagated. According to this the psychologist is called to serve the case of the least powerful and to try to contribute to the equalization of power, knowledge and probably also income.

A first attempt by the Division of Industrial Psychology of the N.I.P. in 1971 to formulate a new ethical code, though welcomed as a substantial improvement, failed to get the necessary support to be put into practice. To avoid a repetition of this situation, the committee in charge—of which I was the chairman—decided to base a new version of the code on an inquiry into the practice and the professional attitudes of industrial and organizational psychologists in the Netherlands.

A questionnaire was sent to all practising psychologists working in this field (about 300 in all). The first part of the questionnaire dealt with the kind of work being done, with problems and conflicts with sponsors and clients, and with the training and professional organization of psychologists. The second part consisted of a series of statements about ethical rules, on which the respondents were invited to scale their responses. The response rate was 65%. A follow-up of the motives for not returning the questionnaire with a sample of the non-respondents showed no systematic factors which could have biased the results. In addition to the postal questionnaire, a stratified sample was interviewed in greater depth about their professional position and ethical problems they had encountered. The questionnaire and the interviews were designed and administered by a project group of students from the Universities of Groningen and Utrecht (see Van Strien, Cools et al., 1973). A steering committee, consisting of seven practising industrial and organizational psychologists, advised the project group about the formulation of the questions and the presentation of results. The formulation of the questions and the feedback of the results were devised in a way to stimulate the critical awareness of ethical problems.

The Present Situation

For a better understanding of the developments, I would like to begin by giving some information about the state of affairs in industrial and organizational psychology in the Netherlands.

A first indication of the impact of industrial and organizational psychology is the number of persons engaged in this field. There has been a rapid increase in the number of industrial psychologists during the last two decades. In 1952 the psychologists engaged in this field totalled less than 30. In 1962 their number had increased to at least 140, and in 1972 to about 300. I have no figures for other countries, but presume that the ratio of psychologists to the number of the working population in the Netherlands to be larger than in any other country, except the USA.

This rapid growth means that the average age of industrial psychologists is relatively low. Thirty per cent of our respondents left university only 4 years ago or less. Until now there has been hardly any unemployment among industrial psychologists. In the next 3 years, however, another 200 students now training to become industrial psychologists will enter the labour market. Indications of unemployment in related professional fields are a cause for concern. This is important in the present context in that it might affect psychologists' self-reliance in standing up for human values.

The position of industrial psychologists is also changing. Until 1960 a majority of them worked as independent practitioners or in independent consultancy firms. Only some large private or state-owned industries, the Civil Service, and the Ministry of Defence had their own psychological departments. In the sixties these internal departments expanded rapidly, and many smaller industrial and non-profit organizations engaged their own psychologists. At present there are at least seven industrial and governmental organizations employing ten or more industrial psychologists. As a consequence of this development, the younger psychologists, especially those who are employed in larger departments are losing their privileged status and their sense of uniqueness. In a way it is even possible to speak of a kind of 'proletarization' of psychologists and other university graduates in industry.

This rapid growth of industrial psychology has mainly been possible as a result of the already mentioned broadening of the scope of professional activities from mainly personnel selection and related activities to organizational psychology in the widest sense. Sixtyfour per cent of our respondents are still engaged for part of their time in personnel selection, and 29% for more than half of their time. In addition to the classical field of selection, however, all kinds of new activities such as training, management development, measurement of motivation and satisfaction, ergonomics, work design, organizational development etc. have found a place within the practice of industrial psychologists.

In the future a further development of these new activities is to be expected. Students tend to focus their studies on these subjects and our respondents express a clear need for refresher courses in these types of work.

From our inquiry personnel selection appears to be the main activity in external, independent bureaux, whereas organizational psychology has been more developed in the internal setting of psychological departments of industrial and other organizations.

130

Another aspect which strikes us, from our inquiry, is the rapidly decreasing membership of the N.I.P., especially among the younger generations. In the last 10 years, membership of the N.I.P. has dropped from at least 90% to about 65% of all psychologists. In fact only half of the psychologists who recently graduated from university enrolled as members. This applies to other psychological fields as well as to industrial psychologists. From personal communications it appears that similar developments are going on in other countries, for instance the UK and the USA.

In the statistical analysis of the results of our inquiry, these four factors (age, external versus internal position, accent on selection versus organizational psychology, and membership of the N.I.P.) were used as the major parameters.

A Multi-relational Model

I should like to summarize and discuss the results of the inquiry and their implications for professional ethics within the framework of a multi-relational model of the position of the psychologist (see van Strien, 1974a). According to this model, the psychological consultant has to deal with the divergent, partly conflicting interests and expectations of (a) his sponsors, (b) the other persons or groups within the client system, (c) the professional system, (d) his own private world and (e) the entire social forces operating in the larger environment. The following diagram represents schematically the systems in which the psychologist is involved or with which he has to deal. All of them exert their own pressures and put their own partly contrasting demands upon the psychologist and, sometimes, bring him into embarrassing conflicts of allegiance. In this account, the temptation to deal with pressures from the larger environment will be resisted and I will concentrate more upon (a) to (d).

In their relation with the client system, psychologists are exposed to increasing pressures. In the field of personnel selection there is a growing public concern

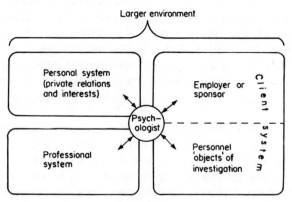

Figure 8.1. A multi-relational model of the position of the psychologist

about the position of the testee and increasing doubt about the rights of the employer to personal information about applicants. In the field of organizational psychology the harmony which characterized industrial relations in the Netherlands in the period after the Second World War is giving way to a growing awareness of conflicting interests. Industrial conflicts and tensions make it ever more difficult for psychologists to remain neutral. Even the claim of the neutrality of established psychology is challenged and social science is accused of having become a tool of management in the service of the powerful. Psychologists who overtly or covertly take the side of the 'bottom part' of the client system tend to get into trouble. Many of our respondents, especially those employed in an internal position, express a deep concern about the possibility of making a significant contribution in their work. The self-respect of some is threatened to such an extent that they have thought about leaving or have actually left their jobs.

The ethical quandaries of the present practice and the increasing critical awareness of the public may be illustrated with three examples of recent conflicts, one from the domain of personnel selection and two from organizational psychology. These have been specially selected because they attracted public attention and were discussed in papers or magazines.

The most notorious case was the handling of applicants by the Psychological Department of the Civil Service (the R.P.D.). The applicants complained that they were not given the opportunity to have an interview about the results, after having been tested, a right that is granted to them even in the old ethical code. In addition to this there were complaints about the use of projective tests, humiliating treatment of applicants, and so on. The question about whether these complaints were well founded is not important at this moment. What matters is that a vehement debate began in which psychologists accused each other of unethical or thoughtless behaviour which led to complaints to the disciplinary committees of the N.I.P.. The Directors of the R.P.D. later resigned as members of the N.I.P.. Questions were raised in Parliament and a committee of inquiry has been set up by the government.

In the field of organizational psychology the most striking incident in the last few years has been the so-called Bello-Project of the Dutch Steel Works and Blast Furnaces. A large-scale investigation of the attitude of workers towards payment systems was undertaken by the Psychological Department, making use of a large number of discussion groups. When this led to a too critical attitude on the part of the employees about the distribution of incomes and other matters of policy, management intervened, and the project was only allowed to continue on a much more restricted basis.

A third incident concerns the reporting of the results of a large-scale survey of the need for more autonomy and influence on the part of workers in the metal industry. The psychologist conducting the investigation failed to make clear arrangements with the sponsors and the management of the organizations involved about the reporting of the results to the respondents on the shop floor. When he expressed the intention to report comparative figures about the situation in the plants involved to the workers, he got into trouble with his sponsors, because they feared industrial relations might be impaired in plants with unfavourable figures. The financing of the project was endangered and the project could be finished only after a considerable delay.

Besides these incidents, which attracted public attention, a great number of incidents and sources of tension were reported in our investigation. Only 28 % of our respondents did not state any ethical problem at all. In the assessment of personnel, the use of tests, the reporting of the results and the abuse of reports still appear to be matters of concern for many psychologists. Attempts to counsel candidates about carrying their application through, in the light of the results, have been opposed by personnel managers. Testing of redundant personnel for lay-off is felt to be another problem.

In organization consultancy the major problem is that psychologists are often brought in at a stage when it is too late to make a significant contribution. This is Davis's point about the researcher being restricted to the margins of a problem; see Chapter 5. Such a situation gives them the feeling that they are only called upon to appease emotions, instead of being able to act as change agents in a meaningful sense. Problems over reporting to non-management personnel, as mentioned in our third example, were repeatedly mentioned in our investigation. Other examples of ethical problems are an assignment to do an investigation into employees' attitude to striking, the use of attitude and morale surveys to manipulate personnel, and the like.

Another concern is work for military organizations or the weapon industry. Quite a few psychologists would for instance question whether NATO is the right channel through which the affiliated governments should sponsor scientific exchange, and in this respect I must confess I had to overcome certain scruples in coming to this conference.

The awareness of ethical problems appears to be strongest among the younger, internal psychologists, working in the field of organizational psychology. Many expressed a strong need for a position more independent of management. The Works Councils, which have been accorded more power by the new law, or steering committees established by them, are seen by a number of psychologists as potential sponsoring bodies. In the opinion of others, unions should be more involved in commissioning investigations by social scientists. In this case a kind of bi-partite sponsorship can be imagined, as already realised in a number of Scandinavian projects, or, if a government body takes part as well, a tri-partite sponsorship (Drew, 1973). In any case, most psychologists wish to act not only as non-directive data gatherers or process catalysts, but also to state their own values.

Person and Profession

For an analysis of the way psychologists as persons and as professionals deal with these kind of problems, we must now turn to the left-hand side of Figure 8.1 on page 130.

Firstly, a few words about the 'personal system'. This heading covers the personal aspirations, values and interests and the political beliefs of the psychologist, the shared opinions in the reference groups he belongs to, the needs of his family, etc. The personal system is seldom explicitly mentioned in discussions about professional behaviour, but it certainly exerts an influence. The statements about desired developments and ethical rules in our inquiry directly pertain to the personal value systems of the respondents. In describing the growth in the number of psychologists, attention has already been drawn to how changes in employment, the loss of uniqueness, and similar factors affecting the personal system, might have an influence on the awareness of and attitudes towards ethical problems.

The 'professional system' comprises professional training, professional organization, institutionalized exchange, professional rules, an ethical code, the promotion of shared interests, etc. In my review of the state of affairs of industrial psychology in the Netherlands, I have already noted the waning interest in the professional organization.

It may be helpful to interpret this phenomenon as an instance of deprofessionalization. In sociology there is quite an extensive literature about professionalization and deprofessionalization which also sheds more light upon the function of a professional code (see for instance Pavelko, 1972; Mok, 1973). It seems possible to distinguish three phases in the development of a profession (van Strien, 1974b).

A. *A pre-professional stage*

In this stage persons endowed with special gifts or knowledge provide their services on a personal basis, often in the service of a lordly or wealthy patron. In this sense many of the present professions are the successors of the priests, the medicine men, the astrologers and the courtly scholars of ancient times. In terms of our diagram there was a direct relation between the personal system of the man of knowledge and the patron.

B. *The stage of professional organization*

A first step towards professionalization was made in the mediaeval guilds. The foundations of the present professional organizations, however, were not laid until the nineteenth and twentieth centuries. After the dissolution of the guilds and the progression of the industrial revolution, there followed an epoch in which the crafts tended to disappear into the proletariat. Forming a solid professional association was the best way for the serving professions to maintain their special position. The promotion of mutual interests, however, was only mentioned as a peripheral aim, the central value being the benefit of the public through high standards of training, exchange of know-how and irreproachably ethical behaviour. The most classical of the professions formed in this way are medicine and law, followed by accountancy, architecture, pharmacy, dentistry and the like. Later on psychologists, social workers, nurses, teachers, football-players, airline pilots and traffic navigators etc. have also formed their own professional organizations. Wilenski (1964) even speaks of the professionalization of everyone. In an incisive treatise the British sociologist Johnson (1972) has shown how behind the noble altruistic appearance can lurk aspirations to protect one's own power position. The possession of a code of professional ethics has been one of the prerequisites for a fully grown profession. In an account of a symposium of the British Psychological Society about Ethics in the Practice of Psychology, there occurs the following quotation by the late Professor Mace: 'I do not think it matters much what our own Society has in its code. The important point is that we should be regarded as the kind of people who have such a thing'. In so far as the ethical code thus served as a mark of professional maturity, it had primarily the character of a code of honour, proclaiming the noble unselfish intentions of the profession. Disciplinary control served mainly to protect the reputation of the profession and was laid in the hands of a board of colleagues. The formation of professional associations means in our diagram of systems that the relation with sponsors or employers is no longer determined by the personal whims of a patron and the bargaining position of the man of learning. The sponsor or employer has now become the client of a professional, who acts as part of a professional system which regulates the relations of its members with their clients.

C. *The post professional stage*

The decreasing membership of the professional organization, apparent from our inquiry, can be interpretated as an indication of what could be called an oncoming post-professional stage. An analysis of the reactions obtained from our respondents shows three different patterns emerging at the moment in the attitude towards professional organizations and professional ethics:

1. *Modernizing the profession.* Psychologists subscribing to this standpoint tend to remain members of the N.I.P. but want to change it from within into a more modern, open professional organization, which serves as a platform and meeting place for all partners involved in the diagram. Related professions should be drawn in as much as possible and walls between professions should be levelled. Professionals should draw together primarily on the basis of their object of concern and field of work and only secondarily on the basis of separate disciplines. In this vision a professional code should take the character of an agreed convention or contract, mutually regulating the conduct of the partners involved in a professional relationship. This means that all parties involved in the client system, including unions and employee organizations, should be consulted in framing rules of conduct and this should be done in a way which is open to public scrutiny. Disciplinary control should not be left to a board of fellow psychologists but be laid in the hands of a body in which all parties involved are represented.

2. *Professionals are as much workers as anybody else.* According to this second viewpoint, the profession should give up its distinct character and be affiliated to, or even incorporated in, other organizations serving the interest of workers. In terms of our diagram the professional system should become, in this view, a sub-system of the labour unions, to serve the common cause of the personnel part of the client system. The number of industrial psychologists holding this view is small but increasing. Some of them are still members of the N.I.P.,

probably with the intention to exert pressure to change it in the desired direction, but they are members of a union at the same time. A number of them are also members of VWO, the Dutch association of scientific workers associated with the World Federation of Scientific Workers, or of the BWA, a more militant twin organization of the VWO. According to this vision there is no need for a specific ethical code for psychologists. Instead, psychologists should, together with representatives of the other interest groups involved, draw up strategic and tactical programmes of action to wrest specific concessions and rights from employers and other persons in power positions. On a more general level they tend to subscribe to some broader manifesto as, for example, the charter for scientific workers of the above-mentioned federation, which states a set of responsibilities in a more exhortative rather than legislative manner.

3. *Relapse into the personal system.* An increasing number of psychologists newly graduated from university have no interest at all in associating themselves with some kind of professional or employees' organization, but merely try to build up good working relations with their colleagues in the direct context of their work. Confronted with ethical problems they will probably seek the advice of their colleagues, but primarily they will act on their own conscience.

In reality of course, the three positions are not as distinct as appears from the description. Often psychologists oscillate between them or try to combine elements of each.

Towards a Client-system Based Professional Code

Because of this divergence of tendencies it will not be easy for industrial psychologists to agree as a profession on a clear strategy towards the client system and the larger environment. Leaving the upholders of the ideal of the old, closed profession on the one hand, and the advocates of a far-reaching deprofessionalization on the other, the main trend in Dutch industrial psychology is to strive for a modernized professional organization, with open relations with the other parties in our systems model.

The way the renewal of the professional code of industrial psychologists is being taken up can be seen in itself as an example of this new open attitude. The industrial and organizational psychologists—members of the N.I.P. or not— were regarded by the committee in charge as their client system, to be consulted about their opinions on ethical propositions. On the strength of the results of the conducted inquiry a draft for the new code has been formulated. Only those statements were included which were endorsed by a substantial majority of the respondents. In a meeting of the section of industrial psychologists the new code was accepted last year on an experimental basis. With the help of an evaluation committee, the users will test the implications over a period of 2 years, after which the necessary reviewing will take place. In the meantime, a number of evaluation hearings are taking place, which are making practising psychologists more willing to submit their work to ethical scrutiny. In this sense the survey and the handling of the results can be considered as a piece of action research.

Within the framework of this report it is not possible to treat the formulations of the new code in detail. The central intention governing professional behaviour of industrial and organizational psychologists is stated to be the furthering of as humane work relations and social conditions as are possible.

This general aim is specified in a way which does not state more detailed rules and caveats, do's and do nots than the old code and most other codes that I am aware of. The primary aim of the code is not to provide the profession with additional or more rigid rules, but to clarify the mutual roles of the partners in the consultancy relation and the rights and responsibilities resulting from them. Considerable attention is given to the handling of information between the partners in our model, this being the precondition for all control and action. People's right to be informed beforehand about the aims of a project and the freedom to refuse participation are stated explicitly, and along with this there is a right to be informed about the results, to read reports delivered to the sponsor of the investigation and to appeal if they feel unjustly treated. In order to further scientific rigour, files of investigations shall be kept in such a way that the considerations which have led to certain conclusions are open to professional scrutiny (a kind of professional audit). Apart from these most salient points, the code of course contains the usual items dealt with in most professional codes such as privacy, confidentiality, validation of methods and the like.

As mentioned in the introduction, the formulation of an ethical code for industrial and organizational psychologists was part of an endeavour to revitalize the ethical awareness and to renew the ethical code of the profession as a whole. Other sections of the N.I.P. were prompted to draft a similar code for their own field of work. At the same time the Standing Advisory Committee on Professional Ethics—of which I am a member—started working on a revised 'General Code' for the psychological profession as a whole, which would be preceded by a 'Preamble', in which the general aims and principles underlying professional behaviour would be stated. The rules laid down in the General Code had to be sufficiently precise and carefully formulated to serve as a basis for disciplinary measures. The Preamble was meant to provide a background philosophy for any dealings in human affairs. The human values involved are of such a fundamental nature that they would apply to other behavioural sciences as well. The question has been raised whether psychologists should draw up a document like this on their own or, better, draw in representatives of the other professions concerned as well. A drawback of the latter approach, however, is that some of the other relevant professions are less organized, which makes it more difficult to consult them; moreover the ethical problems are less strongly felt in most other professions. It was decided that psychologists should proceed with the renewal of their ethics and at the same time initiate contacts with other relevant professions.

The framing of the Preamble and the General Code has already been completed. Drafts were submitted to the last semi-annual conference of the N.I.P.

in June 1974. Taking account of the comments received a final version will later be submitted to the membership for implementation. The function of the renewed code would be:

(a) to stimulate social scientists and their students to pause longer over the ethical and political problems of their work and to consider these at an earlier stage than is now usual.

(b) to induce sponsors and employers to deal more carefully with human problems by presenting the code to them and by discussing the ethical implications and limitations of certain assignments.

(c) to inform job applicants, interviewees, personnel to be involved in change programmes and the like beforehand of their rights, which will help them to better protect their interests.

(d) to stimulate discussion about ethical matters with and within other professions and to further cooperation and joint action.

(e) to make dealing with the human aspects of work relations a matter of public concern; putting the ethical case code before public opinion, and stimulating public discussion about the issues involved can help to exert pressure to terminate malpractices.

The more the ethical code thus extends beyond the boundaries of the professional system from which it originated, and starts to affect the personal system, the different parts of the client system and the larger environment as well, the more it becomes a real client-system based code.

The Quality of Working Life

Coming to the question whether a new code like this will lead psychologists to make a more powerful contribution to the quality of working life, the answer is that it depends on the extent to which it comes to life among psychologists and the other parties in the consultancy relationship.

Starting with the working life of psychologists, taking the new code to heart would mean giving up the entrenched position of being just a professional, a servant of power, a benefactor of the weak and oppressed, or a person who acts on the basis of his own intuition and conscience. By bringing about a dialogue between the personal values of the psychologist, the current values of the profession and society at large, and the values of the different partners of the client system, a step is made towards overcoming the alienation between work and life, theory and practice, subject and object. On the part of the client system this would give those who are the 'objects of investigation' the opportunity to become participants, to have a share in the formulation of the problem and the drawing and implementation of conclusions. This would reduce the alienation in their position and help them in their striving for a better working life.

In the Preamble a set of fundamental values is stated, which clarify the rather general statement about human work relations and social conditions in the code of the industrial and organizational psychologists. These values are: mutual respect and equality among all human beings; right of access to information; fairness in the allocation of resources; self-realization along with mutual responsibility and democratic exercise of power; and, as far as science is involved, objectivity and professional expertness in research, and a consulting relationship in which personal views and interests should never prevail over those of the clients. In the subsequent parts of the Preamble the specific responsibility of the intellectual for the fate of our fast changing society is stressed along with the need for a joint reflection on what should be done. If we call the shaping of society politics, it can be said that the Preamble tries to awaken the political awareness of social scientists. In this sense it can function as an innovative force.

Nevertheless strong reservations still have to be made. You can lead a horse to water but you cannot make it drink. Disciplinary committees can only deal with violation of concrete rules, errors of commission, not with errors of omission. There may be waves of enthusiasm but these will only affect some. Others are apathetic, sceptical or resigned. The divergence within the professional system has already been indicated, which makes it difficult to create a common front. And even if psychologists could draw one line, their power would depend on the commitment of the other parties involved. In my opinion the psychologist's ethics will not bring him far if he has to preach his message in a missionary way. His case is much stronger if there are forces in other parts of our diagram which exert influence in the same direction. The psychologist should, however, proceed with caution. A permanent alliance with a specific party within the client system is not advisable, because the trust of the other parties would be lost. In specific controversies the psychologist should, however, not hesitate to take sides, and to make use of the pressure others are exerting to reach an ethically acceptable solution.

The reality, however, is that this commitment from the other parties is often conspicuously lacking. Clients and the representatives of their interests often do not bother, and public opinion mostly is interested only as long as an issue has news value. Sponsors tend to refrain from giving new assignments to social scientists who have become too exacting or annoying, or even kick them out in the middle of a project. The presence of practitioners in the same or an adjoining field who bother less about ethics often prevents the social scientist from pushing his case as far as he feels he really should. Only when behavioural scientists of all kinds of training and experience, who act as consultants to organizations, present one common front, can real influence be exerted; but this is a far cry from the present situation. Even this influence will be limited, because of the inherent 'softness' of all behavioural science and the accompanying lack of real expert power. Until now the face of the earth has more been changed by technical and economic innovations than by new ideas and insights into human functioning. The impact of behavioural science will certainly grow with the increase of valid knowledge, but it will take a long time for consultants in these fields to make themselves indispensable. Exhortative preambles and rigorous rules of conduct are important prerequisites for a new mentality, but a strong grip on tangible structures is even more important.

Personally, I should like to make the case for the development of a kind of 'dialectical behavioural science' which deals with the social concomitants of structural changes in technology and management as for instance: automation, shift work, new payment systems, dispersal of industries to development areas and so on.

Socio-technical and work design approaches have already drawn attention to the reciprocal relation between the technical and the social aspects of work organization. The logical next step which is now coming closer is framing a multi-system model, in which the economic and the policymaking systems are taken into account as well, the whole within the context of the economic and political macro-environment. The more that is learnt about the relations between changes in structure on each level, the more structural innovations can deliberately be used as the levers of improvements in the quality of working life.

References

Bannister, D. (1973). The shaping of things to come, *Bulletin of the British Psychological Society*, **26**, 293–295.

Clark, A. W. (ed.) (1974). *Experiences in Action Research*, Jossey Bass.

Drew, G. C. (1973). On applied psychology in Britain, *Bulletin of the British Psychological Society*, **26**, 191–197.

Johnson, J. J. (1972). *Professions and Power*, Macmillan.

Mok, A. L. (1973). *Professie en Professionalisering*, Trendrapport SISWO.

Pavelko, R. M. (ed.) (1972). *Sociological Perspectives on Occupations*, Peacock.

Rapoport, R. N. (1970). Three dilemmas in action research, *Human Relations*, **23**, 499–513.

Strien, P. J. van (1974a). Beroepspraktijk en beroepsethiek van bedrijfspsychologen, *Mens en Onderneming*, **28**, 112–125.

Strien, P. J. van (1974b). Deprofessionalisering van de psycholoog? III, *De Psycholoog*, **9**, 87–96.

Strien, P. J. van, Cools, E. *et al.*, (1973). Speelruimte en spelregels, verslag van een enquête over beroepspraktijk en beroepsethiek onder de bedrijfspsychologen in Nederland. Groningen-Utrecht.

Warr, P. B., Cherns, A. B., Jackson, P., Pym, D. (1973). Better working lives, a symposium, *Occupational Psychology*, **47**, 15–36.

Wilenski, H. (1964). The professionalization of everyone. *American Journal of Sociology*, **70**, 137–158.

9

Theories of Motivation

Peter Warr
MRC Social and Applied Psychology Unit
University of Sheffield, England

It is quite essential to increase understanding of motives and their operation if we are to advance knowledge and practice in the area covered by this book. Almost every chapter contains some reference to pressures from society, adaptation to existing conditions, resistance to change, reluctance to work in certain conditions, job satisfaction or dissatisfaction, contemporary values, or changes in employee attitude and outlook. Each of these is a reflection of the operation of complex motivational systems.

The conceptual difficulties in this field are severe, so severe that some prefer instead to term it a graveyard: many good scholars are buried here. Despite that, we clearly need to continue our attempts to devise more adequate models of what people want from work, why they do or do not want certain types of change, what factors influence their satisfaction, and how conflicting personal and organizational goals can be reconciled. In attempting this, we must go beyond merely mapping out motives and their satisfaction, and learn more about the dynamic nature of goal systems: changes in motive strength often need explanation more than the stable existence of particular wants (Steers and Porter, 1974; Warr and Wall, 1975).

The psychological approach to studying people in organizations is seen by some sociologists, anthropologists and others as too narrow because it usually ignores questions of social structure and change. The idea of a few monolithic motives determining the course of events is said to be inappropriate; we need to think in terms of biographical and historical features, cultural influences and technological opportunities.

Such criticism is sound. Psychologists' theories which take personal motives as somehow primary and unchanging are much too limited. In practice however we can incorporate biographical, historical, cultural and technological features within psychological models by considering people's perceptions and assessments of their environments. In this manner we recognize that the context of a person's existence is all-important, but we study it mainly through the individual himself as our unit of analysis. Such a level of analysis is merely one of several that are possible, each painting its own picture of a multi-sided reality.

It is the psychologist's picture of reality with which this chapter is largely concerned. I wish to review a large amount of psychological thinking in an attempt to integrate and evaluate theoretical progress, and will also make a few suggestions about possible lines of development. The approach which I favour has several strands, and it may be helpful to introduce some of them at the outset.

(i) The major features of motivation are in general terms fairly obvious. Through everyday experience and through programmes of research we have already mapped out the broad pattern. What we have not yet done is find a way to put all the well-known features together within an acceptable theoretical structure. We do not necessarily need brand new concepts at the moment. If we could make the current ones work together more adequately, new ideas could emerge from their integration.

(ii) In order to progress towards this objective, we have to give greater emphasis to people's experiences, thoughts and feelings. We need to find improved methods of studying mental processes associated with particular situations or events. This may sound obvious, but there are still a large number of eminent psychologists who would doubt it.

(iii) This requires us to concentrate more upon the location of an action within other actions. We need to develop tools to understand what people do in the context of their past and future intentions and in the context of what they might have done in their present situation. This means that we need to look more at those alternatives which never become realized in overt behaviour.

Issues of this kind will crop up throughout the paper. I shall first introduce some of the terms which I find helpful. The major features of motivation will than be reviewed, suggesting that a theory of motivation which aims to be applicable to work situations has to do justice to all these features. Then we can examine current theories to see how they stand up to this criterion of covering the known components of motivation. Finally, I should like to raise for discussion some changes of emphasis which seem to me to be desirable.

The Concept of Motivation

Let us start with the obvious question: what is a motive? Orthodox definitions contain reference to 'the causes of behaviour' (e.g., Cofer, 1972; Madsen, 1961; Vernon, 1969), 'factors which incite and direct an individual's action' (Atkinson, 1964), 'the determinants of activity' (Young, 1961), 'an idea or concept . . . to explain behaviour' (Bolles, 1967), or the processes 'invoked to account for the initiation, direction, intensity and persistence of goal-directed behaviour' (Weiner, 1972). Authors naturally vary in their emphasis, but there is almost everywhere a claim that motives are determinants of behaviour. Indeed they are—but only sometimes. The concept of motivation must certainly include the possibility that a motive may be reflected in behaviour, but it does not follow from this that a motive and a piece of behaviour always go together. Either of them—motive or behaviour—can occur without the other. We are for instance always wanting things and evaluating possible goals without any observable changes in what we do (cf. Kagan, 1972). Yet psychologists have almost always studied behaviour as their primary subject matter and then gone on to infer motives as hypothetical processes somehow causing that behaviour. It is true that in recent years the approach has been becoming more 'cognitive' (e.g. Dember, 1974; Heckhausen and Weiner, 1973), but the theme is still behaviour first, causes of behaviour second.

This strong professional tradition of being in the behaviour business has had a variety of unfortunate consequences. It has encouraged a heavy dependence upon rigorous control and the measurement of behaviour in limited situations. Recent accounts of mainstream psychologists' work in the field (Appley, 1970; D'Amato, 1974; Wayner and Carey, 1973) are well summarised by D'Amato's observation that 'anyone consulting the reviews . . . for enlightenment regarding the possible basis of human acquired motivation must have come away sorely disappointed. The vast majority of studies cited in these papers relate to animal, and in particular rat, research' (1974, p. 97).

The interest of this conference does not really extend to rats. So let us leave aside the more physiological aspects of motivation and focus instead on motives which involve mental processes with or without immediate behaviour. It is helpful to think in terms of the notion of 'wanting' in this respect. You can want to carry out a whole range of actions without necessarily doing anything at the time; the word 'motive' seems a little odd in those cases when you do not actually do anything. Similarly I would prefer to emphasize the notion of an 'action' instead of always talking about 'behaviour'. The word 'action' is used in everyday speech to imply the operation of thoughts, intentions, evaluations and so on (e.g., Kenny, 1963; Peters, 1958; Taylor, 1964). By definition actions include a mixture of overt behaviour and covert thought. Coming to a conference, for example, requires a series of actions which gain their meaning through intentions and plans and through links with other actions and their associated thoughts.

This chapter will look at motives as 'reasons for action'. To emphasise the experienced features of these reasons for action I shall talk in terms of wants and wanting. Statements about wants are sometimes clearly about evaluation, satisfaction, pleasure, desire and related concepts, but they are sometimes less clearly to do with these. In cases of habit or duty for instance, wants are illustrated by phrases like 'I did it because I always do so' or 'I did it because it's my job'. The point to be made here is that wants, as reasons for action, can be of several different kinds; they do not only operate in the pursuit of pleasure.

Another issue to be considered at the outset is that of the level of our theory (Ryan, 1958, 1970). How specific should the actions be which form the focus of our account? Should we examine someone's tendency to work hard in general throughout the year, or his motivation to work hard at a particular task at a particular time, or both? In a similar fashion, should we concentrate upon fairly stable dispositions such as achievement motivation, authoritarianism, aggressiveness; or should we focus upon more restricted motives in particular circumstances? Motivation theories have varied in their level of specificity, and there is presumably no single correct approach. We do however need to narrow the field down somewhat by defining it in a way which separates it from other areas. My own bias in this is towards restricting motivation theories to more limited episodes of action and wanting and towards identifying the longer-term perspectives as theories of personality, value or attitude (Audi, 1972; Locke, 1975). In this sense, motivation theories will be referred to as 'lower level' and personality theories as 'higher level' approaches. This is of course just a matter of emphasis, and there is no right or wrong about it.

To summarise these introductory comments and preferences, it seems that in discussing theories of motivation our major concern should be with specific actions and a person's reasons for these actions. We should also study his reasons for *not* doing something. Reasons involve thoughts and wants about oneself and one's situation, so that to understand motivation we have to study thinking and wanting whether or not these processes are reflected in behaviour.

Reasons for Actions

Two theories may vary considerably in their scope and yet be of equal validity. This depends on the kind of events which they claim to explain. One theory of motivation may deal only with the behaviour of rats in a maze, whereas another might aim to explain the motivation of schoolchildren in the classroom. These two theories may employ different kinds and numbers of concepts and yet be equally valid within their own domain. In our case we are interested in complex everyday events, particularly those taking place at work, and an interest in this domain means that we must cover a certain minimum number of variables and processes. Theories in our domain need to cover at least nine major possible reasons for action. These types of reason have been known for a long time, partly because of their insistent presence in day-to-day experience, but despite their familiarity they are the building blocks of any theory of motivation in work situations.

These nine reasons will be identified as R1 to R9, where the letter 'R' stands for 'reason for action'. They are as follows:

R1. Intrinsic desirability of an immediate outcome
R2. Intrinsic desirability of consequential outcomes
R3. Social comparisons
R4. Social pressures
R5. Trends in aspiration level
R6. Perceived probability of attainment
R7. Habits
R8. Other wants and actions
R9. The structure of action

Some aspects of each one will be described, and we can then proceed to ask how adequately the currently available theories deal with each of the nine.

R1. *Intrinsic desirability of an immediate outcome.* This is the most central but in some ways the most mysterious feature of motives. Some outcomes are in an irreducible sense pleasant, attractive, desirable, evaluatively positive. Using well-practiced physical work skills or operating at an appropriate level of challenge are of this kind. Intrinsic desirability has for centuries been viewed in terms of 'hedonic tone', and more recently concepts such as 'arousal level' (Berlyne, 1973), 'psychological complexity' (Walker, 1973) or 'level of stimulation' (Eysenck, 1973) have been used to capture its main characteristics. Any theory must be based upon the facts that wanting entails intrinsic desirability of certain outcomes and that people act in order to obtain what they want. By the same token empirical work has to study preferences, interests and evaluations within its area of concern, and a higher-level theory should say something about the nature of these preferences and the variables which affect them.

R2. *Intrinsic desirability of consequential outcomes.* An extension of the first feature is the obvious fact that actions have consequences which themselves vary in desirability. The value of a particular action is in part measured by the desirability of the events which flow from it. In earlier days this was viewed through concepts associated with 'secondary reinforcement', but it is more common at present to talk about the 'instrumentality' of an outcome, how far it is likely to lead to consequential satisfactions.

R3. *Social comparisons.* Actions and the intensity of wants are also strongly influenced through mental comparisons of yourself with other people. There are two main forms of social comparison in this area. The first is in terms of what you should be wanting. There is a sense in which man wants to want; he is regularly looking around for suitable objects of interest, so that wants may be both aroused and satisfied. He can often most easily learn about these objects of interest and possible means of their attainment by comparing himself with other people. If people in the firm down the road are experimenting with flexible working hours, or if colleagues are asking for better canteen facilities, you may well pick up these themes as new ones worthy of attention.

Freud's perspective was that 'cathexes' become attached to different types of object; in part this attachment was thought to arise through processes of social learning. A more recent theme has developed around the notion of 'self-attribution' (e.g., Bem, 1967; Laird, 1974; Schachter and Singer, 1962). The idea here is that people often interpret their feelings and wants with help from the environment. There are two kinds of information which give you cues about what it is that you want. There are internal arousal cues of the kind which are usually easily recognizable, but there are also external cues from the situation and from other people, which define what you should be feeling in that context. It appears that we sometimes learn about our own wants by watching other people.

The second form of social comparison is in terms of your assessment of satisfaction: how well are you doing? It is often very difficult to assess how satisfied you ought to be with a particular level of outcome. Are you satisfied with the boss's level of consideration or should you expect more? Is your pay satisfactory or should you expect more? There are several bases for these judgements about how well you are doing, but in many situations a particularly important one comes from the comparisons you draw with other people. Your assessment of your own satisfaction depends on how satisfied you think others are with comparable rewards and achievements. This point will be taken up again in a later section on equity theory.

R4. *Social pressures.* The fourth set of factors which influence wants and actions is clearly related to the previous one. In many cases where you compare yourself with others there is also an element of influence or persuasion from them. This is sufficiently obvious not to require elaboration, but it may be commented that theories of motivation in organizations pay surprisingly little attention to social influence. This is despite the fact that social influence is almost the defining characteristic of organizations themselves. The operation of social pressures has been stressed in models of wage demands and bargaining (e.g. Brown, 1973; Patchen, 1961) and in studies of group output norms (e.g. Whyte, 1955), but it requires more systematic attention from motivation theorists (cf. Lawler and Suttle, 1973). Note, incidentally, that social pressures go far beyond the informal normative influences so often studied by social psychologists. Under this heading are also included the notions of duty, formal responsibility, coercion and obligations from standards of society (e.g., Vickers, 1973).

R5. *Trends in aspiration level.* This next type of reason for wanting and acting is in terms of comparisons between the past and the present. The intensity of a particular want derives partly from the kinds of actions and satisfactions you have become used to. Recent illustrations of this include Yankelovich's (1974) notion of 'the psychology of entitlement': people at work used to wish that they might find a job with a pension, but they now assume that to be their right. Unemployed people may initially have a strong desire to find work, but repeated discouragements and failures can reduce its intensity considerably (e.g.,

Schweitzer and Smith, 1974). Educated workers whose aspirations for responsibility and involvement are continually frustrated may well stop wanting (e.g., Sheppard and Herrick, 1972).

This central feature of action was studied in the laboratory many years ago by Lewin *et al.* (1944). They examined success and expected success in moderately difficult situations of practical problem-solving or sensori-motor skill (see also Child and Whiting, 1949; Starbuck, 1963). A recurrent theme was that success at a task leads to raised aspiration levels, where these are defined in terms of how high to set the goal on the next attempt. This fact was usually interpreted in terms of a tendency to set up higher and higher goals until success becomes uncertain: many people like to undertake moderately difficult undertakings, and since practice makes these easier, aspirations tend to increase with repeated attempts.

The same point applies to wants and their satisfaction in many other areas. Aspiration levels increase through a process of adaptation: as rewards become familiar, and perhaps more easily attained, people adapt to them and seek out further rewards. Helson (1964, 1973) thought of this in terms of 'adaptation level' and Thibaut and Kelley (1959) wrote in terms of 'comparison level'. This process is not a purely self-contained one, since social comparisons are also involved: your socially-compared inputs to a situation may continue to increase over time so that static reward levels may also become unacceptable for reasons of comparative justice. And other people may be gaining increased satisfactions and acquiring new goals in the same period, thus providing further impetus for change in your own aspirations.

R6. *Perceived probability of attainment.* A sixth reason for doing or not doing something is in terms of expectancy of success. The perceived probability of getting what you want has been noted by many theorists to affect levels of motivation. Aspiration level studies (R5) are clearly relevant here, and Atkinson (1957), Heckhausen (1967, 1968) and McClelland *et al.* (1953) have all produced evidence that aroused achievement motivation is lower in situations of very low and very high perceived probability of success. From quite different perspectives, reinforcement theorists have demonstrated that intermittent schedules of reward (those generating a moderate likelihood of success) are more effective in shaping behaviour than are consistently low or high reinforcement probabilities. Instrumentality theory will be considered shortly; a central feature of this theory is of course the level of expectancy that certain consequences will occur later.

There are at least four kinds of variable which affect expectancies of success. Personal ability levels are obviously important and our self-assessments of these will influence our probability judgements. Individual differences in those aspects of personality to do with internal-versus-external control and optimistic self-reliance are also relevant (e.g., Evans, 1974; Heckhausen, 1973; Turney, 1974; Weiner, 1972). Thirdly, social influence and encouragement can affect how we estimate our chances of getting what we want; and fourthly there are more objective judgements based upon the environment in which we find ourselves. A worker's chances of earning more through extra effort may be restricted by environmental constraints in terms of inadequate equipment, machine-pacing or an ineffective payment-by-results scheme.

R7. *Habits.* As everyday experience makes clear, many of our wants and actions derive strength from the fact that they have become habitual. Allport's (1937) reference to 'the functional autonomy of motives' was a particularly appropriate one. We become accustomed to a particular work routine or to the occurrence of particular events at particular times. A habitual sequence can become important to us, and deviations from it can cause anxiety and concern. By the same token, habitual sequences prevent the exploration of new and possibly more rewarding activities, so that habits affect both the intensity and the content of wants and action.

R8. *Other wants and actions.* A particular action is influenced by other motivational systems in two main ways. In the first case there are often conflicts to be resolved between different possibilities. Choice here naturally depends upon differential salience and priority, and we can view this at different levels of generality and time span. In the short term it may be that social and time pressures determine the choice, but in the longer term there might be a more fundamental hierarchy of priorities. This is for example a key feature of Maslow's (e.g., 1970) theory. Self-esteem is thought to become important as an influence upon thought and action only when basic bodily and security needs have been met to some reasonable degree. Alderfer (1973) has further detailed this idea in his formulation of 'existence–relatedness–growth theory'. This makes rather more precise predictions about the ways in which those three main types of motivational system may influence each other. We may say then that the strength of any one want is in part determined by the degree of satisfaction of other wants.

Most writers on this topic have been satisfied to stress the negative aspects of relations between wants—questions of priority and conflict. We should however also notice that wants influence each other positively—they can augment or recruit each other in the service of a common goal. The goal may be 'common' in the sense that two sources of satisfaction are similar enough to operate as a joint goal at any one moment, but this may also be a question of means–end associations. A longer-term goal can generate and sustain strong sub-goals along the way. The question of relations between actions is the core of my final type of motivational reason, R9.

R9. *The structure of action.* Actions always have some degree of structure: their components are organized at one point in time and across time. In very short-term actions this structure may not be of great significance, and motives there may well function through James's 'ideomotor activities' (McMahon, 1973). But it is wrong to see most actions as larger versions of an ideomotor activity. Quite often the meaning of what you do comes from its embeddedness within larger actions. In long sequences, such as arranging to attend a conference, there is considerable scope for variation. A process of trial-and-error and continuing adjustment of sub-goals takes place as we move towards the attainment of the overall goal (e.g., Nuttin, 1964, 1973); actions are self-correcting.

One way of looking at this is to view actions as being organized around tasks (Ryan, 1958, 1970). A task need not be a self-chosen activity, nor necessarily one which you find attractive. For some reason (coercion, conformity, pleasure, habit or whatever) we take on particular tasks, and these have within themselves some traction which draws us along (Baldamus, 1951). We make and modify plans and we construct programmes of action which will achieve our ends or means to our ends. Satisfaction may in many cases be delayed, and there is a sense in which once we have made a good plan, one likely to succeed, we have already reached a goal without any overt action.

This point is obvious, but it is conceptually very hard to work with. Miller, Galanter and Pribram (1960) did however make a brave attempt. Their approach was coloured by an emphasis on physiological, behavioural and computer characteristics, but their objective was similar to ours; they were 'disturbed by the theoretical vacuum between cognition and action' (p. 11). Into this vacuum they introduced the concept of a plan, defined as 'any hierarchical process in the organism that can control the order in which a sequence of operations is to be performed' (p. 16). Plans are ever-changing in the light of trial and error and they may well incorporate sub-plans with goals that are in themselves undesirable.

Motivation theories have not so far come to terms with this feature of their subject. Man's goals are limited only by his own inventiveness and by his willingness and ability to devise plans and to structure his actions. To incorporate flexibility of this kind into theories of motivation we need to think more about the notion of structure and possible empirical techniques to get at it. These points will be taken up again later.

Some Current Theories

Let us pause and take stock at this stage. Where have we got to? The close interdependence of actions and wants has been stressed. In considering the latter, I have suggested a list of nine types of reason for action, each of which may be influential in any one setting. It was argued that a good theory of work motivation must do some justice to each of the nine.

The nine reasons for action do of course overlap. Social comparisons (reason 3) can affect aspiration levels (reason 5) and perceived probabilities (reason 6). The intrinsic desirability of consequential outcomes (reason 2) and other wants (reason 8) both contain aspects incorporated in the notion of action structure (reason 9). And intrinsic desirability of immediate outcomes (reason 1) plays its part in the development of habits (reason 7). At the moment, however, I feel that we cannot cut down the list below those nine types of factor.

So let us move on to ask how well current theories cover these minimum requirements. In attempting to answer this question theories have been grouped under seven headings. This has been a difficult task, and some of the up-and-coming ones may have been missed out. I have certainly missed out those approaches based entirely upon animal or physiological foundations, and with some reluctance I have also omitted those theories which deal mainly with unconscious motives. All motives are unconscious in the sense that they are latent for long periods, but those which are allegedly unavailable to consciousness present particular problems for the theorist. These will be, for now, left aside, without necessarily denying their existence.

Here then is the list. Each one has been identified by a 'T' for theory:

T1. *Content theories.* One very common approach has been to construct classifications of the major types of dispositional motive. McDougall (1932) argued for the existence of 18 different 'propensities', Murray (1938) thought in terms of 20 'psychogenic needs', and Maslow (e.g., 1973) suggested 14 'being-values'. Such theories of content tend to be at the higher level which were identified at the outset. They cut across lower level theories (those accounting for particular actions), and the groupings which they include are likely to represent contemporary value-systems as well as any unchanging truth. There are undoubtedly some objectively definable needs for food, water and so on, but wants can have as their objectives and sub-objectives almost anything. It seems that classifications of these objectives must be in part arbitrary, but content theories are none the worse for that.

T2. *Hierarchical theories.* Many content theorists do however assume that the arousal of a particular class of motive depends upon the satisfaction of others. The views of Maslow and Alderfer have already been referred to, and Herzberg (e.g., 1966) and Argyris (1973) should perhaps also be mentioned at this point. Whilst the content theories are largely untestable in principle (because they are necessarily arbitrary), the hierarchical models might be open to partial examination if the required longitudinal investigations could be carried out. Cross-sectional, correlational studies tend to reveal small positive links between the satisfaction of different motives, whereas hierarchical theories expect that the more one motive is satisfied the less satisfied will the next one appear. Follow-up studies across time are essential here.

T3. *Aspiration level theories.* Attention has already been drawn to laboratory studies by Lewin in the area of aspiration level and to models by Helson and Thibaut and Kelley. Theories of habituation should also be included under this heading. Most of these (e.g., Solomon and Corbit, 1974; Walker, 1973) assume two processes in opposition to each other, so that repetition of a satisfying action leads not only to its strengthening but also to its weakening at the same time. Another possible approach is through Helson's (e.g., 1973) model of contrast effects. It may be that people evaluate an action and its satisfactions in the light of memories about earlier and more novel events; by contrast to these particularly pleasurable recollections the repeated action may come to be viewed as relatively less desirable than it might otherwise have been.

T4. *Equity theories.* Whereas aspiration level theories emphasise judgmental comparisons with yourself at different times, equity theories emphasise comparisons between yourself and other people. Festinger's (1954) theory of social comparison processes was mainly concerned with the way people evaluate their own abilities and opinions; essentially this was seen as a question of seeking out and responding to suitable comparison situations. Later theories have tended to emphasize judgements about fairness and satisfaction, examining perceived fairness as part of social exchange processes (e.g., Adams, 1963, 1965; Goodman and Friedman, 1971; Pritchard, 1969; Walster, Berscheid and Walster, 1973; Weick, 1966).

The basic tenet of equity theory is that people compare their own inputs to a situation with those of other people and that they make similar comparisons of their rewards. Inputs are typically seen in terms of effort, experience, skill, training, hours of work *et cetera*, and rewards are in terms of the satisfaction or pleasure deriving from pay, status, esteem, material comforts and so on. The major field of application has been that of perceived fairness of different wage levels (e.g., Lawler, 1968, 1971), although other motivational areas are implicitly covered. Homans (1961) applied the notions of equity theory very broadly, thinking in terms of generally-held conceptions of 'distributive justice': people's net rewards in all areas should be proportional to their inputs.

T5. *Achievement motivation theories.* A separate group of models has been particularly concerned with thought and action directed towards meeting internal standards of success. McClelland (e.g., 1961, 1971) has particularly emphasized the higher-level features of dispositional achievement motives and the measurement of individual differences in these. Atkinson (1957, 1964) and Weiner (1972) have refined the central concepts (approach and avoidance motivation, probability of outcomes and incentive value of outcomes) to yield precise predictions about behaviour in experimental situations. These latter approaches have much in common with instrumentality theories, both in line of descent and in their subject matter (e.g., Raynor, 1969).

T6. *Instrumentality theories.* Both perspectives on motivation (T6 and the lower-level T5) are of a rather analytic, microscopic kind. They start from the general proposition that wants are turned into actions when some balance of benefit is thought likely to follow in the foreseeable future, and they proceed by breaking this down into a large number of expectancies and valences. An individual is assumed to weigh these up in deciding how to act, although this comparative calculation is not necessarily conscious or complete. The force to perform an action is in this way seen as a multiplicative function of valence of outcomes and expectancy that they will occur.

Instrumentality theory has received much attention from industrial psychologists, and valuable discussions have been presented by Behling and Starke (1973), Graen (1969), Heneman and Schwab (1972), Miner and Dachler (1973), Mitchell and Biglan (1971), Porter and Lawler (1968), Vroom (1964), Wahba and House (1974) and others (see also Mitchell's discussion in Chapter 10). This is not the place for detailed comment on the theory, but one broad generalization might be appropriate. Its basic components have a long history, even within psychology, and most earlier applications were restricted to situations where possible choices and their outcomes were defined in advance. Betting games where estimates are made of subjective expected utility amongst specified alternatives or situations where people set targets on a predetermined scale both seem particularly appropriate for the application of the theory. However, when it is applied to more open-ended situations in which a wide variety of wants and actions might in principle be considered, there are obvious problems: which reasons for action has the individual evaluated and how does he weight the many components in interaction? Unless instrumentality theory can cast light upon this type of issue it is in danger of remaining either a precise predictive model in very constrained settings or a statement of the generally self-evident: people tend to do what they think will benefit them. I hope that the theory can avoid this dilemma, and will return to the question later.

T7. *Attitude theories.* Social psychologists have constructed many different models in attempts to predict behaviour from attitudes (e.g., Thomas, 1971). In the present context we might view an attitude as a dispositional want-system, and as such some generalized association with action is logically necessary. Yet predictions of behaviour based upon attitude measurements have not been very successful, partly because of simplistic research designs which attempt merely to correlate two rather gross variables and partly because of unexamined contextual influences. Recent work by Fishbein (1967) and Ajzen and Fishbein (1972, 1973) has concentrated upon more restricted attitudes, those towards the act itself, and this part of their model has largely been in terms of instrumentality theory. But they couple that concern with a focus upon normative beliefs (what a person thinks he is expected to do) and his desire to follow those beliefs. As such they go beyond instrumentality theory (introducing R4 as it has been labelled it here), but their tests have tended to rely upon very restricted laboratory situations (e.g., Ajzen and Fishbein, 1974) and to aim primarily at showing that normative beliefs and desires are in fact relevant to these situations. Issues of weighting in realistic settings have yet to be tackled, although a start is being made in the area of market research.

Other social psychological models are also tending in the direction of including additional predictive variables beyond merely a measure of attitude towards an object. Rokeach and Kliejunas (1972), for instance, demonstrate the relevance of 'attitude toward the situation', and Audi (1972), Kelman (1974) and Wicker (1969) have spelled out the need to build up more complex predictions which take account of situational constraints.

The same trend is evident in research into job satisfaction and job performance. The notion of job satisfaction is very closely related to that of attitudes to work, and we are seeing a gradual rediscovery of the fact that in particular circumstances work attitudes and behaviour are linked. Porter and Lawler (1968), for instance, have shown how this is the case with managers when behaviour and rewards are organizationally interdependent. Carlson (1969) illustrated how the recorded association between attitudes and behaviour is increased when personal aptitudes and job requirements are matched. In general, then, there is broad agreement that more attitudinal and situational factors need to be brought into research designs in this area. However, we are still rather uncertain just how to achieve this in practice.

So where are we now? Seven broad types of motivational theory have been listed. These overlap in many ways, though few investigators have so far made use of the overlaps. We should next attempt a brief evaluation of the seven types of theory. This will be done here in terms of their scope, how far they cover relevant features, although other criteria in terms of their content or structure are of course possible.

One aspect of a theory's scope is the actions it refers to. In principle all the types of theory described can apply to many aspects of work and satisfaction. In practical application, however, there has been a strong emphasis on work output. A few voices have been raised in protest against this narrow focus (e.g., Landy and Guion, 1970; Turney, 1974), but hardly anyone has examined from a motivational theory stance such actions as joining a union, lodging a grievance, asking for higher pay, being absent, changing jobs and all the other important activities associated with work. This is a pity, and I wonder what might be done to make amends.

The major question of scope is however about the variables which each type of theory incorporates. I have suggested that for work situations we need to consider a minimum list of nine reasons for action. How far do each of the types of theory cover these nine components? An attempt has been made to answer that question in Table 9.1. A cross occurs where a theory clearly deals with one of the components, and cases of apparent non-application are left blank. The occasional question-mark means what it says—I am not really sure. These crosses, blanks and question-marks are clearly judgements on my part,

Table 9.1. Theoretical coverage of major motivational factors

	T1 Content theories	T2 Hierarchical theories	T3 Aspiration level theories	T4 Equity theories	T5 Achievement motivation theories	T6 Instrumentality theories	T7 Attitude theories
R1 Intrinsic desirability of an immediate outcome	X	X	X	X	X	X	X
R2 Intrinsic desirability of consequential outcomes	X	X			?	X	
R3 Social comparisons				X			X
R4 Social pressures						?	X
R5 Trends in aspiration level		X	X		X		
R6 Perceived probability of attainment				X	X	X	
R7 Habits	X	X	X				X
R8 Other wants and actions	X	X					X
R9 The structure of action		?				?	

and you may well wish to disagree with some of them. Assuming for the moment however that my judgements are broadly correct, we should now ask about the major omissions.

No single theoretical approach adequately embraces all the factors influencing wants and actions. On the face of it the hierarchical theories appear to be most comprehensive, but against that we should perhaps set the lack of detail in these theories: they tend to be broad but somewhat imprecise. Equity theories appear to be the least comprehensive, but these do not really claim to be a complete approach to motivation on their own.

Of the reasons for action, numbers four and nine are the most poorly treated by the theories. These factors (social pressures and the structure of action) have in common an emphasis on the pliability and variability of actions. This seems to be what we have to concentrate on if we are to improve theories in this area.

Three Suggestions

That point will be followed up by setting down three personal suggestions about what we should do next in this field. These request both methodological advances as well as work to resolve the more conceptual difficulties that I have so far been concentrating on.

S1. *Wants, thoughts and intentions.* My first suggestion is a straightforward one, that we should take as given the fact that motivation is a thinking process. There are still far too many papers appearing in the journals which set out to demonstrate that people do have goals, that people are satisfied with their work if it meets their goals, or that people who set high goals are likely to do more. It is as if goals and plans were new possibilities and we were not quite convinced about their existence.

I would like to make two points about this. The first concerns psychologists' feelings about commonsense psychology as practiced by the man-in-the-street. When they are wearing their professional hats, psychologists are likely to express doubt about commonsense explanations of what people do. They look for another set of concepts, and do not accept as evidence for their scientific statements what goes on around them in their day-to-day lives. This process troubles me, and I would like to see scientific psychology develop out of commonsense accounts of actions. Of course we must refine these and generate our own methodologies, but could we not start with the explanations used by laymen? To do this we would begin with concepts like goal, habit, intention, hope, wish and so on, and we would build our theories from there.

The second point about this concerns the level of our theories. At the outset it was noted that 'higher level' theories focus upon more stable dispositions and wide-ranging motives (e.g., McClelland and Steele, 1973). 'Lower level' theories deal more with the explanation of particular actions and events. Both types of theories are needed, but at the present time we should swing more resources behind the development of lower level theories. And when we do that, we cannot avoid consideration of everyday mental processes.

The problem then becomes one of choosing concepts of an appropriate magnitude. I have seen 'wants' or 'reasons for action' as possibly about the right size in this field. This is partly because they are easy-to-use everyday concepts, but partly because some of the discussions arising from, say, instrumentality theory seem to be too microscopic and analytic. To measure the valence of an outcome through the sum of the valences of other outcomes multiplied by their perceived probability is an interesting idea, and clearly it is worth pursuing in some settings. But when we are also looking at many other factors, and when a complex set of observations of a rather microscopic kind is needed to establish each single one of these factors, could we not sometimes take a short-cut by using more direct measures of intensity of wanting? There are similar suggestions in the literature, based on more empirical evidence than that presented here, that some of the elements of instrumentality theory need not be measured in all situations (e.g., Lawler and Suttle, 1973; Schwab and Dyer, 1973; Turney, 1974). I have a hunch that the theory contains more of the essential elements than other models, and that it could be made still more acceptable if it adopted a rather less microscopic focus.

S2. *The structure of motives.* The second suggestion is built around the notion of 'structure'. I have argued that lower level theories must become more involved with the structure of action and thought. We have to develop both concepts and methods of measurement to understand structure better.

So what is this notion of structure? It is basically a question of type and degree of organization (e.g., Warr, 1970). Structure may be observed at one point in time or over a period of time and we should examine both of these. At any one point in time motives may be said to be organized in three main senses:

(a) In terms of interrelationships between elements at about the same level of generality. We could for instance map out the consistencies and inconsistencies in a person's actions, work out correlations between his preferences, or study the pattern of his attitudes and values. This is of course quite a common research approach, although it is more usual at higher than at lower levels.

(b) Organization in terms of hierarchies of levels. What are the links between specific actions and wants and more broad-ranging personal dispositions studied by personality or attitude theorists? This is widely acknowledged as a question of importance, and has been followed up quite a lot in the literature on achievement motivation and self actualization. In other domains it seems to be in need of closer study.

(c) Structure is also a matter of differential importance, and here we have major problems at the level of action. All theories of motivation have to incorporate the fact that certain wants are more salient than others in a particular situation, but so far no theory has made much progress in explaining which component will emerge as more important at any one time. This has for years been recognized as a central problem. Psychoanalytic theory has for instance often been criticized on the grounds that different defence mechanisms are used as explanations in a rather *ad hoc* manner to fit the facts as required. Lewin (e.g., 1935) wrote in terms of paths in psychological space but he was not able to specify which path would in fact be followed in any one situation. Cognitive dissonance theorists predict that people will take steps to reduce dissonance, but they have yet to find ways of determining in advance which means of reduction will be adopted in a particular case of dissonance.

Can we find ways into this problem? I do not myself see anything wrong with psychoanalytic theory's acceptance of different defence mechanisms. Any theory must allow that kind of principle—several different features may all be appropriate in any one situation. But how can we learn which one of the several will in practice become operative? One possibility is to rely more on retrospective studies of particular episodes, and I shall return to this shortly.

The past few paragraphs have been examining structure at one point in time. Structure across time has been the theme of previous sections of the paper. Wants and actions are moulded into shape by situations which extend over time, they are incorporated into means-end segments as part of an overall task with its built-in traction. They have goals which may in themselves be pleasurable or distasteful and whose attainment is often only desired as part of the overall sequence. Furthermore we learn through experience which plans are likely to succeed, and we think our way through problems and difficulties.

It is structure across time which is the particular weakness of current motivation theories, and I wonder where we might turn for help. One obvious possibility which covers many of the themes which have been outlined is the psychology of thinking (e.g., Radford and Burton, 1974). Another is research into the development of motor skills. As Cherns observed in Chapter 1, concepts in that field are similar to the ones we require. A learner may at the outset possess a loosely ordered group of movement sub-routines, each with its own goal. Through processes of repetition and cumulative feedback these constituent acts change as they become located in the correct serial order. As each new act is mastered it becomes supplanted by a higher-order skill that may encompass the earlier one as a sub-routine, but not necessarily in the same form. Spare capacity becomes available to look more at means–end relationships rather than only at particular means of doing something (e.g., Bruner, 1974; Bryan and Harter, 1899; Fleishman and Hempel, 1955).

How can we take up and build upon these notions? My ideas hinge upon the need to follow through people in the course of motivational sequences across time. That brings us to the final suggestion.

S3. *More retrospective models.* One goal of a theory is to allow accurate predictions about what will happen. Whilst still aiming at this as a long-term goal, it may be that in some circumstances we should give greater emphasis to retrospective investigations. The present state of motivation theory seems to me to be one of those circumstances.

It may be quite impossible successfully to predict sequences of actions organized through time and modified on a trial-and-error basis to meet new contingencies. We face too many potential interactions between variables at a time when we know too little about likely combinations and weights. We should also grant the possibility of free will; once this is assumed we have severely restricted our chances of successful complex prediction. Suppose instead that we focused upon certain classes of action which interested us — working hard, joining a union or whatever — and suppose that we conducted extensive retrospective investigations into events in the recent past, perhaps up to the present. We should assist people to provide accounts of their actions, plans, goals and satisfactions, and we could use this material to develop more representative theories which could subsequently be tested predictively as well as retrospectively.

The validity of self-reports and personal accounts as tools for the social psychologist has recently been argued by Harré and Secord (1972), and self-descriptive protocols have been successfully used for some time in experiments on thinking and problem solving (e.g., Newell, Shaw and Simon, 1962, Radford and Burton, 1974). One interesting possibility is that self-report methods might serve further to emphasise the significance of situational features; research has shown how observers tend to attribute a person's action to his dispositional characteristics whereas the person himself more often accounts for the action in situational terms (Jones and Nisbett, 1971).

I have in mind here the development of interview schedules focused upon questions of theory construction. There is of course nothing novel in carrying out interviews, but typically they are employed to obtain data about a specific empirical issue. I am arguing for their greater use in the development of theory. We might start with the nine types of reason for action considered earlier and devise methods to elucidate their relative importance in particular sequences of action. We would aim to understand people in general rather than just one person, but this would be achieved by building up structural information on a person-by-person basis. We would aggregate across people after we had studied sequences and relative weights for each individual. This contrasts with approaches which look for structure in material about the average subject.

One area where a start has been made on retrospective analyses is the evaluation of wages. In judging the fairness of your pay, which of many social comparisons do you give most weight to? Andrews and Henry (1963), Lawler (1965), Patchen (1961) and others have reported differences in fairness estimates depending on the closeness and organizational level of comparison persons. It seems that we could build upon this to gather more detailed information of changes in judgements over time and situations, mapping out the nature and the weight of social comparisons as we go.

A related technique was used by Herzberg, Mausner and Snyderman (1959). They employed patterned interviews to identify feelings associated with certain

158

critical incidents. The incidents were however often a long time in the past and research interest did not really extend beyond a classification of single events and feelings associated with them. Nevertheless the approach was clearly a fruitful one. It may be that we could extend these retrospective self-reports with studies of more recent sequences of actions to acquire deeper understanding of the concept of structure. Such an idea seems a sound one in principle; can we turn in into something useful in practice?

Perhaps I could finish with two quotations which have both made their mark on my thinking:

'It is in the act of valuing that consciousness and behaviour become united' (May, 1967, p. 220).

'Man's own pleasure is in planning and realizing objects not yet obtained' (Nuttin, 1973, p. 272).

If the field of motivation really is the graveyard which some believe, perhaps those could serve as my epitaph.

References

Adams, J. S. (1963). Towards an understanding of inequity, *Journal of Abnormal and Social Psychology*, **67**, 422–436.
Adams, J. S. (1965). Inequity in social exchange. In L. Berkowitz (ed.), *Advances in Experimental Social Psychology*, **2**, 267–299.
Andrews, I. R. and Henry, M. M. (1963). Management attitudes towards pay, *Industrial Relations*, **3**, 29–39.
Ajzen, I. and Fishbein, M. (1972). Attitudes and normative beliefs as factors influencing behavioral intentions, *Journal of Personality and Social Psychology*, **21**, 1–9.
Ajzen, I. and Fishbein, M. (1973). Attitudinal and normative variables as predictors of specific behaviors, *Journal of Personality and Social Psychology*, **27**, 41–57.
Ajzen, I. and Fishbein, M. (1974). Factors influencing intentions and the intention-behavior relation. *Human Relations*, **27**, 1–15.
Alderfer, C. P. (1973). *Existence, Relatedness and Growth*, Collier-Macmillan.
Allport, G. W. (1937). *Personality—a Psychological Interpretation*, Henry Holt.
Appley, M. H. (1970). Derived motives, *Annual Review of Psychology*, **21**, 485–518.
Argyris, C. (1973). Personality and organization theory revisited, *Administrative Science Quarterly*, **18**, 141–167.
Atkinson, J. W. (1957). Motivational determinants of risk-taking behavior, *Psychological Review*, **64**, 359–372.
Atkinson, J. W. (1964). *An Introduction to Motivation*, Van Nostrand.
Audi, R. (1972). On the conception and measurement of attitudes in contemporary anglo-american psychology, *Journal for the Theory of Social Behaviour*, **2**, 179–203.
Baldamus, W. (1951). Incentives and work analysis, *University of Birmingham Studies in Economics and Society*, Monograph A1.
Behling, O. and Starke, F. A. (1973). The postulates of expectancy theory, *Academy of Management Journal*, **16**, 373–388.
Bem, D. J. (1967). Self-perception: an alternative interpretation of cognitive dissonance phenomena. *Psychological Review*, **74**, 183–200.

Berlyne, D. E. (1973). The vicissitudes of aplopathematic and thelematoscopic pneumatology (or the hydrography of hedonism). In D. E. Berlyne and K. B. Madsen (eds.), *Pleasure, Reward, Preference*, Academic Press.
Bolles, R. C. (1967). *Theory of Motivation*, Harper and Row.
Brown, W. (1973). *Piecework Bargaining*, Heinemann.
Bruner, J. S. (1974). The organization of early skilled action. In M. P. M. Richards (ed.), *The Integration of the Child into a Social World*, Cambridge University Press.
Bryan, W. L. and Harter, N. (1899). Studies in the telegraphic language, *Psychological Review*, **6**, 346–376.
Carlson, R. E. (1969). Degree of job fit as a moderator of the relationship between job performance and job satisfaction, *Personnel Psychology*, **22**, 159–170.
Child, I. L. and Whiting, J. W. M. (1949). Determinants of level of aspiration: evidence from everyday life, *Journal of Abnormal and Social Psychology*, **44**, 303–314.
Cofer, C. N. (1972). *Motivation and Emotion*, Scott, Foresman.
D'Amato, D. R. (1974). Derived motives, *Annual Review of Psychology*, **25**, 83–106.
Dember, W. N. (1974). Motivation and the cognitive revolution, *American Psychologist*, **29**, 161–168.
Evans, M. G. (1974). Extensions of a path-goal theory of motivation, *Journal of Applied Psychology*, **59**, 172–178.
Eysenck, H. J. (1973). Personality and the law of effect. In D. E. Berlyne and K. B. Madsen (eds.), *Pleasure, Reward, Preference*, Academic Press.
Festinger, L. (1954). A theory of social comparison processes, *Human Relations*, **7**, 117–140.
Fishbein, M. (1967). Attitude and the prediction of behavior. In M. Fishbein (ed.), *Readings in Attitude Theory and Measurement*, Wiley.
Fleishman, E. A. and Hempel, W. E. (1955). The relationship between abilities and improvement with practice in a visual discrimination task, *Journal of Experimental Psychology*, **49**, 301–312.
Goodman, P. S. and Friedman, A. (1971). An examination of Adams' theory of inequity, *Administrative Science Quarterly*, **16**, 271–288.
Graen, G. (1969). Instrumentality theory of work motivation: some experimental results and suggested modifications, *Journal of Applied Psychology Monograph*, **53**, number 2, part 2.
Harré, R. and Secord, P. F. (1972). *The Explanation of Social Behaviour*, Blackwell.
Heckhausen, H. (1967). *The Anatomy of Achievement Motivation*, Academic Press.
Heckhausen, H. (1968). Achievement motivation research. In W. J. Arnold (ed.), *Nebraska Symposium on Motivation*, 1968, University of Nebraska Press.
Heckhausen, H. (1973). Intervening cognitions in motivation. In D. E. Berlyne and K. B. Madsen (ed.), *Pleasure, Reward, Preference*, Academic Press.
Heckhausen, H. and Weiner, B. (1973). The emergence of a cognitive psychology of motivation. In P. C. Dodwell (ed.), *New Horizons in Psychology II*, Penguin.
Helson, H. (1964). *Adaptation Level Theory*, Harper and Row.
Helson, H. (1973). A common model for affectivity and perception: an adaptation-level approach. In D. E. Berlyne and K. B. Madsen (eds.), *Pleasure, Reward, Preference*, Academic Press.
Heneman, H. G. and Schwab, D. P. (1972). Evaluation of research on expectancy theory predictions of employee performance, *Psychological Bulletin*, **78**, 1–9.
Herzberg, F. (1966). *Work and the Nature of Man*, World Publishing Company.
Herzberg, F., Mausner, B. and Snyderman, B. B. (1959). *The Motivation to Work*, Wiley.
Homans, G. C. (1961). *Social Behaviour, Its Elementary Forms*, Routledge and Kegan Paul.
Jones, E. E. and Nisbett, R. E. (1971). The actor and the observer: divergent perceptions of the causes of behavior. In E. E. Jones, D. E. Kanouse, H. H. Kelley, R. E. Nisbett, S. Valins and B. Weiner (eds.), *Attribution: Perceiving the Causes of Behavior*, General Learning Press.
Kagan, J. (1972). Motives and development, *Journal of Personality and Social Psychology*, **22**, 51–66.

Kelman, H. C. (1974). Attitudes are alive and well and gainfully employed in the sphere of action, *American Psychologist*, **29**, 310–324.

Kenny, A. (1963). *Action, Emotion and Will*, Routledge and Kegan Paul.

Laird, J. D. (1974). Self-attribution of emotion: the effects of expressive behavior on the quality of emotional experience, *Journal of Personality and Social Psychology*, **29**, 475–486.

Landy, F. J. and Guion, R. M. (1970). Development of scales for the measurement of work motivation, *Organizational Behavior and Human Performance*, **5**, 93–103.

Lawler, E. E. (1965). Managers' perception of their subordinates' pay and of their superiors' pay, *Personnel Psychology*, **18**, 413–422.

Lawler, E. E. (1968). Equity theory as a predictor of productivity and work quality, *Psychological Bulletin*, **70**, 596–610.

Lawler, E. E. (1971). *Pay and Organizational Effectiveness*, McGraw-Hill.

Lawler, E. E. and Suttle, J. L. (1973). Expectancy theory and job behavior, *Organizational Behavior and Human Performance*, **9**, 482–503.

Lewin, K. (1935). *A Dynamic Theory of Personality*, McGraw-Hill.

Lewin, K., Dembo, T., Festinger, L. and Sears, P. S. (1944). Level of aspiration. In J. McV. Hunt (ed.), *Personality and the Behavior Disorders*, Ronald Press.

Locke, E. A. (1975). The nature and consequences of job satisfaction. In M. D. Dunnette (ed.), *Handbook of Industrial and Organizational Psychology*, Rand-McNally.

McClelland, D. C. (1961). *The Achieving Society*, Van Nostrand.

McClelland, D. C. (1971). *Assessing Human Motivation*, General Learning Press.

McClelland, D. C., Atkinson, J. W., Clark, R. A., and Lowell, E. L. (1953). *The Achievement Motive*, Appleton-Century-Crofts.

McClelland, D. C. and Steele, R. S. (eds.) (1973). *Human Motivation, A Book of Readings*, General Learning Press.

McDougall, W. (1932). *The Energies of Men*, Methuen.

McMahon, C. E. (1973). Images as motives and motivators: a historical perspective, *American Journal of Psychology*, **86**, 465–490.

Madsen, K. B. (1961). *Theories of Motivation*, Munksgaard.

Maslow, A. H. (1970). *Motivation and Personality*, revised edition, Harper and Row.

Maslow, A. H. (1973). *The Farther Reaches of Human Nature*, Penguin.

May, R. (1967). *Psychology and the Human Dilemma*, Van Nostrand.

Miller, G. A., Galanter, E. and Pribram, K. H. (1960). *Plans and the Structure of Behavior*, Holt, Rinehart and Winston.

Miner, J. B. and Dachler, H. P. (1973). Personnel attitudes and motivation, *Annual Review of Psychology*, **24**, 379–402.

Mitchell, T. R. and Biglan, A. (1971). Instrumentality theories: current uses in psychology, *Psychological Bulletin*, **76**, 432–454.

Murray, H. (1938). *Explorations in Personality*, Oxford University Press.

Newell, A., Shaw, J. C. and Simon, H. A. (1962). The process of creative thinking. In H. E. Gruper, G. Terrell and M. Wertheimer (eds.), *Contemporary Approaches to Creative Thinking*, Atherton.

Nuttin, J. R. (1964). The future time perspective in human motivation and learning, *Acta Psychologica*, **23**, 60–82.

Nuttin, J. R. (1973). Pleasure and reward in human motivation and learning. In D. E. Berlyne and K. B. Madsen (eds.), *Pleasure, Reward, Preference*, Academic Press.

Patchen, M. (1961). *The Choice of Wage Comparisons*, Prentice-Hall.

Peters, R. S. (1958). *The Concept of Motivation*, Routledge and Kegan Paul.

Porter, L. W. and Lawler, E. E. (1968). *Managerial Attitudes and Performance*, Irwin.

Pritchard, R. D. (1969). Equity theory: a review and critique, *Organizational Behavior and Human Performance*, **4**, 176–211.

Radford, J. and Burton, A. (1974). *Thinking: its Nature and Development*, Wiley.

Raynor, J. O. (1969). Future orientation and motivation of immediate activity: an elaboration of the theory of achievement motivation, *Psychological Review*, **76**, 606–610.

Rokeach, M. and Kliejunas, P. (1972). Behavior as a function of attitude-toward-object and attitude-toward-situation, *Journal of Personality and Social Psychology*, **22**, 194–201.

Ryan, T. A. (1958). Drives, tasks and the initiation of behavior, *American Journal of Psychology*, **71**, 74–93.

Ryan, T. A. (1970). *Intentional Behavior, an Approach to Human Motivation*, Ronald Press.

Schachter, S. and Singer, J. (1962). Cognitive, social and physiological determinants of emotional state, *Psychological Review*, **69**, 379–399.

Schwab, D. P. and Dyer, L. D. (1973). The motivational impact of a compensation system an employee performance, *Organizational Behavior and Human Performance*, **9**, 215–225.

Schweitzer, S. O. and Smith, R. E. (1974). The persistence of the discouraged worker effect, *Industrial and Labor Relations Review*, **27**, 249–260.

Sheppard, H. L. and Herrick, N. Q. (1972). *Where Have All the Robots Gone?* The Free Press.

Solomon, R. L. and Corbit, J. D. (1974). An opponent-process theory of motivation. I, Temporal dynamics of affect, *Psychological Review*, **81**, 119–145.

Starbuck, W. H. (1963). Level of aspiration, *Psychological Review*, **70**, 51–60.

Steers, R. M. and Porter, L. W. (1974). The role of task-goal attributes in employee performance, *Psychological Bulletin*, **81**, 434–452.

Taylor, C. (1964). *The Explanation of Behaviour*, Routledge and Kegan Paul.

Thibaut, J. W. and Kelley, H. H. (1959). *The Social Psychology of Groups*, Wiley.

Thomas, K. (ed.) (1971). *Attitudes and Behaviour*, Penguin.

Turney, J. R. (1974). Activity outcome expectancies and intrinsic activity values as predictors of several motivation indexes for technical-professionals, *Organizational Behavior and Human Performance*, **11**, 65–82.

Vernon, M. D. (1969). *Human Motivation*, Cambridge University Press.

Vickers, G. (1973). Motivation theory—a cybernetic contribution, *Behavioral Science*, **18**, 242–249.

Vroom, V. H. (1964). *Work and Motivation*, Wiley.

Wahba, M. A. and House, R. J. (1974). Expectancy theory in work and motivation: some logical and methodological issues, *Human Relations*, **27**, 121–147.

Walker, E. L. (1973). Psychological complexity and preference: a hedgehog theory of behavior. In D. E. Berlyne and K. B. Madsen (eds.), *Pleasure, Reward, Preference*, Academic Press.

Walster, E., Berscheid, E. and Walster, G. W. (1973). New directions in equity research, *Journal of Personality and Social Psychology*, **25**, 151–176.

Warr, P. B. (ed.) (1970). *Thought and Personality*, Penguin.

Warr, P. B. and Wall, T. D. (1975). *Work and Well-being*, Penguin.

Wayner, M. J. and Carey, R. J. (1973). Basic drives, *Annual Review of Psychology*, **24**, 53–80.

Weick, K. E. (1966). The concept of equity in the perception of pay, *Administrative Science Quarterly*, **11**, 414–439.

Weiner, B. (1972). *Theories of Motivation: from Mechanism to Cognition*, Markham.

Whyte, W. F. (1955). *Money and Motivation*, Harper and Row.

Wicker, A. W. (1969). Attitudes versus actions: the relationship of verbal and overt behavioral responses to attitude objects, *Journal of Social Issues*, **25**, 41–78.

Yankelovich, D. (1974). The meaning of work. In J. M. Rosow (ed.), *The Worker and the Job*, Prentice-Hall.

Young, P. T. (1961). *Motivation and Emotion*, Wiley.

10

Applied Principles in Motivation Theory

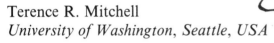
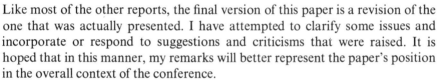

Terence R. Mitchell
University of Washington, Seattle, USA

Like most of the other reports, the final version of this paper is a revision of the one that was actually presented. I have attempted to clarify some issues and incorporate or respond to suggestions and criticisms that were raised. It is hoped that in this manner, my remarks will better represent the paper's position in the overall context of the conference.

The major thrust of the paper is an attempt to integrate, at the applied level, a number of highly divergent theoretical interpretations of motivation. Hence, while Peter Warr (Chapter 9) laid out the ways in which many of our theories were different, this paper will attempt to show some similarities. Also, where he dealt with theory, this will emphasize practice. Finally, it is probably useful to point out that the conceptual level of analysis will be the individual worker. This emphasis contrasts with many of the other papers [e.g., Albert Cherns (Chapter 1) or Lou Davis (Chapter 5)] which emphasized an organizational or social perspective.

The literature on motivation is immense and does not easily fit into a simple classification. However, one can discern some underlying dimensions upon which we can order various approaches to the topic. One such dimension is the degree to which a theory views man as a rational, mechanistic type as opposed to a more emotional, irrational individual. The former approach suggests that man is in some way 'out for himself' while the latter implies a more 'caring for others' philosophy. At the extreme end of the mechanistic pole is operant conditioning and Skinnerian behaviourism. On the opposite end is the participative management approach stemming from the human relations and human potential movements. Somewhere in the middle is a class of rational cognitive theories such as equity theory, exchange theory or expectancy theory. While these three general views of man's motivation are different in many ways they also have some striking similarities at the level of practical application. It may be that by describing these approaches in more detail we can reconcile and synthesize these applications into an agreed upon set of principles.

Skinner's Operant Conditioning

Many of us in the organizational area have never considered Skinner's work as really applicable to organizational settings. Note, in fact, that Warr's paper omits the behavioural analysis as a major motivational approach. Somehow our area is too complex to be handled by what is viewed as a rather simple mechanistic approach to human behaviour built on data generated in the laboratory from animals. However, in *Beyond Freedom and Dignity* (Skinner, 1971) Skinner describes and advocates the utilization of Skinnerian principles for the social design of our institutions and our culture. This work is not to be taken lightly. Numerous researchers in our own field are now writing on this topic. A number of studies have set up reinforcement schedules in work organizations and have found supportive results (e.g., Yukl, Wexley and Seymore, 1972). Symposia at last year's Academy of Management and the American Psychological Association meetings were devoted to the application of Skinner's ideas to the work setting.

What, in fact, does Skinner have to say that is important for understanding work behaviour? Well, there are two major components of the theory that are important: environmental determinism and reinforcement. To understand these components we must briefly describe Skinner's underlying ideas. Two types of behaviour are attributed to the human organism, respondents and operants. The former type of behaviour is assumed to occur as a function of direct stimulation. An example given by Skinner occurs when a person sneezes. These behaviours are attributed to their survival value and have played only a minor role in Skinner's research.

The operant behaviour, which is emitted in the absence of any apparent external stimulation, has been the major unit of investigation. When this type of behaviour is followed by consequences which change the likelihood of its occurrence again under similar conditions, these consequences are called a reinforcer. Food, for example, is a reinforcer to a hungry organism; anything the organism does that is followed by the receipt of food is more likely to be done again whenever the organism is hungry. Some stimuli are called negative reinforcers; those consequences which reduce the likelihood of behaviour occurring. 'Thus, if a person escapes from a hot sun when he moves under cover, he is more likely to move under cover when the sun is again hot. The reduction in temperature reinforces the behaviour it is 'contingent upon'—that is, the behavior it follows' (Skinner, 1971, p. 27).

The central and most important characteristic of this approach is the complete omission of any reference to the consciousness of the organism. A reinforcer is a stimulus which increases or decreases the probability of a response. A reinforcer does not 'feel good' or 'bad' but it is defined simply in terms of its effects on observable behaviour. This is environmental determinism. Using this approach Skinner has developed what he calls schedules of reinforcement in which the frequency and timing of rewards are specified. In general, positive reinforcement works better than negative reinforcement and reinforcers should occur immediately after the behaviour. Thus, through schedules of reward and punishment one can 'shape' people to behave in a fashion deemed desirable.

The application of these ideas to employee motivation would require a number of steps. First the desired behaviours would need to be specified. Is motivation the number of hours worked? The amount of energy expended? While a problem of agreement exists here it also exists for our other theoretical approaches. Second, we must determine what is positively and negatively reinforcing for individual employees as well as their current rate of motivation. Third, we would apply a selected reinforcement schedule. According to the theory, motivated behaviour would increase.

Expectancy Theory

Perhaps the theory most prevalent in today's literature on motivation is expectancy theory (Heneman and Schwab, 1972; Mitchell and Biglan, 1971; Mitchell, 1974). This approach suggests that an individual's behaviour and attitude are a function of the degree to which the behaviour or attitude is instrumental for the attainment of some outcomes and the evaluation of these outcomes (Vroom, 1964). The important idea is that the theory is based on a rational man model. The individual is believed to process large amounts of information in a rational manner and behave in a fashion that will maximize his return.

One supposedly exerts a certain amount of effort on the job based on three factors: (i) the degree to which effort is seen as leading to good performance, (ii) the degree to which good performance is instrumental for the attainment of some outcomes, and (iii) the evaluation or valence of these outcomes. Symbolically,

$$W = E\left(\sum_{i=1}^{N} I_i V_i \right)$$

W = amount of work (effort)
E = expectancy: i.e. the degree to which effort leads to successful performance
I_i = the instrumentality of performance for the attainment of the ith outcome
V_i = the valence or importance of the ith outcome
N = the number of outcomes

This equation is meant to represent the force on the individual to exert effort.

Thus a person intends to work hard if (i) he thinks his effort will lead to good performance (E) and (ii) he believes that good performance will lead to valued outcomes $\left(\sum_{i=1}^{N} I_i V_i \right)$.

A number of reviews of this literature are currently available (e.g., Mitchell, 1974) and will not be covered here. However, a fair summary of these data would suggest that almost all the investigations show at least moderate support for the expectancy rationale.

Participative Management

The word 'participative' in management theory means many different things. While there would surely be disagreement on specific definitions of each aspect, there are some broad statements with which most people would agree. In general, participation implies that there is shared decision making. People contribute according to their competence and not necessarily by position. These ideas are prevalent in much of the literature on job enrichment and organizational development. Another major aspect of the participative approach is that communication channels are open in all directions resulting in greater and more accurate information flow. Thus decision making is not only accomplished at the correct level but also with the proper information at hand. Finally, there is the idea that participation increases motivation through employee involvement. One can argue that the individual will have a greater commitment to specific decisions and the organization as a whole when he takes part in deciding how the system will function. Underlying all of these ideas is a philosophy that man is concerned for self-actualization. Participation supposedly works because it provides the employee with a chance to express himself, to become involved with the direction of the organization, to use his skills and abilities to their fullest potential.

So, on the one hand we have an alternative which suggests that man is completely governed by environmental contingencies. On the other extreme is a very loose theory (mostly composed of applied principles) which evolved from a view of human nature depicting man as a wanting, willing individual who behaves according to needs, desires, attitudes and feelings. These positions appear highly divergent, with an expectancy approach somewhere in between. The next two sections will attempt to show the similarities between an expectancy theory and each of the other two approaches in terms of their practical applications. A final section will point out commonalities for all three approaches.

Expectancy and Skinner

You will recall that a reinforcement analysis dealt with rewards and the frequency with which these rewards are distributed. One can easily see the theoretical correspondence between the impact of a reinforcer (positive or negative) and the valence of an outcome. The more positive the reinforcement the more highly valent (e.g., attractive) it would be. There should be correspondence between the environmental event and our cognitive assessment of it. There are also similarities between the idea of 'frequency of reinforcement' and the subjective probability (i.e., expectancy) of a behaviour leading to an outcome. Supposedly, the more frequently we were reinforced the higher our subjective probability estimate of the relationship between the reward and the behaviour.

In a thorough analysis of how these two theories can be integrated into one overall approach Jablonsky and DeVries (1972) point out the practical principles on which both approaches would agree. These are:

(i) Avoid using punishment as a primary means for controlling behaviour. In most cases positive reinforcement is equally effective and may avoid some negative side effects of punishment such as the need for surveillance. When undesirable behaviour occurs it should be ignored.

(ii) Minimize the time lag between the behaviour and the response. If physical rewards are not immediately available, one can bridge the gap by verbal mediation.

(iii) Apply positive reinforcers in a systematic way. This can be done through a careful analysis of what is favourable or unfavourable to individuals, what is their current response rate, and the establishment of specified reinforcement schedules.

(iv) Specify the desired behaviour clearly, in operational terms.

The individual must know both what is desired and what is not desired. Thus we can see considerable correspondence in terms of both the theoretical constructs and the implementation of these theories.

Expectancy and Participation

A similar analysis can be made for expectancy theory and participative management. Listed below are four general principles on which these two theories should agree both in theory and in practice. It should be mentioned that these four points are conceptually different from the four described above. The similarities between Skinner and expectancy theory are more explicitly stated at both the theoretical and applied levels. However, since participative management is a rather loose body of theory and application, I have attempted to show how the *underlying rationale* for participation would be similar for expectancy theorists and those believing in participative management.

Organizational contingencies are clearer with participation

Numerous studies have shown that including people in the decision making process clarifies the expectation about what leads to what. Leavitt (Leavitt and Mueller, 1967, p. 483), for example, presents data showing that feedback and information exchange 'increases the accuracy with which information is transmitted'. This accuracy can be directly incorporated into expectancy theory. Supposedly, through participation, the subject should know fairly well which behaviours are likely to be rewarded and which ones are not. The effort-performance relationship should be clearer and hopefully higher in magnitude under a participative system. By definition, the higher the expectancy, the greater the predicted effort (with outcome values held constant). We suggest, therefore, that clarified contingencies should lead to greater effort.

Participation increases the likelihood that employees will work for outcomes they value

A second way that participation may directly influence the components of expectancy theory is through the values that workers have for organizational outcomes. More specifically, through the process of participation, employees may be able to help set work standards, negotiate on working conditions and influence the reward structure. According to our equations, they would therefore ascribe high valences to the outcomes that are contingent on their effort. Thus employees would be better able to choose rewards they value highly. Again, by definition, the higher the valences, the greater the effort (when expectancy is held constant).

Participation increases the effect of social influence on behaviour

There are numerous studies from the group dynamics literature which relate participation and influence. The greater the communication or cohesiveness, the greater the influence. Vroom's review (1964, p. 229) emphasized that participation increases 'the strength of group norms regarding execution of the decisions, and the worker's "ego involvement" in the decisions'. Since both communication and cohesiveness are integral components of the participative approach, it would be expected that increased social influence would also occur.

These ideas have also been built into the expectancy motivational model by other authors (Dulany, 1968; Fishbein, 1967; Graen, 1969; Mitchell and Knudsen, 1973; Mitchell and Nebeker, 1973). These people have argued that one can treat 'meeting the expectations of others' as an outcome and include it in the $E(\Sigma IV)$ formula. However, there seems to be a distinction between what one could call internal and externally oriented motivation. Rewards such as salary, promotion or even intrinsic satisfaction are essentially oriented towards the question 'what do I get', while meeting the expectations of others seems to be theoretically different in that you are supposedly providing rewards for others as well as yourself. For these reasons, most theorists have included a second component in the expectancy model. One measures the degree to which effort meets the expectations of others weighted by the value of meeting these expectations. Note that we can include the expectations of peers, family, supervisors, etc. in this social component. Again, both theory and practice would correspond.

Participation increases the amount of control that a person has over his own behaviour

Supposedly, through the process of participation, there will be an increase in the degree to which an individual can influence and control those areas over which he has expertise. In this sense, the decisions would be made at the 'appropriate' level. Motivation is supposed to increase under these conditions.

What would this suggest for expectancy theory? Well, you will recall that the job effort model actually predicts the individual's intention to behave in a certain fashion. More specifically, we predict that an individual intends to choose that level of effort which he believes will maximize the receipt of valued outcomes. However, it is often the case that a person may not have control over the degree to which he could carry out his intentions. So, for example, one might intend to spend two hours working with the boss but end up working twice that long or half that long depending upon the boss's intentions. In general then, we would predict that the more control an individual has over his behaviour, the higher the correlation between predicted effort and observed effort. If an individual is highly motivated *and* is able to carry out his intentions because he has control over what he does, we would expect that he would do a good job.

Although we have not covered the empirical support for these four propositions let it be said that most of these ideas have been tested and supported and reports of these findings are available elsewhere (Mitchell 1973). It does appear as if many of these hypotheses generated from expectancy and participative approaches would lead to similar predictions. This brings us to our final attempt at integration: what sorts of principles do all three theories agree upon?

Predictive Commonalities for all Three Approaches

Rewards are more effective than punishment. Participative theorists believe that striving towards a goal is better for motivation than having people do things because of their fear of punishment. Somehow it is better to do something because you want to. A Skinnerian would argue for positive reinforcement on practical grounds suggesting that less surveillance is needed and that it is easier to maintain the proper behaviour. No reference would be made to wants or to fears. However, the prediction is similar.

Both social group processes and the formal reward system can influence behaviour. For the Skinnerians, any environmental event which increases the likelihood of a response would be positively reinforcing. Both social reinforcers (e.g., praise from a peer) and formal rewards (e.g., a pay rise) can have a major impact on behaviour. For expectancy and participative theorists social rewards are also important. An individual will exert effort not only because he believes it may lead to more money but also because he thinks his peers expect it of him. Again, our predictions would be similar in that all three approaches would incorporate social processes into their analysis.

To optimize the appropriate behaviour, rewards should be suited to the individual. The agreement here is striking in its formal inclusion in all three theories. An individual analysis is a central point; what is reinforcing, highly valent or actualizing will be different for different people. Flexibility in our reward systems would be appropriate from all three points of view.

Feedback in the form of rewards and punishments should be given frequently and consistently. The individual learns organizational contingencies through feedback. If we wish to encourage or shape various behaviours it is best accomplished through clear, explicit and frequently administered feedback.

Summary and Conclusion

In analysing the above list a number of comments seem appropriate both in terms of my own personal feelings as well as those expressed by other conference participants. First, John Rowan suggested that these principles are fairly trivial and Albert Cherns stated that every motivation theory would make the same predictions. The reaction seemed to be that these principles were not very startling.

These are important comments. If in fact one believes that these principles are self-evident then it reflects quite negatively on our knowledge about why people behave the way they do. One possible test of this idea is to examine various work design or structuring programmes to see if they are incorporated. Not a single paper presented at the conference dealing with such programmes, explicitly or implicitly included all of these principles. To dismiss them out of hand seems rather premature.

Also, to suggest that all theories of motivation include these principles is simply wrong. The Dual Factor theory, the Need Hierarchy, Theory X and Y, Equity Theory and Exchange Theory all omit at least one of these principles. Although one might make similar inferences from some of the more general statements included in these theories, most of them fail to specifically address themselves to any of these issues.

Finally, it was suggested by a number of participants (e.g., Cherns, Lawler) that an attempt to generate a 'general' theory of motivation may be fruitless: different theories will apply in different situations. This may be true. However, parsimony would at least demand that integrations be attempted. At this point I would personally be reluctant to abandon the pursuit of such an approach.

However, the attempt at integration presented here was clearly at the level of applied principles. We should not discount the theoretical differences. Both the expectancy and participative approaches refer to internal cognitive variables as the causes of behaviour while Skinner does not. This distinction is important. It suggests that while our different approaches may generate similar predictions their explanations of the causes of behaviour are diametrically opposed. Understanding requires more than prediction. Thus, while our similarities are easily incorporated into operating technologies, there is still much heated debate as to the underlying causes of the predictions. Since this controversy bears directly on much of our philosophizing about man, it will undoubtedly influence how technologies of behaviour are implemented.

Acknowledgement

This research was partially supported by the Office of Naval Research Contract NR 170-761, N00014-67-A-0103-0032 (Terence R. Mitchell, Principal Investigator).

References

Dulany, D. E. (1968). Awareness, rules and propositional control: a confrontation with s-r behavior theory. In D. Horton and T. Dixon (eds.), *Verbal Behavior and General Behavior Theory*, Prentice Hall.

Fishbein, M. A. (1967). Attitude and the prediction of behavior. In M. A. Fishbein (ed.), *Readings in Attitude Theory and Measurement*, Wiley.

Graen, G. (1969) Instrumentality theory of work motivation: Some experimental results and suggested modifications. *Journal of Applied Psychology Monograph*, **53**, Whole No. 2, Part 2.

Heneman, H. G., III, and Schwab, D. P. (1972). An evaluation of research on expectancy theory predictions of employee performance. *Psychological Bulletin*, **78**, 1–9.

Jablonsky, S. F. and DeVries, D. L. (1972). Operant conditioning principles extrapolated to the theory of management, *Organizational Behavior and Human Performance*, **7**, 340–358.

Leavitt, H. J., and Mueller, R. A. H. (1967). Some effects of feedback on communication. In E. A. Fleishman (ed.), *Studies in Personnel and Industrial Psychology*, Dorsey Press.

Mitchell, T. R. (1973). Management and Participation: An Integration. *Academy of Management Journal*, **16**, 670–679.

Mitchell, T. R. (1974). Expectancy models of job satisfaction, occupational preference and effort: a theoretical, methodological and empirical appraisal. *Psychological Bulletin*, **81**, 1053–1077.

Mitchell, T. R., and Biglan, A. (1971) Instrumentality theories: Current uses in psychology. *Psychological Bulletin* **76**, 432–454.

Mitchell, T. R. and Knudsen, B. W. (1973). Instrumentality theory predictions of students' attitudes towards business and their choice of business as an occupation. *Journal of the Academy of Management*, **16**, 41–51.

Mitchell, T. R. and Nebeker, D. M. (1973). Expectancy theory predictions of academic performance and satisfaction. *Journal of Applied Psychology*, **57**, 61–67.

Skinner, B. F. (1971). *Beyond Freedom and Dignity*, Alfred A. Knopf.

Vroom, V. H. (1964). *Work and Motivation*. Wiley.

Yukl, G., Wexley, K. N., and Seymore, J. D. (1972). Effectiveness of pay incentives under variable ratio and continuous reinforcement schedules. *Journal of Applied Psychology*, **56**, 19–23.

11

The Loci of
Work Satisfaction

Ralph Katz and John Van Maanen
Massachusetts Institute of Technology, USA

There is perhaps no area in the social sciences fraught with more ambiguity, conflicting opinion or methodological nuance than that of work satisfaction. Yet, paradoxically, there are few areas more researched. Even a casual glance at the voluminous literature should be enough to convince the most hardened generalist that work satisfaction is indeed a complex, cumbersome and many sided concept for which simple schemes do not exist. However, despite years of study, there is continuing controversy about the applicability of any particular theory of work satisfaction across even a modest range of tasks, organizations and work settings.

Fundamentally, the difficulties are conceptual. Work satisfaction is treated for the most part as if it were unidimensional, somehow amenable to measurement and representation by a single number. And a potpourri of theoretical emphases exists from which one may choose to locate the source or sources of satisfaction. For example, satisfaction may be seen to be contingent upon the individual's idiosyncratic internal need structure; the specific set of job tasks performed by the individual; the interpersonal norms and values generated in the workplace; the managerial processes that direct activities; the organizational policies regarding rewards; and so on including all combinations of the above. Hence the dilemma: either the satisfaction formulation is too general, without practical implication; or the calculus is too specific, misleading in diverse work situations.

Moreover, research in the area is characterized by loose definition, duplicity and a sort of swashbuckling, *ad hoc* correlational approach in which statistical significance replaces social significance. From this morass, support for virtually any position regarding the determinants of satisfaction can be marshalled: the proverbial dustbowl of empiricism. It is not surprising therefore that the applications that characterize the field are often exaggerated, atheoretical and faddish in the extreme. This view has been developed in critiques by Strauss (1963), Carey (1967), Hackman and Lawler (1971), Perrow (1972), and Gomberg (1973).

Of late, job redesign efforts have been heralded with almost messianic fervour as the solution to a supposed widespread discontent with routinized, meaningless and dead-end jobs. Spirited accounts from this perspective have been provided by Davis and Taylor (1972), Sheppard and Herrick (1972), HEW Task Force Report (1973) and Jenkins (1974). Earlier, democratization and humanization of the work *milieu* was the solution to what was regarded primarily as a morale problem. And in the now much ridiculed Frederick Taylor era, incentive rewards and the standardization of work procedures were viewed as the solution to a productivity-based satisfaction problem. While the influence of these latter two approaches has waned over time, both are still with us today.

These three points of view can be labelled for our purposes 'human resources', 'human relations', and 'human rewards', respectively. They represent the major research and theoretical paradigms popularized in the United States over the past 60 or so years. However, evolutionary progress toward understanding the nature and consequences of work satisfaction seems dubious, for no one model is applicable to all settings nor has any one framework subsumed the others. Furthermore, each tends to isolate and concentrate reform around a rather narrow set of conceptual variables consistent with the overall perspective of a particular paradigm. To a large degree, applications-oriented researchers in the field resemble Pirandelian players, each trapped within a programmed role, assuming the problem dimensions and offering his own pet solution.

Without addressing in detail particular analytic perspectives on work satisfaction such as Morse (1953), Dubin (1956), Herzberg *et al.* (1959), Adams (1965), Porter and Lawler (1968), Smith, Kendall, and Hulin (1969), Hulin and Blood (1969), Locke (1970) and others, it seems clear that the applicability of any approach depends on situationally specific, individually divergent issues. And, as Crozier (1964) and Karpik (1968) have demonstrated so insightfully, satisfaction cannot be viewed in isolation from the complex institutional and sociological settings to which satisfaction reports are directed.

If the ultimate purpose of our theorizing is the construction of better organizations where satisfaction is one of the evaluative yardsticks (along with effectiveness, adaptiveness and so on), then it is imperative to determine how different design features (work structures, reporting relationships, pay systems, etc.) affect specific aspects of work satisfaction. At a very general level, the important design features coincide with elements central to the three paradigms of human resources, relations and rewards. In other words, the problem revolves around the determination of which, if any, of these models best describes the sources of satisfaction and then a translation of the theoretical implications of such findings into practical programmes. It is to this end that the research reported here was directed.

Specifically, in this study we attempted to move away from traditional conceptualization of work satisfaction (i.e., unidimensional and individualistic) by demonstrating empirically the situationally dependent nature of the concept, denoting clearly the linkages attaching satisfaction attitudes to workaday realities. Thus we shift mental gears and metaphorically depict work satisfaction as a multidimensional concept best idealized not by a single level, but rather by a characteristic shape. It is easy to imagine for instance, an organizational surround wherein two employees report identical levels of satisfaction yet experience their jobs in radically different ways. One employee may be influenced predominantly by the salary and advancement aspects of the job while the other may be most influenced by the challenge, action and variation features of the job. In such a situation, the two employees have the same level of work satisfaction even though each have very different shapes.

In the deductive argument to follow, a model is outlined which identifies three quite separate origins of work satisfaction, within variables to do with properties of the job, interaction context and organizational policy. Each of the loci is shown to be analytically distinct and related to conceptually objective design variables. From this formulation emerges a substantially different notion of trans-situational change programmes designed to influence work satisfaction.

Methodology

Sample: Four government organizations (two municipalities, one county and one state) participated in the study. These governments represent a rather loose confederation of various service departments operating within a defined geographical territory (e.g., police and fire departments, public utilities, hospitals, social work agencies, sanitation departments, planning departments, etc.). Within each organization a stratified random sample was determined. Of the total sample of 3500 selected employees, 88% participated in the study. The stratification was based on proportionate sampling from eight Equal Employment Opportunity Commission (EEOC) job categories representative of the mix of occupations available in public sector organizations: administrative, technical, professional, protective service, paraprofessional, clerical, skilled craft and maintenance. For further discussion of the sample characteristics, see Van Maanen and Katz (1974).

Instrument: A survey questionnaire consisting of some 300 items was administered in February, 1974 to groups of public employees ranging from five to 50 persons. For the present analysis, we shall confine our remarks to three portions of the instrument: (i) the Minnesota Satisfaction Questionnaire developed by Dawis and Weitzel (1970); (ii) a truncated version of the Yale Job Inventory described in detail by Hackman and Lawler (1971); and (iii) a series of presumably objective design measures regarding various contextual properties of the work situation surrounding the respondent. A brief explanation follows.

Work satisfaction. A modified version of the Minnesota Satisfaction Questionnaire (MSQ) was used to measure the level of employee satisfaction. This instrument, comprising 100 items, was divided conceptually into 25 four-item indices, each related to a specific aspect of satisfaction (e.g., recognition, supervision, compensation, security, promotion and so on). Overall satisfaction was defined simply as the mean of all items. Each item asked the respondent to indicate on a five-point, Likert-type scale [ranging from very satisfied (5) to very dissatisfied (1)] how the respondent presently felt about a particular work feature. The instrument was selected from among a number of alternative questionnaires primarily because we wanted to span as wide a variety of work characteristics as possible. For a recent use and analysis of this instrument, see Wanous (1974).

Design characteristics. A crucial factor in this study was to determine the 'objective' characteristics of the jobs in which the respondents were assigned. To accomplish a portion of this task, the Yale Job Inventory was utilized. The items selected provide a reasonably accurate (insofar as self, peer, supervisor and outside observer ratings of the job converge) description of five so-called core-dimensions—skill variety (the degree to which the job requires different activities calling for the use of different skills); task identity (the degree to which the job requires the completion of a whole process); task significance (the degree to which the job has a perceivable impact on other people); autonomy (the degree to which the job provides an employee with freedom, independence and discretion in scheduling and carrying out work assignments); and feedback (the degree to which an employee receives information from the job as to the effectiveness of his work). Based on these five dimensions, a Motivating Potential Score (MPS) for each job was calculated [MPS = (skill variety + task identity + task significance) × autonomy × feedback from job]. Each of the above indices (with the exception of the MPS) consists of the mean response to at least three different seven-point, Likert-type items (i.e., each item asked the respondent to indicate the extent to which one of the above-specified attributes was present or absent on one's job). For a further description of the Job Inventory, see Hackman and Oldham (1974).

A number of specific items concerning other presumably objective design characteristics of the respondent's work experience were included in the instrument package. These items concerned authority, work assistance, pay, promotion, communications and the like. These design items were not thought to be inclusive of all relevant objective organizational features. Rather they were selected on the basis of covering different but representative areas that might affect employee attitudes. Four of these properties are utilized in this paper: (1) feedback from agents: the degree to which the employee receives information on his performance effectiveness from co-workers and supervisors (see Hackman and Oldham, 1974); (2) assistance from co-workers: the degree to which the employee requires help (or provides help) in carrying out day-to-day responsibilities; (3) promotion fairness: the degree to which advancement procedures in the employee's department are standardized (i.e., apply equally to all employees); (4) pay equity: the percentage difference between what the employee is paid at present and what others performing the same job outside the organization are paid. With the exception of pay, seven-point, Likert-type items similar to the Job Inventory were used for measurement.

Data analysis: Prelude to results. There are two critical data analysis problems. First, the diverse elements of expressed satisfaction must be represented as parsimoniously as possible. Second, the affective elements must be shown to be influenced significantly by the various design features of the organizational environment.

Two separate non-metric methodologies (hierarchical clustering and multidimensional scaling) are used conjunctively to address the first problem—deriving an economical satisfaction configuration. The clustering technique—Johnson's (1967) hierarchical algorithm—is used to reveal just how the different satisfaction items group together. The multidimensional scaling routine—TORSCA, as described by Torgerson (1965)—is used to reveal the underlying structure of the response set (i.e., the dimensions elicited by satisfaction items). In other words, clustering details an evaluative set which is constructed over a scaled perceptual set.

Operationally, the responses to the MSQ are combined to form an overall 25 by 25 correlation matrix to which the Johnson scheme is applied (to uncover compact clusters), and satisfaction measures calculated simply by averaging the items located in each cluster. In order to denote where the dimension-free clusters reside in psychological space, the same correlation matrix is used to scale the items into a dimensionalised Euclidean field.

Since there have been numerous factor analytic studies based on satisfaction data, it is important to denote the advantages of these procedures before continuing. Unlike factor analysis, both the scaling and clustering algorithms are non-metric (that is, input data are not assumed to be ordered in a ratio or interval fashion) and there are no linearity requirements. The correlations in the input matrix are treated simply as measures of the similarity between items. The derived solution is therefore invariant for any monotone transformation of the original correlation matrix (that is, one need know only that a given correlation is greater or less than another). Furthermore, the clustering technique develops dimension-free hierarchies within clusters. One does not have to determine dimensions before constructing clusters, nor does one have to determine whether dimensions are orthogonal, oblique or whatever. Finally, non-metric procedures typically yield fewer dimensions in their final solutions than metric alternatives, thus providing greater simplicity.

Once the attitude clusters are located and defined, the second problem can be solved by use of canonical and partial correlation. Canonical correlations

178

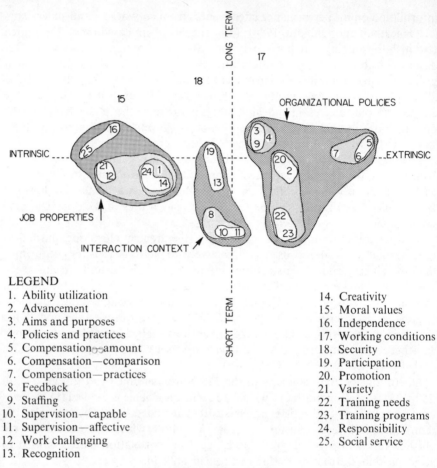

Figure 11.1. Satisfaction map

LEGEND
1. Ability utilization
2. Advancement
3. Aims and purposes
4. Policies and practices
5. Compensation—amount
6. Compensation—comparison
7. Compensation—practices
8. Feedback
9. Staffing
10. Supervision—capable
11. Supervision—affective
12. Work challenging
13. Recognition

14. Creativity
15. Moral values
16. Independence
17. Working conditions
18. Security
19. Participation
20. Promotion
21. Variety
22. Training needs
23. Training programs
24. Responsibility
25. Social service

furnish a relational measure between two component sets (each composed of two or more variables), in this case the discovered satisfaction clusters and the objective or design variables. Partial correlations, on the other hand, allow various elements in the two sets to be isolated while controlling on the remaining variables. For a further discussion of these techniques see, McNemar (1969) and Blalock (1970).

Findings

The results of the satisfaction mapping routines are presented diagrammatically in Figure 11.1. The horizontal and vertical axes represent a two dimensional solution of the scaling algorithm and the contour lines drawn around various items portray the clustering solution. It is important to note that the two-dimensional solution space reproduces clearly the original relationships uncovered by the hierarchical groupings. Thus, two dimensions are sufficient to display the embedded clusters revealed by the Johnson procedure. Solution spaces of higher dimensionality were calculated but did not substantially improve the goodness of fit.

The horizontal dimension in Figure 11.1 ranges from items dealing with social service, independence and challenging work to items concerning pay, advancement and training. This appears to approximate the intrinsic and extrinsic varieties of satisfaction. The vertical axis is somewhat more problematic. The items range from the pleasantness of working conditions and security at one end of the continuum to supervision and feedback at the other. Intuitively, this resembles something akin to a temporal based dimension—the long-run, short-run element involved in work satisfaction. This interpreted psychological map asserts consequently that individuals, when presented with this stimulus set comprised of satisfaction items (MSQ), distinguish perceptually among those items that are intrinsically or extrinsically satisfying and those that are pertinent in the long or short run.

Three distinct clusters are depicted in Figure 11.1 *via* the contour lines enclosing certain satisfaction items. The hierarchical nature of the clustering is depicted by contours embedded within other contour zones (shaded areas). Thus, the three major clusters—which we will refer to as loci—are represented by the three non-embedded contours. Except for a very few items that could not be grouped mathematically or meaningfully, all items fall into one of the three clusters—labelled job properties, interaction context and organization policies. Importantly, the items within each locus correspond to the paradigmatic variables of the human resources (job properties), human relations (interaction context), and human rewards (organization policies) models discussed previously.

It is important to specify that the satisfaction mapping cannot be used to classify individuals as being either high or low on any dimension. Nor does it imply that an individual derives his satisfaction primarily from characteristics unique to one end of a dimension. Rather, it is the loci, stretched out along both dimensions, that capture the measure and shape of one's reported satisfaction. Whether or not the three loci are conceptually distinct, arranged in a dominant order or are related homomorphically to design features of the environment are questions to which we now turn.

Table 11.1 presents correlations between each design feature and overall satisfaction scores and the three satisfaction loci. These should be interpreted in terms of their meaning within the logic of the study rather than in terms of statistical significance; with a sample as large as this one ($N \geq 2514$ for all tables) almost all non-zero correlations are statistically significant. The material in the table suggests that each design feature of the studied organization is associated with overall satisfaction. As shown in the left-hand column, the core job dimensions, interaction properties and policy measures are correlated highly with global satisfaction. Indeed even in the other columns of the table, where satisfaction is divided into the three clustered components (loci), the relationship remains relatively strong, except perhaps for pay equity.

Table 11.1 Correlations of design features with overall satisfaction and the three
satisfaction loci

	Correlations with:			
Design feature	Overall satisfaction	Interaction context	Job properties	Organizational policies
Task variety	0.28	0.19	0.50	0.13
Task identity	0.24	0.18	0.27	0.16
Task significance	0.23	0.19	0.35	0.14
Autonomy	0.40	0.32	0.50	0.22
Feedback from job	0.36	0.33	0.38	0.28
Feedback from agents	0.48	0.56	0.36	0.37
Co-worker assistance	0.36	0.41	0.25	0.37
Fairness of promotion	0.51	0.38	0.31	0.32
Pay equity	0.16	0.11	0.11	0.15

At first glance, it would appear that separate loci are nondiscriminating and that only a single overall measure of satisfaction is necessary. Yet the canonical correlation coefficient is $+ 0.67$, suggesting a substantial association between the three design characteristics and the three satisfaction loci. And, most importantly, the canonical analysis indicates that all variables must be included in the equation with approximately equal weight.

In order to crystallize the structure, partial correlations between the design factors and satisfaction loci are presented in Table 11.2. The loci held constant in each column are indicated at the top, and the partial correlations with each locus singly are shown in the body of the table. These are unambiguous. The five task dimensions are related only to the job properties loci. Feedback from agents and co-worker assistance are related solely to the interaction context loci. And promotion fairness and pay equity are associated with only the organizational policy loci. Therefore, each satisfaction locus can be related to a specific design feature and, as discovered by the canonical correlation analysis, all are important.

The results presented here were built upon a very heterogeneous sample of people working at considerably different jobs within differing organizations and departments. On the supposition that we might be levelling out important distinctions, the analysis was repeated for each organization, each department, and each EEOC classification separately. The findings in all instances were nearly identical to the results summarized above.

Implications

The thrust of the foregoing section suggests that we are dealing with an intricate, albeit relative, phenomenon. Work satisfaction, in the abstract, is interwoven

Table 11.2. Partial correlations of design features and satisfaction loci

Control loci:	Job and organizational	Interaction and organizational	Job and interaction
Design feature	Interaction context	Job properties	Organizational policies
Task variety	−0.10	0.54	−0.21
Task identity	0.02	0.20	−0.02
Task significance	0.00	0.32	−0.10
Autonomy	0.06	0.43	−0.15
Feedback from job	0.10	0.21	0.00
Feedback from agents	0.42	0.00	0.00
Co-worker assistance	0.28	0.04	0.07
Fairness of promotions	0.04	0.05	0.42
Pay equity	0.01	0.01	0.12

with job, interaction and policy threads, each of which contribute independently to the detail and strength of the fabric. On the surface, it may appear that Schein's (1970) cogent argument for a 'complex man' approach to the study of individuals in organizations is the most appropriate. Yet it may be useful to think also of human behaviour as being quite simple, but because most individuals work in very complex physical, social and political environments, their actual behaviour appears extremely complicated. In a similar vein, Simon (1969) draws an analogy with an ant traversing a beach ribbed with waves of sand: the ant's path might appear complex, although the ant's actions were directed at only the simple objective of returning to the nest. The crooked trail we see reflects the complicated environment in which the ant's task is carried out rather than a truly complex behaviour pattern.

This approach inverts the traditional psychological viewpoint in which the vast complexity of man's behaviour is seen to lie within him (emphasizing needs, motives, values and other individual differences). The assumption that behaviour is simple (indeed rational) may ultimately prove more fruitful. For such a perspective directs our attention to the variable characteristics of the situations in which people's work lives are embedded rather than to the relatively fixed personality dimensions of individuals called out in work settings. In part, our argument is that satisfaction is a function of situational surroundings accompanying the doing of work rather than a function of the psychological predispositions or demographic characteristics of the worker. While such influences cannot fully be put aside, we feel that it is far more important to identify environmental relationships to satisfaction than the more frequently used intrasubjective relationships. In this way any resulting change strategies can be grounded upon concrete phenomena observable in the work place. Furthermore, the addition of individual need preferences only slightly and non-significantly altered the reported patterns of the objective characteristics' relationship to satisfaction attitudes. While perhaps in cases of very high or very low need preferences, substantial effects may be observed, the usefulness of this approach seems questionable.

Regardless of theoretical slant on the determinants of behaviour, one implication is common to both the complex situation approaches. Put simply, there can be no one correct managerial strategy to influence employee satisfaction which works for all persons, across all situations and at all times. This is not a moot point. If one examines the myriad of programmes designed to combat alienative or dissatisfying aspects of the work experience, myopic and limited perspectives predominate. Both researchers and change-oriented practitioners tend to emphasize one philosopher's stone at the expense of others. Thus each satisfaction paradigm—whether human resources, relations or rewards—utilizes a very different set of assumptions about appropriate remedies.

What has been neglected in the unfolding of these attitude studies is the humble fact that whatever one's framework for viewing the roots of work satisfaction, support for that position is likely to be forthcoming. As Table 11.1 indicates, each cluster of objective traits correlates reasonably well with overall satisfaction. But as Table 11.2 so clearly demonstrates, these objective features are theoretically distinct. This situation is compounded by the pervasive tendency for those jobs ranking high (or low) on one objective feature to rank high (or low) on the other features, a sort of Marxian corollary suggesting that the better jobs in terms of their design (autonomy, variety, feedback) are also better paying, more likely to lead to advancement and enjoy privileged inter-actional benefits. However, a deeper probe of this somewhat commonsensical result reveals that this need not be the case. For example, professional jobs within the municipal government sample ranked high on all task properties, yet ranked low on all the interaction and policy dimensions (Van Maanen and Katz, 1974). In other words, focusing strictly on empirical correlations when dealing with this component variable called satisfaction can often be misleading.

We are arguing in effect that when one designs a change programme aimed at influencing work satisfaction, explicit attention must be paid to all three explanatory paradigms—human resources, relations, and rewards. One without the others may lead to substantial difficulties. Certainly there is a corres-pondence among the elements of the three models, but the effects of each can be isolated. Furthermore, each framework implies a quite different course of subsequent actions. If, for illustration, the source of dissatisfaction can be attributed to job characteristics (e.g., little variety or task identity), the appro-priate remedy would not involve a human relations programme to improve hierarchical communications or a policy change revising training techniques for employees working the target job—although these remedies could perhaps have positive secondary consequences. Rather the solution is one that involves changing directly the nature of the task. On the other hand, if there is a wide discrepancy between what employees are asked to give on the job and what they get in terms of reward, the solution is not job enrichment, but payroll enrichment.

Focusing on the work itself (by constructing more meaningful jobs where possible) may be the most effective method by which to improve satisfaction in the public sector, providing of course that substantial dissatisfaction can be attributed to only this area and sufficient latitude for improvement exists. Policies need not be revised extensively, and unlike many industrial jobs where technology almost precludes significant enlargement of various jobs (the proverbial Chaplinesque assembly lines), public bureaucracy routines are subject to vast changes. It may be that paper, people, and service tasks do not resist redesign efforts in the same fashion as steel, machinery and production tasks.

At least in most public offices a priority ranking may be established when attending to programmes designed to increase work satisfaction. First, jobs themselves must be investigated to determine whether or not improvements are called for from a human resources standpoint. Second, the interaction context should be examined along more or less traditional human relations dimensions. Third, the overall policies of the organization should be studied to trace down sources of reward dissatisfaction. But what is critical about this simple scheme is that it proceeds logically, from the most flexible potential change target to the least flexible or presumably the most resistant to change.

Several cautions should be added here however. The best plan in any organization is the most comprehensive. All three loci of work satisfaction must be considered. Furthermore, the discussion thus far assumes a somewhat stable environment. Yet, organizations are dynamic systems and changes in one area invariably have repercussions in other areas. Similarly, the loci equation implies a dynamic. A most basic example will suffice. Suppose a particular job is redesigned such that more responsibility and autonomy are provided. Over time, the employees working the enlarged jobs may justifiably become more dissatisfied with organizational policies such as a promotional system resting on seniority or a payment scheme resting on seniority—policies with which employees were probably once reasonably satisfied. Clearly, there are tradeoffs in the loci formulation, resembling perhaps something like a hydraulic system in which in change in one variable entails a change in another. Additionally, there is little reason to suspect that even the most enlarged jobs will not eventually become routinized and boring as employees become proficient at their redesigned tasks or that revised benefit packages will not lose their attractiveness at some future time. Hence longitudinal considerations must be included when advocating a tactic of improving work satisfaction.

To summarize, we have demonstrated empirically that the loci of work satisfaction fall approximately into three clusters related primarily to objective features of one's occupational situation. And based on these objective characteristics of working life, individual satisfactions develop which are conceptually, if not always operationally, independent. Of course, different people will

184

emphasize different loci, but we believe that in most situations, such emphasis will reflect collectively legitimated interpretations of the work-set and setting. It follows that stronger theory and more appropriate applications will result if we no longer concentrate on psychological explanations of the social, but rather allow the social to provide an account of the psychological.

Postscript

There are several troublesome issues associated with this brief portrait of work satisfaction. First, better objective descriptions of work situations are required. If the approach presented above is to have analytic and practical value, we need reasonably accurate measurement techniques by which to characterize and compare work environments—particularly along the woefully neglected organizational policy dimension. Perhaps some potentially valuable indices may come eventually from researchers who are presently attempting to construct simplified typologies of the structural characteristics of organizations (e.g., Perrow, 1967; Child, 1972; Pugh et al., 1969; Evan, 1963) and those examining classification schemes for characterizing career sequences (Schein and Bailyn, 1974; Evans, 1974; Van Maanen and Schein, in progress).

Second, the further delineation of experiential or psychological states associated with each set of satisfaction loci is a necessity. Assistance in this task is likely to come from the cognitive modelling work directed towards building mental maps or the underlying dimensionality associated with various aspects of psychological space (Carroll, 1969; Green, 1969; Gould and White, 1974). Hence, we must reveal the mental images people carry with them of their work and workplace (images formed primarily via socialization processes and filtered information flows). This difficult task of measurement is necessary if we are to advance beyond this speculative stage—recognizing of course that the act of measurement may itself screen out aspects of the very thing we are trying to capture with our rulers.

Third and most importantly, we must begin to develop integrated change programmes that combine human resources, relations and reward features such that applied solutions promoted by change agents fit the various problem parameters. In other words, greater specificity and dimensionality is required in all programmes designed to effect work satisfaction. And if this difficult shift is to be made lasting, sequential and dynamic strategies must be invented.

Acknowledgement

This material was collected for a large diagnostic study conducted by the authors for the National Training and Development Service, Washington D.C. under an Economic Development Administration Grant. We should like to extend our appreciation to NTDS project director, Peter Gregg, for his most able assistance throughout the research.

References

Adams, S. (1965). Inequity in social exchange. In L. Berkowitz (ed.), *Advances in Experimental Social Psychology*, volume 2, Academic Press.

Blalock, H. (1972). *Social Statistics*, (2nd edition), McGraw-Hill.

Carey, A. (1967). The Hawthorne studies: A radical criticism, *American Sociological Review*, **32**, 403–416.

Carroll, J. D. (1969). Analysis of individual differences in multidimensional scaling via an N-way generalization of Eckart-Young decomposition, Bell Telephone Laboratories, Murray Hill, New Jersey.

Child, J. (1972). Organizational structure and strategies of control: A replication of the Aston study, *Administrative Science Quarterly*, **17**, 163–177.

Crozier, M. (1964). *The Bureaucratic Phenomenon*, University of Chicago Press.

Davis, L. E., and Taylor, J. C. (1972). *Design of Jobs*, Penguin Books.

Dawis, R. N. and Weitzel, W. (1970). The measurement of employee attitudes, Technical Report No. 3001, ONR Contract No. N00014-68-A-0141-003.

Dubin, R. (1956). Industrial workers' worlds: A study of the central life interests of industrial workers, *Social Problems*, **3**, 131–142.

Evan, W. (1963). Indices of the hierarchical structure of industrial organizations, *Management Science*, **9**, 468–477.

Evans, P. (1974). The price of success: An accommodation to conflicting needs in managerial careers. Unpublished Ph.D. Dissertation, Massachusetts Institute of Technology.

Gomberg, W. (1973). Job satisfaction: Sorting out the nonsense, *AFL-CIO American Federationist*, 14–19.

Gould, P., and White, R. (1974). *Mental Maps*, Penguin Books.

Green, P. (1969). Non-metric approaches to multivariate analysis in marketing, University of Pennsylvania Working Paper.

Hackman, J. R., and Lawler, E. E. (1971). Employee reactions to job characteristics, *Journal of Applied Psychology*, **55**, 259–286.

Hackman, J. R., and Oldham, G. R. (1974). The job diagnostic survey: An instrument for the diagnosis of jobs and the evaluation of job redesign projects, *Technical Report Number 4*, Department of Administrative Science, Yale University.

Herzberg, F., Mausner, B., and Snyderman, B. B. (1959). *The Motivation to Work*, Wiley.

HEW Task Force Report (1973). *Work in America*, Massachusetts Institute of Technology Press.

Hulin, C. L., and Blood, M. R. (1968). Job enlargement, individual differences and worker response, *Psychological Bulletin*, **69**, 41–55.

Jenkins, D., (1974). *Job Power: Blue and White Collar Democracy*, Penguin Books.

Johnson, S. C. (1967). Hierarchical clustering schemes, *Psychometrika*, **32**, 241–254.

Karpik, L. (1968). Expectations and satisfaction in work, *Human Relations*, **21**, 327–350.

Locke, E. (1970). Job satisfaction and performance: A theoretical analysis, *Organizational Behavior and Human Performance*, **5**, 484–500.

McNemar, Q. (1969). *Psychological Statistics* (4th edition), Wiley.

Morse, N. (1953). *Satisfaction in the White Collar Job*, University of Michigan Press.

Perrow, C. (1967). A framework for comparative organizational analysis, *American Sociological Review*, **23**, 194–208.

Perrow, C. (1972). *Complex Organizations: A Critical Essay*, Scott Foresman.

Porter, L. W., and Lawler, E. E. (1968). *Managerial Attitudes and Performance*, Irwin.

Pugh, D. S., Hickson, D. J., Hinings, C. R., and Turner, C. (1969). The context of organizational structure, *Administrative Science Quarterly*, **15**, 91–114.

Schein, E. H. (1970). *Organizational Psychology* (2nd edition), Prentice Hall.

Schein, E. H., and Bailyn, L. (1974). Life career considerations as indicators of quality of employment. Paper presented at *Symposium on Quality of Employment Indicators*, sponsored by Bureau of Social Science Research.

186

Sheppard, H. L., and Herrick, N. (1972). *Where Have All the Robots Gone?*, The Free Press.
Simon, H. (1969). *The Science of the Artificial*, Massachusetts Institute of Technology Press.
Smith, P. C., Kendall L. M., and Hulin C. L. (1969). *The Measurement of Satisfaction in Work and Retirement: A Strategy for the Study of Attitudes*, Rand-McNally.
Strauss, G. (1963). The personality-versus-organization hypothesis. In H. Leavitt (ed.), *The Social Science of Organizations: Four Perspectives*, Prentice-Hall.
Torgerson, W. S. (1965). Multidimensional scaling of similarity, *Psychometrika*, **30**, 379–393.
Van Maanen, J., and Katz, R. (1974). Work satisfaction in the public sector, Technical Report, National Training and Development Service, Washington, D. C.
Van Maanen, J., and Schein, E. H., People through organizations: The negotiated career, Department of Labor Monograph Series, in preparation.
Wanous, J. (1974). A causal-correlational analysis of the job satisfaction and performance relationship, *Journal of Applied Psychology*, **59**, 139–144.

12

The Person and the Situation in Job Satisfaction

Lorne M. Kendall
Simon Fraser University
British Columbia, Canada

The theme of this conference, personal goals and work design, raises the general question of assessing the interaction between characteristics of workers and the context in which they are found. Are satisfaction and satisfactoriness best predicted and understood in terms of linear, compensatory, non-interactive models? If true, then human engineering that ignores individuals' individual differences can steam ahead with work designs which are optimal for the universal person. But, if major influences are interactive we may be forced in the direction of more personalized work design, worker placement, and training in order to optimize the attainment of personal and organizational goals.

As theorists and practitioners we may be forced into the language of qualification, sounding at times like the cagey politician keeping out of corners—yes, but it depends on the type of person, he is not the one for that situation. Not at all like the flamboyant language of universals used in pre-election promises, and in global theories.

The importance of person × situation (P × S) interactions as major determinants and predictors of attitudes and behaviour has been raised on many occasions (Bieri, Atkins, Briar, Leaman, Miller and Tripodi, 1966; Brunswik, 1956; Ekehammar and Magnusson, 1972; Ekchammar, Magnusson and Ricklander, 1974; Endler and Hunt, 1966, 1969; Helson, 1959; Hunt, 1965; Lewin, 1939; Magnusson, Gerzen and Nyman, 1968; Mausner, 1955; Miller, 1963; Murphy, 1947; Sells, 1963).

Bowers (1973) recently criticized the current tendency to give primacy to the situation in accounting for personality, a reaction to an earlier overextended trait emphasis, and he argues for an interactionist position which denies primacy of either traits or situation in the determination of personality. Bowers summarizes 18 studies in which P × S interactions could be assessed and found that in 14 the interaction of person × settings accounted for more variance than either main effect. Certainly such outcomes encourage the continued pursuit of interaction models, even though little guidance is provided to focus attention on particular dimensions of situations.

In fact, although there may be allowance made for the importance of context in conjunction with personal factors, and even non-additive interactions may be proposed, explicit empirical evaluation of interaction effects are not frequent in organizational studies. At least two tough nuts must be cracked before we get to the meat of P × S interactions. First, there is the problem of finding suitable statistical models and computational gyrations to assess interaction effects without giving special preference to main effects. (See Frederiksen, Jensen, and Beaton, 1972, for a good presentation of some alternative models for analysis of interactions which appear differentially sensitive.)

Some past efforts to establish the empirical importance of interactions have been discouraging. For example, the work on moderator variables (e.g., Frederiksen and Melvill, 1954; Saunders, 1956) and predictability (e.g., Ghiselli, 1956, 1960) represents struggles with interaction effects, primarily among personal variables, which have not provided much encouragement. Interaction effects, when found and replicated, are often judged too small to offset costs (e.g., Wiggins, 1973).

The second major difficulty lies in comprehensive representation of crucial dimensions of situations, a problem of a taxonomy of situational features and their measurement. It is one thing to find that a person behaves differently in two settings, but the more important point is to find which aspects of the situations are related to the behaviours. This requires an ability to learn more about a situation than is presented in mere behavioural terms.

Up to this point I have presented a general case for measuring situational variables and studying P × S interactions. The following will focus on job satisfaction and its correlates. First a theoretical position is advanced to the effect that job satisfaction is a social judgement made in relation to a specific context and is affected in particular by P × S interactions. Consequently, measurement of job satisfaction must provide for individual frames of reference. Next, some of the problems and suggested strategies for measuring situations are presented. Finally, an empirical analysis illustrates some of the methodological problems encountered in an attempt to assess the importance of interaction effects. Some implications of this are discussed.

The Nature of Satisfaction and Its Measurement

In an extensive investigation of the measurement of satisfaction Smith, Kendall and Hulin (1969) took the position that job satisfaction is a feeling toward discriminable aspects of job situations. These feelings are a function of characteristics of the job judged in relation to a personal standard or frame of reference. Potentially important components of the frame of reference for evaluation of job features include personal characteristics like skills, expectations, values, and aspirations (which may be indexed by things like background and experience of the worker and which may contribute substantially to an adaptation level), and situational variables which may represent social norms as well as reality constraints in terms of alternatives available in a given situation (perhaps indexed by characteristics of the company and community in which a person works and lives).

The feelings of an individual about various aspects of his job are not absolute. If you ask a person 'How is your car?', he may reply with a question, 'Compared to what?'. With respect to income, at least above a certain minimum, a given wage is a source of satisfaction, a source of dissatisfaction, or irrelevant to an individual, depending upon how much other available jobs might pay, upon what other people of comparable training, skills, and experience are obtaining in the same labour market, upon what the same individual has earned in the past, and upon the financial obligations he has assumed. (See Locke and Whiting, 1974, for a recent example of this type of interaction.)

It is the discriminable characteristics of the job and the interaction of personal factors and the situation which are taken into account when satisfactions are assessed. This position has important implications for the measurement as well as the prediction of satisfaction which are detailed in Smith, Kendall and Hulin (1969). It was shown there that the Job Descriptive Index (JDI) and some global ratings using cheerful and unhappy 'faces' as anchors had very good discriminant validity and also good convergent validity with measures designed to make explicit to some extent at least the frame of reference of the raters. These studies used a triadic method of scoring job descriptions where an aspect of job receives a positive score if it is characteristic of a 'best' job and, in addition, is not characteristic of a 'worst' job. In particular, it was found that the complete frame of reference, involving comparisons with both best and worst anchors, was necessary to achieve acceptable discriminant validity. Scores based on a comparison of present jobs with only a 'best' job (or only a 'worst' job) failed badly in discriminant validity and produced primarily method variance.

The argument is that job attitudes arise when job characteristics are judged in relation to the interaction of personal and situational factors which provide the ingredients for an individual's frame of reference or personal standard. Following from this formulation we should use personal and situational factors, and the interaction ($P \times S$) in prediction studies of satisfaction. While it is true that absolute pay may predict Pay Satisfaction moderately well it seems more likely that pay considered in relation to community norms is more directly relevant to satisfaction with pay.

Measurement of Situational Factors

The importance of measuring situational dimensions has been argued earlier. There are several approaches to the problem of isolating relevant dimensions of the situation but the problem is far from solved. Frederiksen (1972) discussed the need for a taxonomy of situations and argued for the development of factors representing clusters of situations that tend to evoke the same responses. Such factors would constitute the categories in a taxonomy of situations, using the criterion of similarity of behaviours elicited rather than the criterion of similarity with respect to attributes.

Magnusson and his colleagues have studied the dimensionality of the individual's perceptions of situations by means of similarity judgements and multidimensional scaling. This stimulus analytic approach focuses on the dimensions of the subjective or perceived situation as compared to a response analytic approach (where data refer to situational behaviour, as in the proposal of Frederiksen discussed above). Magnusson and Ekehammar (1974) compared these two approaches and found high congruence of outcomes but also found some discrepancies which led to the conclusion that one should distinguish clearly between situation perception factors and situation reaction factors in research on the psychological significance of situations. Ekehammar, Schalling and Magnusson (1974) also reported high congruence between the two methods.

Ekehammar and Magnusson (1973) reported that situations as a whole are used as stimuli and suggest that the individual's total experience of a situation gives it its significance for a person. They argue for the use of similarity ratings which permit judges to deal with a total situation.

Another approach, and the one used in the study reported later, is to start with objective data describing the actual physical and demographic features of the situation, similar to what Murray (1938) called 'alpha press'. It can be argued that it is such information about the community within which a person lives and works which provides the most immediate and familiar standards against which to compare features such as the wages received for particular skills in relation to what other available jobs pay, and the adequacy of income in relation to the cost of available facilities, goods, and services which have become desirable.

Census data have been used to develop composite scores which appear to index socially relevant aspects of situations. Hagood, Davilensky and Beum (1941) reported an early study of regionalism and index construction using factor analysis of county data. Tryon (1955) was able to group political subdivisions of the San Francisco Bay area successfully using cluster analysis of census data. Cultural patterns were studied using factor analysis of census data by Cattell, Breul and Hartman (1952) and Hofstaetter (1951, 1952). Factor analysis of census data was used to establish dimensions for the description, comparison, and classification of cities by Kaplan (1958) and Price (1942), and of counties by Johnson (1958) and Jonassen (1961). Also see Hadden and Borgatta (1966).

MaCurdy (1971) used a set of 18 composites based on census data for school districts in British Columbia, Canada, to predict psychiatric admission rates and diagnosis and found canonical correlations as high as 0.82 with a total canonical redundancy of 15% (Stewart and Love, 1968). Clearly situational variables derived from census data tap information of psychological significance and contribute to predictions.

Prediction of Satisfaction Using Interactions

The following analysis illustrates an attempt to assess the importance of P × S interactions using personal and situational measures developed in conjunction with the Cornell Studies of Job Satisfaction (Smith, Kendall and Hulin, 1969). The advantage of using this data base is that a large heterogeneous sample of workers was available from a wide range of situations. The sample used consisted of 1727 male workers chosen representatively from 21 plants in diverse businesses and industries located in 16 counties (or Standard Metropolitan Statistical Areas) representing a broad range of communities throughout the United States. There was no missing data on any of the variables used in this analysis.

Selected personal factors

Information on personal background, experience, and qualifications that could be relevant in influencing one's frame of reference and particularly the adaptation level are often correlated so it is usually possible to condense such data by means of techniques like factor analysis. Often the quality of the resulting composite measures is improved (Burkett, 1964; Gleason and Staelin, 1973) and still they adequately represent the major variance from the domain. For example, a principal component analysis of 44 personal background items from the Cornell Studies produced a substantial simplification and condensation of the initial data and the resulting ten composites appeared to make sense.

In the present analysis it was necessary to limit severely the number of variables from the personal and situational domains to keep the number of possible predictors, including first order interactions, to a manageable size. Therefore only five personal variables were selected which it was felt might contribute substantially to personal standards used in judging a particular job, or which represented current status with respect to rewards and attainment. The variables were: (i) *job level*; (ii) *education*; (iii) *income*; (iv) *economic maturity*, a composite representing evidence of concrete planning to meet future obligations. It appears related to an important variable identified by Ferguson, (1958, 1960); (v) *obligations*, a composite involving relatively long term obligations based on number of dependents, being married, and attempting to own a home.

Selected situational factors

Only six situational measures were selected because of the need to limit the total number of predictors. Four of these were obtained from factor analysis of 55 census variables for 370 counties sampled in the United States. The six situational measures were: (i) *prosperity and cost of living*, a composite of high income, good housing, high per capita expenditures for retail and food sales, high school enrollment, high rents, high farm value, etc.; (ii) *decrepitude*, a composite of old age, poor health, few new homes, and low birth rate; (iii) *urban growth*, a composite involving population influx with attendant housing problems suggested by a high incidence of newer homes, few vacant dwelling units, and many apartments; (iv) *slum conditions*, a composite which presents a picture of overcrowded and poor housing, a high percentage of non-whites, infrequent home ownership, low education, and a low percentage of males in the work force; (v) *unemployment*; and, (vi) *unionization*, a composite derived from factor analysis of 25 company variables for 1230 companies, involving unionization, manufacturing, relatively large local plant size, and pension contributions provided mostly by the company.

One point to emphasize is that the situational variables selected for the most part represent the much broader context of the community rather than more immediate features of the work situation itself. Factors like organizational climate would need to be included in any attempt at complete assessment of the role of situational variables.

Criteria

A total of seven criteria were selected for prediction, all being variables felt to involve social judgements where relative evaluations were required that would be influenced by personal and situational standards. It was expected that interactions between personal and situational variables would contribute significantly to prediction of these criteria for the reasons discussed previously.

The Job Descriptive Index provided four measures of satisfaction with specific aspects of jobs (work, pay, promotion opportunity, and coworkers) which showed good convergent and discriminant validity in an extensive programme of validation using a sample of 988 subjects in a wide range of situations (Smith, Kendall and Hulin, 1969). Two global measures of satisfaction with Job in General (JIG) and Life in General (LIG), based on a 'faces' rating scale and subjected to similar validation were also used. Another variable selected as a criterion was a question on Desired Income (to be fully satisfied with income).

Analysis

The question to be answered from the analysis is whether P × S interactions contribute significantly to prediction of any of the seven selected criteria. The question is not whether interactions add significantly to main effects but rather are they important in their own right. In principle it should be appropriate to use multiple regression where cross-product terms are used to represent interactions (Cohen, 1968; Ezekiel and Fox, 1959; Saunders, 1956; Wilson, 1973). Now we hit a snag. There are technical problems encountered when attempting to answer the desired question and the usual practice is to answer the alternative question instead, a strategy biased against interaction effects. Wilson (1973) presents several suggestions for identifying interaction effects but problems remain. The main effects may sometimes look very good because they steal some of the action of interaction terms. Although all variables, including interactions, may operate concurrently and in concert, the value assumed by a particular main effect variable could be determined primarily by its interactions with other variables.

There are other problems too arising from possible colinearity of interaction and main effect terms, and from the arbitrary scaling of variables without true zero points. A purist would wisely retreat into inactivity at this point but I will resist this temptation.

A stepwise multiple regression was used. In effect, all possible predictors, main effects and interactions, are put in competition to select a small team of predictors which would do about as good a job as the total set. Evaluation of importance can be based on whether a selected predictor would be missed if it were dropped from the team. The contribution of a given variable is assessed in relation to the other selected variables so the evaluation is relative to a particular team. Even with this approach caution is required when attempting to interpret relative contributions when predictors are intercorrelated (see Darlington, 1968, for a presentation of some of the cautions).

Thirty-one predictors entered the stepwise regression. It is difficult, if not impossible, to produce a unique selection of a given-sized best subset of predictors so the goal becomes a search for a good set but not necessarily the best. It can be argued that a logical selection of predictors, guided by a strong theory, would be preferable when interactions are involved. For example, Ghiselli (1968) distinguished static and dynamic classes of variables, static ones (like intelligence) being thought more likely to contribute to prediction in an additive fashion, and dynamic ones (like indicators of motivation) being thought more likely to operate interactively.

We have some hunches but nothing that could be called strong theory, so an empirical procedure was used to eliminate predictors. Seven separate stepwise regression analyses were run, one for each criterion. The competition for team membership was opened with all 31 contenders given a chance to help predict each of the seven criteria in turn. Variables were dropped one at a time if their deletion resulted in no significant decrease in multiple correlation. Deletion of predictors was stopped when the t value for the decrement in the unshrunken multiple correlation, R_0, reached at least 3.0 for each of the remaining predictors, indicating that the removal of any further predictors would produce a significant loss in prediction.

Results

The multiple correlations ranged from substantial (0.69) to trivial (0.19) although all were unquestionably different from zero. The magnitudes are of less importance, however, than the identity of the surviving predictors, and the decrements in R_0 resulting from deletion of any of these survivors.

A summary across all seven criteria provides a basis for some general observations about the classes of predictors retained. Personal variables were retained 8 times, situational variables 0 times, P × P interactions 5 times, and P × S interactions 16 times. Taken at face value these results suggest that P × S interactions are indeed important contributors to the prediction of attitudes. If the sums are prorated to allow the the different number of possible predictors in each set then the outcome is less dramatic, but still the P × S interactions contribute at an important rate compared to the personal and P × P data sets (13% for P × S, compared to 23% for personal and 14% for P × P data sets).

The most striking feature of the results is that although deletion of any retained predictor would result in a significant decrease in R_0, the actual decrement for any given deletion was usually very small. For example, four variables were retained as predictors of Work Satisfaction. The multiple correlation was 0.43. If either Job Level or Economic Maturity were dropped there would be a significant but small decrease in R_0 of 0.036 or 0.038 respectively. Thus it can be argued that, considered in relation to the four predictors selected, Job Level and Economic Maturity are of about equal importance. To give up either one would produce about equal losses in validity. In comparison it was found that the interaction of Income × Unemployment was less important than either of the first two predictors mentioned but equal in importance to the interaction of Obligations × Unemployment. Deletion of either interaction term resulted in decrements in R_0 of 0.023 or 0.026 respectively.

A similar pattern was observed with other criteria. Six variables were retained to predict Pay Satisfaction with R_0 being 0.53. The predictors, with associated decrements in R_0 shown in parentheses, were: Job Level (0.008); Income (0.018); Job Level × Income (0.004); Economic Maturity × Decrepitude (0.008); Economic Maturity × Urban Growth (0.048); Economic Maturity × Unemployment (0.018); Obligations × Prosperity (0.027). The interaction of Economic Maturity × Urban Growth appears to be quite important. This could be related to a judgement based on expectations and plans for the future and suggests that active financial planning for the future in a situation where there is a rapid growth and change is very much related to satisfaction with pay. A negative sign associated with the Obligations × Prosperity interaction suggests that the combination of high obligations in an area of high prosperity but also high prices is a bad combination in terms of judging satisfaction with pay. This combination could very well identify circumstances where there is just not enough bread to go around.

As a final example, Desired Income was highly predicted ($R_0 = 0.69$) by five variables (associated decrements in R_0 are shown in parentheses) which are:

Job Level × Education (0.010); Education × Obligations (0.015); Income × Prosperity (0.012); Income × Unemployment (0.013); and Economic Maturity × Urban Growth (0.004). The Education × Obligations interaction is of interest suggesting high expectations resulting from conventional indoctrination regarding the instrumental value of education (Mann, 1953) in conjunction with high obligations. More is expected and probably more is needed also.

Discussion

The stepwise regression procedure does not produce any simple answer to the question posed concerning importance of P × S interactions with respect to predicting attitudes. However, the overall results are consistent with the conclusion that these interactions are important in this context. Replication is the necessary means of checking hunches generated from the present study. The large sample size used gives some reason to expect that the relations found would cross-validate without difficulty.

Ambiguities arise because of the complications in regression analysis when there are many predictors available and when there is considerable redundancy among the predictors. The results described above probably give a fair representation of the operation of the particular sets of selected predictors. But other sets could be obtained which might work just about as well. In fact similar levels of prediction were obtained from use of only the five main effects of personal variables alone. Nevertheless, prediction using the P × S interactions worked equally well. Empirically we are left at an impasse to be resolved perhaps only by invoking our own particular biases. It is tempting to side with the result that supports interactions. We know that people are always in some context so it could be argued that main effects of personal variables alone predict effectively because they reflect the results of P × S interactions.

Perhaps the most important point to be made is this. The insensitivity of the predictions to loss of a single member of a predictor team serves as an important reminder that in real life behaviour and attitudes are often overdetermined. Many factors operate concurrently and to alter or remove any particular factor may result in little change in the criterion, its status being buffered by the overdetermined constraints of many other factors. When we study a very restricted range of predictors we may be misled as to their importance in the wider scope of things, forgetting that we have considered their importance in relation to only a limited set of competitors.

References

Bieri, J., Atkins, A. L., Briar, S., Leaman, R. C., Miller, H. and Tripodi, T. (1966). *Clinical and Social Judgment. The Discrimination of Behavioral Information*, Wiley.
Bowers, K. S. (1973). Situationism in psychology: An analysis and a critique, *Psychological Review*, **80**, 307–336.

196

Brunswik, E. (1956). *Perception and the Representative Design of Psychological Experiments,* University of California Press.
Burkett, G. R. (1964). A study of reduced rank models for multivariate prediction, *Psychometric Monograph,* No. 12.
Cattell, R. B. (1949). Dimensions of cultural patterns of factorization of national characters, *Journal of Abnormal and Social Psychology,* **44,** 443–469.
Cattell, R. B., Breul, H. and Hartman, H. P. (1952). An attempt at more refined definition of the cultural dimensions of syntality in modern nations, *American Sociological Review,* **17,** 408–421.
Cohen, J. (1968). Multiple regression as a data-analytic system, *Psychological Bulletin,* **70,** 426–443.
Darlington, R. (1968). Multiple regression in psychological research and practice. *Psychological Bulletin,* **69,** 161–182.
Ekehammar, B. and Magnusson, D. (1972). Anxiety profiles based on both situational factors and response factors. *Reports from the Psychological Laboratories,* University of Stockholm, Number 376.
Ekehammar, B. and Magnusson, D. (1973). A method to study stressful situations, *Journal of Personality and Social Psychology,* **27,** 176–179.
Ekehammar, B., Magnusson, D. and Ricklander, L. (1974). An interactionist approach to the study of anxiety, *Scandinavian Journal of Psychology,* **15,** 4–14.
Ekehammar, B., Schalling, D. and Magnusson, D. (1974). Dimensions of stressful situations, *Reports from the Psychological Laboratories,* University of Stockholm, Number 414.
Endler, N. S. and Hunt, J. McV. (1966). Sources of behavioral variance as measured by the S-R inventory of anxiousness, *Psychological Bulletin,* **65,** 336–346.
Endler, N. S. and Hunt, J. McV. (1969). Generalizability of contributions from sources of variance in S-R inventories of anxiousness, *Journal of Personality,* **37,** 1–24.
Ezekiel, M. and Fox, K. A. (1959). *Methods of Correlation and Regression Analysis,* 3rd edition, Wiley.
Ferguson, L. W. (1958). Industrial psychology, *Annual Review of Psychology,* **9,** 243–266.
Ferguson, L. W. (1960). Ability, interest, and aptitude, *Journal of Applied Psychology,* **44,** 126–131.
Frederiksen, N. (1972). Toward a taxonomy of situations, *American Psychologist,* **27,** 114–123.
Frederiksen, N., Jensen, O. and Beaton, A. (1972). *Prediction of Organizational Behavior,* Pergamon.
Frederiksen, N. and Melvill, S. D. (1954). Differential predictability in the use of test scores, *Educational and Psychological Measurement,* **14,** 647–656.
Ghiselli, E. E. (1956). Differentiation of individuals in terms of their predictability, *Journal of Applied Psychology,* **40,** 374–377.
Ghiselli, E. E. (1960). The prediction of predictability, *Educational and Psychological Measurement,* **20,** 3–8.
Ghiselli, E. E. (1968). Interaction of traits and motivational factors in the determination of the success of managers, *Journal of Applied Psychology,* **52,** 480–483.
Gleason, T. C. and Staelin, R. (1973). Improving the metric quality of questionnaire data, *Psychometrika,* **38,** 393–410.
Hagood, M. J., Davilensky, N. and Beum, C. O. (1941). An examination of the use of factor analysis in the problem of subregional determination, *Rural Sociology,* **6,** 216–233.
Hadden, J. K. and Borgatta, E. F. (1966). *American Cities: Their Social Characteristics,* Rand McNally.
Helson, H. (1959). Adaptation-level theory. In S. Koch (ed.), *Psychology: A Study of a Science,* Vol. 1, McGraw-Hill.
Hofstaetter, P. R. (1951). A factorial study of culture patterns in the United States, *Journal of Psychology,* **32,** 99–113.

Hofstaetter, P. R. (1952). Your city—revisited: A factorial study of culture patterns, *American Catholic Sociological Review*, **13**, 159–168.

Hunt, J. McV. (1965). Traditional personality theory in the light of recent evidence. *American Scientist*, **53**, 80–96.

Johnson, G. H. (1958). A search for functional unities: An analysis of United States county data. Unpublished doctoral dissertation, New York University.

Jonassen, C. T. (1961). Functional unities in eighty-eight community systems, *American Sociological Review*, **26**, 399–407.

Kaplan, H. B. (1958). An empirical typology for urban description. Unpublished doctoral dissertation, New York University.

Lewin, K. (1939). Field theory and experiment in social psychology: Concepts and methods, *American Journal of Sociology*, **44**, 868–896.

Locke, E. A. and Whiting, R. J. (1974). Sources of satisfaction and dissatisfaction among solid waste management employees, *Journal of Applied Psychology*, **59**, 145–156.

MaCurdy, E. A. (1971). An ecological study of hospitalized mental disorders in British Columbia, Unpublished master's thesis, Simon Fraser University.

Magnusson, D. and Ekehammar, B. (1974). Perceptions of and reactions to stressful situations. *Reports from the Psychological Laboratories*, University of Stockholm, Number 410.

Magnusson, D., Gerzen, M. and Nyman, B. (1968). The generality of behavioral data I: Generalization from observations on one occasion, *Multivariate Behavioral Research*, **3**, 295–320.

Mann, F. C. (1953). A study of work satisfaction as a function of the discrepancy between inferred aspirations and achievement, *Dissertation Abstracts*, **13**, 902.

Mausner, B. (1955). Studies in social interaction: I A conceptual scheme, *Journal of Social Psychology*, **41**, 259–270.

Miller, D. R. (1963). The study of social relationships: Situations, identity, and social interaction. In S. Koch (ed.), *Psychology: A study of a Science*, Vol. 5, McGraw-Hill.

Murphy, G. (1947). *Personality: A Biosocial Approach to Origins and Structure*, Harper.

Murray, H. A. (1938). *Explorations in Personality*, Oxford.

Price, D. O. (1942). Factor analysis in the study of metropolitan centers, *Social Forces*, **20**, 449–455.

Saunders, D. R. (1956). Moderator variables in prediction, *Educational and Psychological Measurement*, **16**, 209–222.

Sells, S. B. (1963). Dimensions of stimulus situations which account for behavior variance. In S. B. Sells (ed.), *Stimulus Determinants of Behavior*, Ronald.

Smith, P. C., Kendall, L. M. and Hulin, C. L. (1969). *The Measurement of Satisfaction in Work and Retirement*, Rand McNally.

Stewart, D. and Love, W. (1968). A general canonical correlation index, *Psychological Bulletin*, **70**, 160–163.

Tryon, R. C. (1955). Identification of social areas by cluster analysis: A general method with an application to the San Francisco Bay area, *University of California Publications in Psychology*, **8**, No. 1.

Wiggins, J. S. (1973). *Personality and Prediction: Principles of Personality Assessment*, Addison-Wesley.

Wilson, K. V. (1973). Linear regression equations as behavior models. In J. R. Royce (ed.), *Multivariate Analysis and Psychological Theory*, Academic Press, pp. 45–73.

13

Change in Command and the Behaviour of Subordinate Leaders

Paul M. Bons   and   Fred E. Fiedler
University of Washington and   *University of Washington*
U. S. Military Academy, West Point   *Seattle, USA*

Research on leadership behaviour has been intensive since World War II, and in particular since the identification of the well known Ohio State University dimensions of Consideration and Initiation of Structure. Only recently has there been a growing concern with identifying the determinants of these behaviours. Up to now the implicit assumption has been simply that an individual is consistently considerate or structuring, that is, that the tendency to behave in a considerate or structuring manner is a characteristic of his personality. At the same time, it has, of course, been recognized that people behave differently under various conditions. Thus, under pressure and stress, most leaders become less considerate (e.g., Greene and Organ, 1973) and their members demand more authoritarian leadership (e.g., Hamblin, 1958; Mulder and Stemerding, 1963). One recent set of studies specifically attempts to identify those contingencies in the situation which determine behaviour (see House, 1971; Kerr, Schriesheim, Murphy and Stogdill, 1974), although they do not address the role which personality differences will play.

There is considerable evidence, however, that the leader's behaviour is determined in part by his personality and in part by the situation, and that personality and situation interact in determining certain types of behaviour (Fiedler, 1967; Bowers, 1973; Sarason, Smith and Diener, 1975).

This paper takes a new look at the situational determinants which need to be considered in understanding the behaviour of leaders in small military units and how this may influence the working lives of their subordinates. The framework within which we will consider this problem is the Contingency Model of Leadership Effectiveness, a theory of leadership which has been developed over the last 20 years (Fiedler, 1967; Fiedler and Chemers, 1974), and which provides a well researched basis for investigating leader behaviour in terms of the situation and the leader's own characteristics.

The Contingency Model

This theory holds that the effectiveness of a task group or of an organization depends upon two main factors: the leader's motivational system and the degree to which the situation gives the leader control and influence. The first of these factors distinguishes two types of leaders who have different motivational structures and, therefore, exhibit different types of behaviours in anxiety-arousing and uncertain situations. According to the model, the relationship-motivated person under these conditions needs to relate to others and is primarily concerned with maintaining good interpersonal relations while the task-motivated person is primarily concerned with accomplishing the task.

Leaders are classified on the basis of the Least Preferred Coworker (LPC) score which is obtained by first asking an individual to think of all persons with whom he has ever worked, and then to describe the one person with whom he has been able to work least well. The description of his least preferred coworker is made on a short bipolar, eight-point scale of the semantic differential format; for example:

Friendly: :   :   :   :   :   :   :   : Unfriendly

               8   7   6   5   4   3   2   1

Uncooperative: :   :   :   :   :   :   :   :Cooperative

                 1   2   3   4   5   6   7   8

High LPC leaders, that is, individuals who describe their least preferred coworker in relatively positive terms, are seen as primarily relationship-motivated. Low LPC persons, those who describe their least preferred coworker in very unfavourable terms, are basically task-motivated.

Relationship-motivated people seem more open, more approachable, and more like McGregor's 'Theory Y' managers, while the task-motivated leaders give the impression of being more controlled themselves and engaging more in controlling others, even through they may be as likeable and pleasant as their relationship-motivated colleagues. Our current evidence suggests that the LPC score, and the personality attributes it reflects, are about as stable as most other personality attributes. Changes do occur but in the absence of major upsets in the individual's life, they tend to be gradual and relatively small. Retest reliabilities for mature military leaders have been above 0.70 over 6 to 8 month periods.

The second parameter in the contingency relationship is 'situational favour-ableness' (Fiedler, 1967). A favourable situation gives the leader more control and influence over his group, whereas an unfavourable situation reduces the degree to which he can predict the consequences of his behaviour. Nebeker (1975) has shown that situational favourableness can be redefined as a measure of uncertainty and that a situation which promotes unpredictable outcomes tends to be stressful and anxiety arousing.

Traditionally, the measure of situational favourableness in the Contingency Model has been defined as a composite of variations of three subscales. These are, first, the degree to which the leader is, or feels accepted and supported by his members (leader–member relations); second, the degree to which the task is clear, programmed and structured as to goals, procedures, measurable pro-gress and success (task structure); and third, the degree to which the leader's position provides him with power to reward and punish and thus obtain compliance from his subordinates (position power).

However, it would appear that other elements of the leader's environment might produce similar uncertainty. Among the most important elements in the leadership situation, which contributes to the leader's control, influence, and security, is his relationship with his own superiors. His fate and his career depend in large part on his ability to 'read' and satisfy his boss. A stable relation-ship with his superiors will enable him to make fairly accurate predictions about the superior's reactions to his work as well as the backing and support he is likely to receive from him under various conditions.

Where his boss's own tenure is uncertain, and particularly, when he gets a new boss, the uncertainty level and anxiety of most leaders is likely to rise a good deal: 'What kind of person is this new man?', 'What will he expect of me?', 'Will I be able to get along with him?'. Until now, the Contingency Model has not taken account of changes in superiors or in command structure in determining the favourableness of the situation. We shall here consider specifi-cally the consequences of these changes on the performance and behaviour of relationship-motivated (high LPC) and task-motivated (low LPC) squad leaders.

Two clusters of behaviours will be considered in this study. These are: (i) relationship-relevant, consisting of considerate and rewarding types of behaviours, and (ii) task-relevant, which consist of controlling, structuring and punitive types of behaviours.

Method

Sample. This study dealt with 115 squad leaders of a newly mobilized infantry division. Most of the squad leaders were in the grade of sergeant (E5 or E6) and had been in the US Army an average of approximately 7 years. Experience ranged from 1 to 22 years. In their leadership position they com-manded an infantry squad of from three to ten men with a mission of training for combat readiness. These squad leaders, in turn, reported to a platoon leader, typically a young lieutenant, and to a platoon sergeant, who normally exceeded him in experience by several years. The General Intelligence score for this sample was 103.7 with a range from 82 to 123.

Tests and questionnaires. The officers, non-commissioned officers and enlisted men of the division were tested the first time shortly after their unit was organized and a second time approximately 6 to 9 months later, after completion of the advanced Army Training Test, signifying the unit's combat readiness. Officers and non-commissioned officers were given the questionnaires separately from the enlisted men. All were assured of the confidentiality of the data, and were told that their cooperation was voluntary.

Questionnaires included the LPC scale, a measure of group atmosphere and a variety of measures on which the leaders described themselves and their superiors, and on which each individual, leader and non-leader, described the behaviour and perceived power of his superior. For each leader, therefore, we have a description of his relationship and task-related behaviour as perceived by his men. In addition, superiors also rated their subordinate leaders on a variety of performance behaviours. We thus have a number of behavioural measures on each leader as he is seen by his subordinates and as he is seen by his own superiors.

The seven dependent measures used in this study, along with sample items from each, follow:

Behaviours rated by subordinates

Person-oriented behaviour—He is friendly and approachable. He puts suggestions made by the group into operation.

System-oriented behaviour—He lets group members know what is expected of them. He encourages the use of uniform procedures.

Rewarding behaviour—Getting you promoted. Giving you high efficiency ratings.

Administrative-punishing behaviour—Putting you in the stockade. Reducing your pay or demoting you.

Person-punishing behaviour—Putting you on extra duty. Chewing you out.

Behaviours rated by superiors

Task-performance behaviour—He carries out administrative actions required of him as a leader of a unit in keeping with Standard Operating Procedures and regulations.

Person-performance behaviour—He knows and understands the personal problems of his subordinates and considers their suggestions and feelings.

Along with the measure of task versus relationship motivation previously discussed (the LPC scale), data were collected about changes in the squad leader's supervisors during the 6- to 9-month interim period. This change in boss serves as the other primary independent variable in this study. With two immediate supervisors (the platoon leader and the platoon sergeant) a possibility exists for three categories of change. These are:

(a) squad leader remains with the same platoon leader and platoon sergeant (No change);

(b) either the platoon leader or platoon sergeant changes but not both (1/2 change);

(c) both the platoon leader and platoon sergeant change (Max change).

The question naturally arises as to causality. Does the change in supervisor(s) cause change in behaviour, or does certain change in behaviour in the leader cause his supervisor to be replaced. Preliminary analyses revealed that there were no meaningful differences on any dependent behavioural measures between relationship-motivated and task-motivated leaders at the first test. This strengthens the argument that behaviour change results from change in command structure rather than the reverse.

Results

Although not of direct concern to the present discussion, it should be noted that relationship-motivated (high LPC) leaders were seen by both superiors and subordinates as significantly more person-oriented than task-motivated leaders. This occurred regardless of the change in supervisor(s), and is a finding which is fairly typical in studies of this nature (Fiedler, 1972). There was also a general decrease in punitive behaviour on the part of squad leaders as a result of boss change regardless of leader motivation. While statistically significant, the decrease is rather slight in absolute terms, and as we shall see, depends in part on the personality of the leader as well as experience.

We also found a decrease in rated performance on the part of experienced leaders whose superiors were changed. This did not occur for lesser experienced leaders. The reason for this finding may well lie in the fact that the new boss's expectations may be too high in view of the short time in which he has worked with the squad leader. That is, the superior may be comparing him to his former subordinates who had learned to please him, and the present squad leader may look less competent in comparison. The fact that no significant differences were observed and reported by subordinates in either system-oriented or person-oriented behaviours would tend to support this interpretation, in that it is relatively more difficult for a squad leader to 'hide' behaviours from his subordinates than from his superiors.

By far the most interesting findings concern the changes in the leader's method of dealing with disciplinary problems, that is, his punitive behaviour. As will be recalled, leaders were rated by their squad members on their use of personal and administrative measures of punishment. Figures 13.1 and 13.2 show the results for experienced and inexperienced leaders. It should be recalled that a point falling above the dashed line indicates an increase in use of the

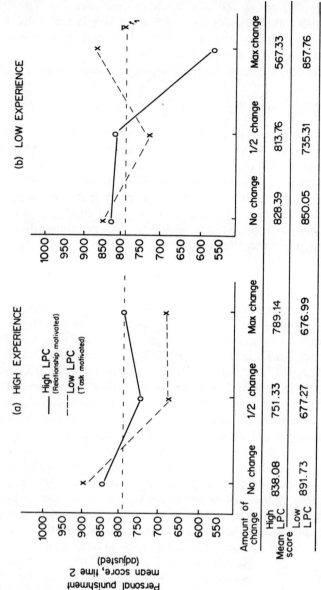

Amount of change		No change	1/2 change	Max change
Mean score	High LPC	838.08	751.33	789.14
	Low LPC	891.73	677.27	676.99

(a) HIGH EXPERIENCE

High LPC
(Relationship motivated)

Low LPC
(Task motivated)

Personal punishment
mean score, time 2
(adjusted)

(b) LOW EXPERIENCE

	No change	1/2 change	Max change
	828.39	813.76	567.33
	850.05	735.31	857.76

Figure 13.1 Person-punishing behaviour as a function of LPC and change in boss for given levels of leader experience

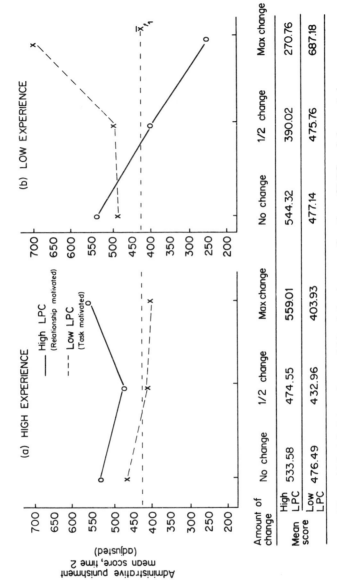

Amount of change		No change	1/2 change	Max change	No change	1/2 change	Max change
Mean score	High LPC	533.58	474.55	559.01	544.32	390.02	270.76
	Low LPC	476.49	432.96	403.93	477.14	475.76	687.18

Figure 13.2 Administrative-punishing behaviour as a function of LPC and change in boss for given levels of leader experience

particular punitive behaviour since time 1 (the first time of testing). Thus, Figure 13.2 shows that relationship-motivated leaders who are experienced tend to increase the use of administrative types of punishment when superiors change, while task-motivated leaders tend to decrease their use under a new boss.

The opposite is the case for leaders with low experience. Here, the task-motivated leaders in conditions of maximum change drastically increased the use of administrative as well as personal types of punishment while the relationship-motivated leaders equally dramatically reduced their use of punishment under new supervisors. Leaders who remained under the same superiors showed a tendency to become somewhat more punitive.

The inexperienced task-motivated leaders appear to feel a strong need to control their men, perhaps in order to impress the new boss with the ability to handle the unit. Relationship-motivated leaders, however, essentially give up punishment as a method of controlling their units, perhaps in order to maintain and strengthen the emotional support from their subordinates now that the support from superiors has become more tenuous and uncertain.

In summary, then, changes in leader behaviour due to change in the leader's superiors are primarily related to punishment. The direction of change is dependent upon the motivational style of the leader. For this sample, there were no significant shifts in the use of rewards, system-oriented (structuring) or person-oriented (consideration) behaviour under new supervisors as a function of the squad leader's motivational style.

Conclusion

Several important points need to be made in considering the implications of this study. The finding that the high LPC leaders are seen by both superiors and subordinates as having better relations with subordinates supports previous studies of this type. The data indicating that all leaders, regardless of motivation, are less likely to use informal, personal-punishing methods when working for a new boss is new and may reflect the strain which a change in higher level supervision brings about.

Important in the present context, however, is the finding that a change in superiors has different effects on relationship- and task-motivated leaders, and that this effect is further modified by the leader's experience in several important cases. The Contingency Model, and research on the meaning of the Least Preferred Coworker score (Fiedler, 1972), has repeatedly pointed out that differences in the behaviour of high and low LPC leaders occur in favourable and in unfavourable situations. This study provides a more detailed picture of the specific behaviour changes which take place when the leader's command environment is altered.

For this sample, although subordinates did report an overall effect of relationship motivation on person-oriented behaviour, changes in behaviour primarily occur in the way the leader approaches disciplinary problems. In marked contrast to previous studies, we can see here the effect of experience, and the accompanying feeling of security which the experienced leader is likely to have as he attempts to deal with his men. The inexperienced leader, however, is more likely to push the panic button when he has to deal with a completely different set of superiors. The task-motivated leader, for instance, apparently tightens the discipline. He is more likely to reprimand and to chastise those who fail to perform well or who overstep the rules. Essentially, he wants control.

On the other hand, when the inexperienced, and equally insecure leader who is relationship-motivated finds himself deprived of his old boss's emotional support, he essentially foregoes administrative punishment, probably to retain the support of his subordinates. For the experienced leader, who has gone through all this before, punitive behaviour is relatively unaffected by these changes.

The intriguing question which confronts us in this study is the reason why punitive behaviour, rather than considerate behaviour or structuring behaviour should be affected by these changes. Is this the only salient behaviour which the subordinates see, or is this the major basis for the leader's interaction with his subordinates? As our data indicate, the leader's task-relevant behaviours, at least as seen by his superiors, do not change greatly as a function of leader motivation and command environment changes; and his considerate behaviour, as we have already pointed out, appears to be quite stable, with high LPC leaders exhibiting more interpersonal behaviours across all situations. The major changes seem to occur in the behaviour of the task-motivated leader who presumably wants to maintain the effectiveness of his unit. However, where there are major changes in his supervisors, the relationship-motivated leader in effect withdraws from his role as disciplinarian.

This is an interesting problem with major implications for maintaining performance. It is obvious that a simple rule on how to behave is not likely to resolve the difficulties in this area. Current efforts to change leader behaviour generally centre around such 'rules' (i.e., training). If, on the other hand, specific leader behaviours are a result of the leader's motivational style only in interaction with situational variables, attempts to change leader behaviour may be made more successful by restructuring the situation rather than by attempting to reshape his personality.

References

Bowers, K. S. (1973). Situationism in psychology: An analysis and a critique, *Psychological Review*, **80**, 307–336.

Fiedler, F. E. (1967). *A Theory of Leadership Effectiveness*, McGraw-Hill.

Fiedler, F. E. (1972). Personality, motivational systems, and behavior of high and low LPC persons. *Human Relations*, **25**, 391–412.

Fiedler, F. E., and Chemers, M. M. (1974). *Leadership and Effective Management*, Scott, Foresman & Co.

Greene, C. N. and Organ, D. W. (1973). An evaluation of causal models linking the received role with job satisfaction, *Administrative Science Quarterly*, **18**, 96–103.

Hamblin, R. L. (1958). Group integration during a crisis. *Human Relations*, **11**, 67–76.

House, R. J. (1971). A path goal theory of leader effectiveness. *Administrative Science Quarterly*, **16**, 321–338.

Kerr, S., Schriesheim, C. A., Murphy, C. J., and Stogdill, R. M. (1974). Toward a contingency theory of leadership based upon the consideration and initiating structure literature. *Organizational Behavior and Human Performance*, **12**, 62–82.

Mulder, M. and Stemerding, A. (1963). Threat, attraction to group and need for strong leadership, *Human Relations*, **16**, 317–334.

Nebeker, D. M. (1975). Situational favorability and environmental uncertainty: An integrative study. *Administrative Science Quarterly*, **20**, 281–294.

Sarason, I. G., Smith, R. E., and Diener, E. (1975). Personality research: Components of variance attributed to the person and situation. *Journal of Personality and Social Psychology*, **32**, 199–204.

14

Psychological Aspects of Shift Work

Pieter J. D. Drenth, Gerlof Hoolwerf
Free University of Amsterdam
and
Henk Thierry
University of Amsterdam, Holland

It was customary some years ago to expect that shift working would increase during the 1960's to allow employers to make maximum use of capital investment (e.g., Banning, *et al.*, 1961). In practice this has not come about. For example, the percentage of Dutch production workers (over 18 years old, excluding coalminers) employed on shifts has remained steady. The figures are as follows: 1957, 17.5%; 1960, 19.2%; 1963, 17.7%; 1966, 18.3%; 1969, 19.8%.

These proportions nevertheless represent a significant minority of employees, and the Ministries of Economic and Social Affairs in the Netherlands have recently sponsored a large investigation into shift working. The study consists of three sub-projects. The first is a macro-economic part, done by the Erasmus University in Rotterdam, in which an analysis is made of the effects on the national income of optimal shift working. The second is a micro-economic part, carried out by the Advisory Bureau Berenschot, which focusses on individual companies. Thirdly, there is an industrial psychological study, examining the influence of psychological variables on the development of shift work. This chapter reviews the results of the psychological sub-project. Another report is by Hoolwerf, Thierry and Drenth (1974), and the first two sub-projects have been described by Iwema and Hoffman (1974) and de Jong and Bonhof (1974).

210

Background to the Research

It is clear that shift work is unpopular. Many people who work shifts dislike the irregular hours, tolerating them only reluctantly (Mott *et al.*, 1965). Downie (1963) has suggested that shift workers' more positive statements about their hours reflect a process of adaptation over time—they have become adapted to the unpleasant features of their routine. Banks (1956) stresses that many shift workers become resigned to the routine as inevitable in their own situation. The reluctance of day workers to move into a shift schedule can perhaps partly be explained by a general resistance to change. There are research results which indicate that the longer one has worked on shifts, the less the dissatisfaction (Smith and Vernon, 1928; Mott *et al.*, 1965; Griew and Philipp, 1969). This could be due to a natural selection process: those who cannot adjust gradually leave, and those remaining are by definition less dissatisfied. In the case of young unmarried men, the desire not to miss their free evenings increases their resistance to shift work (Downie, 1963), all the more since girls usually work during the day (Taylor, cited in Sergean, 1971). In addition to these age differences, other personal and environmental factors are also related to the attitude towards shift work. Tradition and residential area (Sergean, 1971), social level (Philips, 1958), professional competence (Mott *et al.*, 1965), as well as intelligence (van Loon, 1958) all appear to be important.

We have found it helpful to examine the effects of and attitudes towards shift work in terms of five different sets of factors. These are reviewed next.

Social factors. Here we have in mind the influences of shift work upon social life. It is apparent that the shift worker is at a potential disadvantage, particularly for activities which take place during the hours when the regular day worker is usually free (van Alphen de Veer, 1958; Banning *et al.*, 1961; Mott *et al.*, 1965; Sergean, 1971). His social life is necessarily restricted.

Home-life factors. There are a number of direct, unpleasant consequences for the shift worker's home life, such as not being able to have regular meals with the children, the wife being home alone, the decreasing participation in what is happening in the family. Events of this kind are tied to a kind of daytime schedule (Banning *et al.*, 1961; Banks, 1956; Mott *et al.*, 1965; Philips, 1958; Wyatt and Mariott, 1953). Indirectly, there are also annoying aspects associated particularly with the evening and night shift: one comes home at an 'abnormal' time, must sleep and eat at 'abnormal' hours, and so on. This can present a range of extra problems for the wife and the family (Wedderburn, 1967).

Health factors. The effects of shift work on physiological and physical conditions have been studied extensively (e.g., Rutenfranz, 1967; Taylor, 1969; Vernon, 1940). These studies were concerned not so much with the shifts as such, but with the changing of shifts. It was found that the 'adaptation process', the stabilization of a 24-hour rhythm of blood pressure, body tempera-

211

ture and reaction times, took longer than was generally expected. Several kinds of shift work cycles have been proposed on the basis of these data, but practical problems arise from the wide differences in individual reactions; these differences are also related to the kind of work undertaken (Sergean, 1971).

An important complaint by shift workers concerns the problems of sleeping (Aanonsen, 1964; Wyatt and Mariott, 1953; van Loon, 1958). Considered absolutely, the shift worker does not seem to sleep much less than the regular day worker. However, it appears that the quality of sleep is more important than the amount, and qualitative changes in sleep patterns may accompany shift work (Menzel, 1962). In a similar way, eating habits are influenced considerably by shift changes (Wyatt and Mariott, 1953; Sergean, 1971).

It is important to recognise that health is an overall reaction to the total situation. Shift work entails more than merely working unusual hours. There may be associated differences in working conditions, the work itself, the kind of supervision and so on. This fact may partly explain differences in research results from studies comparing the health of shift and day workers. Dirken (1966), Raffle (1967), de la Mare and Shimmin (1964) find only limited differences between shift and day workers. Wyatt and Mariott (1953), Thijs-Evensen (1958), Pierach (1955) and Banning et al. (1961) refer to harmful influences or to the exacerbation of psychosomatic complaints, but Sergean (1971) contends that there is little evidence for this.

Financial factors. Shift workers almost invariably receive a shift bonus or premium. Sergeant (1971) expresses the opinion of many investigators when he states that the bonus is the most important if not the only attraction of shift work for the workers. This idea is widely shared by management, who place strong emphasis on money as the exclusive compensator for the discomforts caused by shift work. We shall return to this point later.

Organizational factors. It is extremely difficult to extract generalizable conclusions about the effects of shift work on work performance, absenteeism, accidents, labour turnover and so on. This is because of the wide differences between situations in terms of other factors such as working conditions and job requirements. Pure and entirely controlled comparisons are not practicable.

There is very little research into differences in accident rate (Oginsky, 1966; Vernon, 1918) or in labour turnover. Absenteeism differences have been more studied, but the problems of comparability across situations and across measures of absence mean that results are inconsistent. Jardillier (1962) and Walker and de la Mare (1971) found that shift workers were absent more frequently, especially on the night shift. Aanonsen (1965) and Taylor (1967) reported that day workers had higher levels of absenteeism, but Banning et al. (1961) concluded that there were no differences. Analysis of data more finely by various shifts does not yield a clear picture (Shepherd and Walker, 1956; Sergean and Brierley, 1968).

The effects of shift work on the performance of employees and on the general

212

production levels of a company have of course also been studied in detail (dc la Mare and Walker, 1968; Wyatt and Mariott, 1953; Banning *et al.*, 1961; Bjerner and Swensson, 1953; Ulich, 1957). The general impression is that there is no reason to suppose that the qualitative and quantitative aspects of production differ strongly between shift and non-shift work.

The Design of the Research

Most studies have concentrated upon the shift worker himself. We felt that it was important in our research to complement such material with responses from other people involved in the worker's life. In particular we wished to examine the views of wives and supervisors.

It is likely that the husband's opinions and attitudes will be influenced by those of his wife, and the latter should themselves be obtained. We have already seen that shift work disturbs a 'normal' day schedule, leading to problems of organization and disturbing the peace of the home. Further, it might be expected that the night shift or changes in shifts have undesirable consequences for the wife's health, sleep and eating patterns. Wyatt and Mariott (1953) and Banning *et al.* (1961) report clearly negative feelings and unpleasant consequences for the wives. The latter investigators especially analysed the relationship of shift workers with their children. The older school-age children, much more than the younger ones (who are more often home when the father is present during 'abnormal' hours), have to be primarily attended by the mother, with all the problems which this can create.

Furthermore, it is of course also important how the wife feels about the shift work allowance in relation to the possible negative consequences of shift work. For she is often the one who regulates the household and the budget. She is also in the best position to determine how easily the family could do without the additional allowance. Her opinion will be an important factor in the choice to work on shifts or to return to the regular day schedule.

We also wished to examine the position of the first-line supervisor. For the shift worker, much more so than for the day worker, he is the key figure in communications with higher authorities, with other groups of workers, and with the events taking place in the company more widely. It is apparent that shift workers may be required to take more decisions and responsibility, but it remains an open question whether higher management adequately delegate this responsibility to shift employees. The views and reactions of the supervisor are thus of considerable interest.

The research obtained data from shift workers ($N = 493$) and regular day workers ($N = 541$), as well as from wives ($N = 422$) and supervisors ($N = 86$). Information was also obtained from higher management, but this will not be described in the present selective review. The total sample was approximately 1600 respondents, with employees drawn from 14 companies. Of these companies three were in the textile industry, four in food and allied products, three in metal working, two in construction, one in paper and one in the printing industry.

Separate questionnaires were developed for each group of respondents, asking for biographical data, factual information about jobs and hours, attitudes towards different hours and work schedules, general work satisfaction and certain leadership and power variables. In the present report we will describe only some of the results and statistical analyses.

Some Research Results

Shift workers and day workers

We were somewhat surprised to find that there were few differences between shift workers and regular day workers in biographical features. There is no difference in education level and average age. Slightly more shift workers are married and their average number of children is slightly greater. Furthermore, they have been working for the company for a shorter time. Their wives have a second job less often, and the shift workers are more frequently in a junior position of leadership. They have relatively more often been a member of the works council.

The opinions and attitudes of both groups towards the work situation were also rather similar. Both liked the company in general and immediate supervision the most, and the wage, stress and communication factors the least. There was however a marked contrast in their views about shift work. The comparison of their overall feelings is shown in Table 14.1. The difference between patterns of reaction by day workers and shift workers is statistically significant at the 1 % level. It is clear that the regular day worker has a considerable resistance to shift work, and (not shown in this table) the more so to the extent that he has a greater probability of working evening and night shifts. Shift workers' feelings are more favourable, although they prefer the day to the night shift. Older shift workers tend to be less dissatisfied than younger ones. The family situation does not appear to influence attitude towards shift work. It does however influence the attitude of the regular day worker: married day workers have

Table 14.1. Overall feelings about shift work of day workers and shift workers

Reaction to shift work	Percentage of day workers	Percentage of shift workers
Very pleasant	1	10
Rather pleasant	2	30
Neutral	8	30
Rather unpleasant	21	16
Very unpleasant	68	14

Table 14.2. Opinions about shift work held by day workers (solid line) and shift workers (dotted line)

Opinions about shift work	Strongly agree 5 4 3 / Strongly disagree 2 1	Statistical Significance
Stress		
Bad for health		—
Lack of sleep		5%
Too many worries		1%
Interference in personal life		1%
Free time		
More free time		1%
Isolation		
Less contact with foremen		—
Less contact with other supervisors		—
Less contact with management		—
Little contact between day and shift workers		—
Shift workers hear company news later		5%
Relations with supervisor		
Relationship with supervisor is better		1%
Foremen consider more personal problems and wishes		—
More appreciation by foreman		5%
Freedom in work		
More responsibility		1%
More freedom in work		5%
More influence in assignment of tasks		—
Better interrelations		1%
Feelings of special position		
Shift workers more willing to sacrifice something for the company		1%
Shift workers work harder		1%
Shift workers do more unpleasant jobs		1%
Shift worker is a special type		—
Day workers are more highly regarded		1%
Shift workers are more money minded		1%
Night shift		
On the nightshift it is more possible to do your job well		—
On the night shift work is less busy		—

greater resistance to shift work than unmarried ones. Furthermore, the less experience with shift work and the longer the time spent on a day schedule, the more resistance the day worker has to shift work.

Respondents were asked a variety of more detailed questions about shift work. Some of these are summarized in Table 14.2, where the response scale runs from strongly agree (5) through neutral (3) to strongly disagree (1). In summary of the material in that table we can say that the shift worker experiences his working schedule and the associated living situation as unpleasant. He has sleeping problems, and views shift work as detrimental to his health and interfering with his pattern of life. The only advantage is the somewhat greater responsibility and closer relationship with the other workers. This general picture emerges even more strongly from the regular day workers' answers. Particularly interesting are the opinions about the possible special position of shift workers. Although shift employees value their own status more than do the day workers, the latter regard their shift-work colleagues less highly and see them as more money-minded.

Table 14.3. Advantages and disadvantages of shift work, as seen by day workers (solid line) and shift workers (dotted line)

Aspect of shift work	Advantage — Disadvantage (scale 5 4 3 2 1)	Statistical Significance
Shift bonus		1%
More free time		1%
More quiet work		—
More responsibilities		1%
Extra job		1%
Alternation of shifts		1%
Varying free time		1%
Time to start work		1%
Work on saturday		5%
Contact with friends is more difficult		—
Wife has to cook more frequently		1%
Difficulties in family		1%
Less social life		—
Sleeping problems		1%

More detailed opinions were investigated through responses to the fourteen features listed in Table 14.3. People were now asked to rate each feature on a scale from 'big advantage' (5) through 'neutral' (3) to 'big disadvantage' (1). The features have been ordered in the table from positive to negative, and it can be seen that the shift worker generally judges the situation more favourably than the regular day worker. It is also clear that very few features are in fact seen as advantages (scoring higher than an average of 3). Some remarks should be made about the use of free time. The regular day worker sees shift work as being detrimental to his social life, and he expects that shift work will leave him less time for his hobbies. The shift worker is a little less negative, but he does express his negative feelings on this point also.

Actual use of free time and participation in clubs was determined for both groups. It appears that shift workers' reports and certainly day workers' expectations about shift work are rather inconsistent with the facts. The shift worker is no less a member of clubs and devotes as much time to this aspect of social life as does the day worker. Similarly, shift workers do not spend less time on hobbies and do not have different hobbies than day workers, even though they complain that they have less time for them.

Statistics about the possible effects of shift work on absenteeism have also been collected and interpreted in this study. Distinctions were made between 'short absences', 'long absences', 'number of times absent' and 'number of days absent'. The general conclusion from the material is that there is little difference in absenteeism between regular day and shift workers, nor between two-shift and three-shift workers. Both for day workers as well as for shift workers, it appears that age has a negative relationship with absenteeism.

One of the most important advantages, and in the eyes of the management also one of the most effective compensations, is the shift work bonus. The regular day workers find, relatively speaking, the size of the bonus the most acceptable. The shift workers are somewhat more negative, and within this group the three-shift workers are the most negative. Further, it appears that the willingness to work on Saturday and Sunday both of shift and of regular day workers does increase somewhat with a greater bonus, but it remains unattractive for both categories, the most for the day worker. In other words money helps, but not much.

It did appear that the majority of the shift workers were unwilling to finish with shift work if this would require financial sacrifices (67% no versus 33% yes). Of those who were willing, the majority would only accept cessation if the sacrifice remained rather small (less than 2-weeks' bonus). Both the shift workers and the day workers slightly preferred money to spare time, if they were to receive extra compensation, but the shift workers show a stronger preference for the monetary reward.

Employees' wives

Both categories of wives generally have a negative view of shift work, although the wives of the regular day workers are more negative than shift workers' wives. Moreover, the latter are more inclined to think that one gradually becomes accustomed to shift work. Also, with respect to the possible consequences, it is noteworthy that the wives of day workers generally have a more negative perception or expectation in comparison with the actual experiences and opinions of the shift workers' wives.

It seems that prior objections are more serious than those based on experience. Of course it is not impossible that resignation and/or habituation play a role. It may also be that one has become used to the shift work bonus, and therefore rationalizes the disadvantages and inconveniences. Nonetheless it should be noted that the opinions of the shift workers' wives remain predominantly negative. More than 70% felt that life would be more pleasant with the day schedule.

Concerning the advantages and disadvantages, the same picture emerges (see Table 14.4). The wife of the day worker is generally more negative than the

Table 14.4. Advantages and disadvantages of shift work as seen by the wives of day workers (solid line) and the wives of shift workers (dotted line)

Aspect of shift work	Advantage / Disadvantage	Statistical Significance
Shift bonus		1%
More free time		1%
More quiet work		—
More responsibilities		—
Extra job		1%
Alternation of shifts		—
Varying free time		—
Time to start work		1%
Work on saturday		—
Contact with friends is more difficult		—
Wife has to cook more frequently		1%
Difficulties in family		1%
Less social life		—
Sleeping problems		1%

wife of the shift worker, the greatest difference being in the evaluation of the shift work bonus. This greater concern with money of the shift worker's wife is also evident in the choice she makes between money and free time; she clearly prefers the former.

If one further considers the fact that the willingness of the shift worker's wife to make financial sacrifices in order to return to a day schedule is much less than the willingness of the day worker's wife for her husband to change to shift work for the same monetary benefits, the hypothesis becomes more plausible: that the wife of the shift worker has become accustomed to the extra money and does not want to do without it, and that she consequently minimizes her objections.

First-line supervisors

The foremen of day workers and shift workers agree with each other in their evaluation of most of the features of shift work shown in Table 14.5. No significant differences are found. In general, however, the day work supervisors are

Table 14.5. Advantages and disadvantages of shift work, as seen by foremen of day workers (solid line) and foremen of shift workers (dotted line)

Aspect of shift work	Advantage 5	4	3	Disadvantage 2	1
Shift bonus					
More free time					
More quiet work					
More responsibilities					
Extra job					
Alternation of shifts					
Varying free time					
Time to start work					
Work on saturday					
Contact with friends is more difficult					
Wife has to cook more frequently					
Difficulties in family					
Less social life					
Sleeping problems					

more negative. It is noteworthy that the supervisor of the shift worker is more negative than the shift worker himself. The relationship for the day schedule is the reverse: the day worker is more negative than his supervisor. Seen overall, the order from least to most negative is: shift worker—supervisor of shift worker—supervisor of day worker—day worker.

The expectations of the supervisors about workers' reactions to shift work do not appear to differ much from the actual opinions and reactions. In other words, the supervisors appraise the attitudes of their subordinates fairly accurately. However, there is one clear exception: the evaluation of and the importance attached to the shift work bonus. The shift work supervisor significantly overestimates the appreciation of this monetary reward in comparison with the shift worker, and the same is true for the day worker and his supervisor.

Discussion and Conclusions

In this last section important points of the study will be summarized and some conclusions about a desirable policy with respect to shift work will be drawn. Shift work is undesirable to many, especially to those who at present work on a regular day schedule. The wives sometimes experience the disadvantages even more than their husbands. The first-line supervisors are generally well informed about the views of their subordinates, but they tend to overestimate the possible compensatory function of the extra money.

We should not overlook the fact that 40% of the shift workers report that they find shift work to be rather or very pleasant. This clearly deviates from the attitude of the regular day workers, of whom 89% view it as unpleasant to very unpleasant. These data lead one to assume that actual experience and process of adjustment is an important factor in the evaluation of shift work.

It may be helpful to link this point with the one made by den Hertog (Chapter 4) and Davis (Chapter 5). They noted how people learn to accept the conditions of their employment, although the prospect of change is initially unattractive. This may in part arise from the fact that employees have only a limited anticipation of the consequences of work structuring or job design. Adjusting to change is not simply a question of changing attitudes, it also involves learning more about the implications of the new procedures.

One important feature of shift work is the influence, predominantly experienced as negative, of the shift rhythm: the interrupted sequence of the evening and night, and the frequent shift changes. In general, however, the shift worker's attitude towards shift work is clearly related to his total experience of the work situation and work climate: he can form a judgement based on a wide range of job features including the hours worked. This is in contrast with the regular day workers, whose attitudes towards shift work related to their views about more limited characteristics of this kind of work: they may form more stereotyped impressions of shift work based only on judgement of the hours worked.

Money is a compensation for shift work, but it does not remove the disadvantages. The objectionable aspects of the shift situation continue to exist, and the attitude of most shift workers does not become positive. Only their willingness to work in shifts is 'bought'. The management philosophy is clearly to be typified as 'the compensation for the inconveniences by extra income'. In addition, there is the fact that both the first-line supervisor and higher management strongly overestimate the importance of the financial reward in the views of the workers.

We definitely have the impression that policy concerning shift work has until now been based on a simple balance model. On one side are thought to lie the inconveniences and disadvantages, and on the other side so much compensation (and it usually occurs to no one to think in other than money terms). These are adjusted so that the 'scale' becomes approximately balanced. From a psychological point of view, it is doubtful whether this approach is correct. In the first place, money has a camouflaging function. The actual objections are not considered, and the sources of inconvenience are left undisturbed. Moreover the bonus can become a wrong motive to choose shift work. The bonus also has an habituating effect, and can result in an unrealistic evaluation of the work situation.

True compensation should be intrinsic. Objections should be lightened by the introduction of measures to improve the situation or should be balanced by advantages that can be classified on the same psychological dimension as the disadvantages.

In the first place we might consider a number of simple steps that directly tackle the objections against shift work. These might include the following:

Arranging for better transportation during unusual hours of the evening and night.
Improving cafeteria facilities.
Improving housing conditions through better sound-proofing.
Increasing knowledge about the company by means of better information and communication systems.
Increasing the quality of leadership by special selection and training of first-line supervisors.

In the second place, special attention should be paid to the selection and guidance of the shiftworker himself. A number of personal qualities and environmental and family conditions can be listed as probably being related to a better acceptance of shift work, and accordingly to better performance and tenure. Additionally, there seems to be much more room for allowing people greater choice of both the kind of shift and of their coworkers than is usual at present. Experiments with greater freedom of choice should be encouraged.

In the third place, a number of measures with respect to the work and working conditions themselves can be considered. One may think of granting shift workers a greater responsibility for production decisions, of greater freedom to choose the pace of work, the schedule of rests, the work procedure, or of a delegation of the assignment of tasks within the group, the quality control procedures, or the system of distribution of the part-finished products to the worker or the group.

This plea for an increase in the responsibility and an enrichment of the job for the shift worker does not imply the undesirability of these measures for the normal day worker. The point is that these aspects are seen as particularly attractive features of shift work, and also that shift work by its very nature offers special opportunities for changes of this nature.

Of course a shift work bonus should be given. But we should ask companies to consider seriously what is the policy that lies behind this emphasis on monetary compensation. It can be expected that after such attempts as mentioned above have been made to remove objections or to create as many intrinsic advantages as possible, certain objections will still remain. In that case, the bonus should be maintained. It can then be admitted, however, that it does not remove the objections, but that it offers prospects of a number of advantages outside the work situation.

In the fourth place, one should not be too afraid of different experiments, if necessary on a local level. Most experience and empirical evidence refers to the classical two-, three- or four-shift systems. It would be interesting to gather some systematic data with respect to quite different shift systems. Possibilities here include different shift schedules, larger blocks of free time, varying length of shifts, varying working times, longer or more frequent vacations, the formation of reserve teams, etc. Information on the reactions of the worker, physiologically as well as psychologically and socially, could be of great value for future decisions.

Finally, it should be clear that this study again has shown that shift work is generally not appreciated, and that disadvantages and objections strongly exceed the positive aspects. It seems likely that this will be the case at least as long as the society remains oriented towards a day schedule, and as long as society's pattern of life continues to mark out the evening or night worker as exceptional. The introduction of shift work is not just an economic measure, but affects strongly the people involved. Accordingly, whenever the introduction of shift work is considered, the economic arguments should be reviewed in the context of likely influences upon the quality of life both at work and outside work.

References

Aanonsen, A. (1964). *Shiftwork and Health*, Scandinavian University Books.
Alphen de Veer, M. R. van (1958). Enkele psychologische aspekten van het werken in ploegendienst, *Mens en Onderneming*, **12**, 357–364.
Banks, O. (1956). Continuous shift work: The attitudes of wives, *Occupational Psychology*, **30**, 65–85.
Banning, W., Bonjer, F. N., Bast, G. H., Jong, J. R. de and Werff, H. M. A. van der (1961). *Ploegenarbeid*, Contactgroep Opvoering Productiviteit, Den Haag.

222

Bjerner, B. and Swensson, A. (1953). Shiftwork and rhythm, *Acta Medica Scandinavia*, **278**, 102–107.

Dirken, J. M. (1966). Industrial shift work: Decrease in well-being and specific effects, *Ergonomics*, **9**, 115–124.

Downie, J. N. (1963). *Some Social and Industrial Implications of Shiftwork*, The Industrial Society.

Griew, S. and Philipp, E. (1969). *Workers' Attitudes and the Acceptability of Shift Work in New Zealand Manufacturing Industry*, Research Paper of the New Zealand Institute of Economic Research.

Hoolwerf, G., Thierry, H. and Drenth, P. J. D. (1974). *Ploegenarbeid: een Bedrijfspsychologisch Onderzoek*, Vrije Universiteit, Amsterdam.

Iwema, R. and Hoffman, L. (1974). *Macro-economische Consequenties van Ploegenarbeid*, Stichting Het Nederlands Economisch Instituut, Rotterdam.

Jardillier, P. (1962). Etude de 14 facteurs influant sur l'absentéisme industriel, *Le Travail Humain*, **35**, 107–116.

Jong, J. R. de and Bonhof, W. (1974). *Bedrijfseconomische Aspecten van de Ploegenarbeid*, Utrecht.

Loon, J. W. van (1958). Enkele fysiologische aspecten van het werken in ploegendienst, *Mens en Onderneming*, **12**, 347–356.

Mare, G. de la and Shimmin, S. (1964). Preferred patterns of duty in a flexible shift-working situation, *Occupational Psychology*, **38**, 203–214.

Mare, G. de la and Walker, J. (1968). Factors influencing the choice of shift rotation, *Occupational Psychology*, **42**, 1–21.

Menzel, W. (1962). Physiology and pathology of shiftwork, *Arbeitsphysiologie*, **14**, 304–318.

Mott, P. E., Mann, F. C., McLoughlin, Q. and Warwick, D. P. (1965). *Shift Work, the Social, Psychological and Physical Consequences*, University of Michigan.

Oginsky, A. (1966). Comparative research on three-shift work: Morning, afternoon and night, *Proceedings of the Fifteenth International Congress on Occupational Health*.

Philips Studiegroep (1958). *Medische, Maatschappelijke en Psychologische Gevolgen van Ploegenarbeid*, Eindhoven.

Pierach, A. (1955). Night work and shift work among healthy and unhealthy workers, *Acta Medica Scandinavia*, **307**, 159–166.

Raffle, P. A. B. (1967). Automation—another change in working environment, *Abstracts of World Medicine*, **41**, 657–670.

Rutenfranz, J. (1967). Psychological aspects of night and shift work, *Arbeitsmedizin*, **2**, 17–23.

Rutenfranz, J. (1971). Probleme der schichtarbeit, *Informationsdienst für Werksärzte*.

Sergean, R. (1971). *Managing Shift Work*, Gower Press.

Sergean, R. and Brierley, J. (1968). Absence and attendance under non-continuous three-shift systems of work, *Nature*, **219**, 536.

Shepherd, R. D. and Walker, J. (1956). Three-shift working and the distribution of absence, *Occupational Psychology*, **30**, 105–111.

Smith, M. and Vernon, M. D. (1928). A study of the two-shift system in certain factories, *IFRB Report* number 47, HMSO, London.

Taylor, P. J. (1967). Shift and day work: a comparison of sickness absence behaviour at an oil refinery from 1962 to 1965, *British Journal of Industrial Medicine*, **24**, 93–102.

Taylor, P. J. (1969) The problems of shiftwork, *Journal of the Royal College of Physicians*, **3**, 370–384.

Thijs-Evensen, E. (1958). Shiftwork and health, *Industrial Medicine and Surgery*, **27**, 493–497.

Ulich, H. (1957). Zür Frage der Belastung des arbeitenden Menschen durch Nacht und Schichtarbeit, *Psychologische Rundschau*, **8**, 42.

Vernon, H. M. (1918). An investigation of the factors concerned in the causation of industrial accidents, *Health of Munition Workers Committee, Memorandum* number 21, HMSO, London.

Vernon, H. M. (1940). *The Health and Efficiency of Munition Workers*, Oxford University Press.

Walker, J. and Mare, G. de la (1971). Absence from work in relation to length and distribution of shift hours, *British Journal of Industrial Medicine*, **28**, 36–44.

Wedderburn, A. A. I. (1967). Social factors in satisfaction with swiftly rotating shifts, *Occupational Psychology* **41**, 85–107.

Wyatt, S. and Mariott, R. (1953). Night work and shift changes, *British Journal of Industrial Medicine*, **10**, 164–172.

15

Conference Review: Issues of Understanding

Edward E. Lawler, III
University of Michigan, USA

This paper will approach the topic of personal goals and work design by focusing on three questions: (i) What do we know? (ii) What don't we know? and (iii) What do we need to know? The problems are essentially issues of person–environment fit, all revolving around how well work situations fit human beings, given their needs, values and abilities. Questions such as whether changes in the work ethic demand a new approach to job design are characteristic of the kind of person–environment fit questions that many people at the conference felt to be in need of an answer. Before dealing with that issue, I would like to say a few words about what constitutes a good person–environment fit.

The discussions at the conference have been marked by a kind of schizophrenia about what constitutes a good fit between the employee and his organization. Some speakers have tended to use employee satisfaction as the criterion of whether a good fit exists; others have used individual or organizational effectiveness as the criterion (see Cummings and Salipante, Chapter 3). There is, of course, no 'right' answer about what is the appropriate criterion. However, I do think it is important that research on this problem attends to both criteria. The case for attending to organizational effectiveness is easily made. Our whole style of life depends upon organizations performing effectively. Hence in considering changes in job design we need to know what impact they will have on organizational effectiveness. This is not to say, however, that all changes which are actually made need to be ones that promise increased organizational effectiveness. We may in some cases want to make changes which will lead to no change or to a decrease in organizational effectiveness. For example, we may want to enrich jobs in a particular situation because it will lead to increased personal growth and development even though it will reduce productivity (e.g., Rowan, Chapter 7). We cannot, however, make informed decisions about job and organization design changes unless we know how they will influence effectiveness. Because of its centrality to our style of life this is one area where it is crucial that informed decisions about the trade-offs involved be made. Thus, even someone who is primarily concerned about increasing the quality of work as expressed by employees needs to pay attention to organizational effectiveness.

The case for focusing on job satisfaction and other measures of the quality of work is less frequently made but no less important than that for focusing on organizational effectiveness. We cannot make informed change decisions without this information unless we are willing to say that it does not matter what effect jobs and organizations have on individuals. This position is absurd, given that organizations exist to serve the needs of individuals and that organizational effectiveness is valued because it means organizations are doing a good job of serving the needs of people outside the organization (e.g., customers, stockholders). It hardly seems logical to ignore the satisfaction of employees while trying to design organizations that are maximally effective in satisfying the needs of people outside the organization. In short, where there are conflicts between what is optimal for organizational effectiveness and what is optimal for employee satisfaction, we need to know how various organizational designs affect both the individual and the organization if we are to make intelligent trade-offs between the two.

What We Know

Now let us consider what we know about individuals and their relationship to work. First, I think we know much more than could be summarized by several conferences like this one. Papers like those presented by Cummings and Salipante (Chapter 3), Katz and Van Maanen (Chapter 11), Mitchell (Chapter 10) and Warr (Chapter 9) have pointed this out already. Warr's paper is particularly interesting from this point of view since, although he is critical of the work on motivation theory, the nine points he uses to evaluate motivation theory are based upon a considerable amount of knowledge. In a sense, unless we knew a lot he could not have pointed out those issues which motivation theories fail to deal with adequately.

This optimism about what we know raises an interesting question. If we know so much about people, why have so many speakers at the conference expressed dissatisfaction with what we know? The answer lies in the kind of knowledge we do have. In general, it is knowledge of relationships, some of which are causal and some of which are correlational, and knowledge of the kind of mental processes that go on in people. As Mitchell points out, at a general level we know what process must go on for an individual to be motivated (that is, valued reward must be tied to behaviour). We know the relationship between satisfaction and such outcome variables as absenteeism and turnover. We also know on the general level what causes employee satisfaction.

Given that we know all these things and many more, why are there feelings of discouragement about what we know? A crucial reason for this is contained in Cherns' paper (Chapter 1). It has to do with the problem of individual differences. Because of them, statements about what we know must stay at a general level otherwise we end up making statements which are true for only a portion of the people in the world. To return to motivation, as long as we say 'tie valued reward to performance' we are on reasonably safe grounds, but as soon as we try to specify what rewards are valued we are in trouble. Tying pay to performance, for example, does not motivate some employees (Lawler, 1971). Thus, when we try to put the content flesh on the process bones we run into individual difference problems. Some researchers have chosen to ignore these differences and to charge ahead. My opinion, however, is that awareness and specification of these differences is one of the most important contributions of psychology. Thus, to some extent it is because we know so much about how individuals differ that we end up being discouraged about our ability to understand them. Needless to say, I do not think we should be discouraged; rather we should accept these differences and make them an important part of our work.

What We Do Not Know

Let us now turn to the issue of what we do not know. Obviously we lack a tremendous amount of knowledge, and I could not begin to come to grips with all of it here. What can be done is mention a few things people think we know that in fact we do not know. Cherns' paper raises the issue of whether peoples' attitudes toward work are changing. During the last few years it has become popular to assume that they are. The simple fact of the matter is that we simply cannot tell whether satisfaction is increasing or decreasing and whether the work ethic is increasing or decreasing. This is for a very simple reason: we do not have the historical data needed to answer the questions. With a few exceptions we began collecting reasonable data on these issues only recently and as a result we will not have good data on them for many years (Quinn, Staines and McCullough, 1974). Most of the discussions during the last few years on how the quality of work life can be improved have centred on what employees want, or on what their strongest needs are. This conference is no exception, as the papers of Katz and Van Maanen (Chapter 11) and Rowan (Chapter 7) illustrate. The case for and against job enrichment, autonomous work groups, participation, etc. is made on the basis of how important such things as autonomy, pay, and interesting work are to employees.

Many people claim that the evidence shows pay to be less important than

228

some rewards which satisfy higher-order needs, while others claim the reverse (Work in America, 1971). Unfortunately we simply do not know what is true, and we lack the methodology to find out what is true (Lawler, 1971). The psychometric issues involved here will not be examined, other than to say that we lack good approaches to finding out what reward or rewards an individual values most and least. What we can tell, as has already been stressed, is that people differ widely in what they want and we can identify which individuals value each reward the most and the least. Thus, both the proponents and opponents of job enrichment can find people to support their views, since some people clearly do not want it while others clearly do (Lawler, 1973).

We do know, as Vansina (Chapter 6) and Cherns point out, that a number of things are changing in society which seem to have implications for job and organizational design. For example, the changes in our educational system which are taking place seem to suggest that people are changing. Not only is the education level of the average man increasing but he is receiving an education that is based more on the principles of self control, autonomy, and individualization. Given that education level correlates with the nature of people, it seems logical that jobs must alter to keep up with the changes in people that are probably taking place. Yet we still lack good evidence on the nature of these changes in people.

We also do not know just how many people are misplaced in their present job and organizational settings. We do have evidence that it is a significant number and definitely worth worrying about, and we also have evidence that a common reason for the misfit is that the people are placed in jobs that are not sufficiently challenging for their needs, skills, and abilities (Porter, Lawler and Hackman, 1975). One way of looking at this is shown in Figure 15.1.

This figure is largely a guess, but it captures my view of the present situation. It shows that most jobs are low on challenge and that many people prefer challenging jobs. The result is that many people end up in jobs that do not fit their needs. In terms of Figure 15.2, very few people fall into what is identified as the region of fit, while many end up in what is identified as the region of under-utilization. It is not hard to see why so many basically similar jobs have

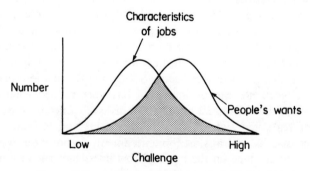

Figure 15.1. A possible pattern of challenge in work

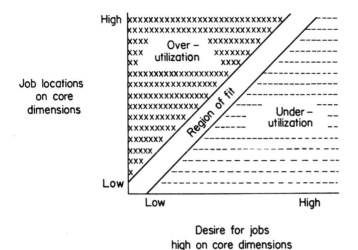

Figure 15.2 Person–environment fit

been designed. The paper by Davis (Chapter 5) nicely captures this. The technology combined with the designers' perceptions of people tend to produce jobs which are low on the core dimension of jobs—autonomy, variety, task identity, and feedback (Hackman and Lawler, 1971). Given the differences which exist among people, the existence of many similar jobs creates a misfit problem. People differ and therefore jobs and organizations must differ if people are to end up in settings which fit them. This point highlights one of the reasons why selection is a necessary but not sufficient condition for everyone to have a job that is appropriate for him or her. Selection cannot guarantee a good person–environment fit unless the jobs are there to start with, and Figure 15.1 suggests that they are not available. Hence we must change the nature of jobs and organizations. How are we to do this? The question can be answered by looking at what we need to know.

What We Need to Know

We clearly need better measurements of the effectiveness of the new organizational and job designs that have been proposed. Noticeably missing at this conference, and as Cummings and Salipante (Chapter 3) note in the organizational behaviour literature, are good attempts to assess the many action research projects which have been done. In all reports the action part is very visible but the research side is not. There are many reasons why this is so, but one that may be crucial has to do with the people who do organizational change. They are not as committed to measuring the effectiveness of what they do as they are to doing it. The result is that they are in a poor position to convince others that their own particular approach to designing jobs and organizations is in fact superior. Further, we are in a poor position to learn things from past experiences in organizational and job redesign that will help us improve our designs. In other words, little self-correction and learning is possible.

Let us look for a moment at what needs to be measured if we are to do a good job of assessing any new approach to organizational and job design:

(i) We need to measure the nature of the individuals so that we can determine the degree to which our results are a function of the individuals who are employed there.

(ii) We need to measure the impact of the changes on the individuals' need satisfaction, mental health, physical health, absenteeism, and turnover.

(iii) We need to measure the productivity and cost effectiveness of these organizations.

(iv) We need to measure the nature of the technology in the work place.

(v) We need to measure the nature of the union-management relationships and the nature of the union organization.

(vi) We need to measure the structure of the organization and the environment in which it operates.

Only if we measure all of these things and perhaps more will we be able to answer questions concerned with the effectiveness of different approaches. It is realized only too well how difficult this kind of research is. It not only requires interdisciplinary teams, it requires advancing the state of the art in several disciplines. For the last two years at the University of Michigan we have been working on some of these measurement issues. We have formed a team made up of accountants, industrial engineers, psychologists, sociologists, and anthropologists, and are developing a measurement package. In developing this standardized package we have had to tackle some tough problems. For example, we have had to develop a cost accounting system for absenteeism and labour turnover. We felt this was necessary because so many new job designs do not strongly affect productivity and other traditional economic measures. Thus, we must measure new things in order to correctly gauge their impact. In short, we feel it is wrong to accept management's traditional measures of effectiveness since they are designed in ways that emphasize only short term productivity and this is not what many new approaches are likely to influence. It is our responsibility to measure all the effects of every new design even if they are not ones that management normally deals with and asks us to measure. Unless we do this we cannot expect management to consider the variables we think are important and to alter the way they reach conclusions about the effectiveness of different approaches.

In order to test the adequacy of our measurement package and to test the effectiveness of some new designs, we have become involved in assessing a number of organizational experiments. In four of these, someone else is doing the organizational redesign and we are studying their changes. The use of an outside assessor is an important development in organizational change research, since it adds considerable credibility and a different perspective to the assessment. In four other locations we are acting as change agents and are measuring our own effectiveness. Our goal is to add a number of other sites to our programme so that in a few years we will have standardized data on the effectiveness of a number of different approaches to organizational and job design that take into account the differences among people and organizations. We need these data in order to make informed decisions about which designs we should adopt and indeed about which new technologies we want to use. Only with these data can we, as Cherns has suggested, decide that we do not want certain kinds of technology and thereby become the masters of technology rather than the victims of the technological imperative.

In addition to data on the effectiveness of designs we badly need new approaches that take into account the differences among individuals. There seems to be little recognition in the literature on organizational change of the very great importance of individual differences. One result of this has been that most suggested solutions to the problem of poor individual-organization fits have been universalistic in nature. That is, they assume a high degree of similarity among people and go on to suggest that everyone be given participative supervision, an enriched job or some other 'work humanization treatment'. This of course is what traditional approaches to management have always done. The only difference is that traditional management approaches have suggested other ways of treating people (e.g., simplification of jobs, use of extrinsic rewards and punishments). Some change is needed in the design of jobs if the distribution shown in Figure 15.1 is to be brought into balance. However, if all jobs were changed we would end up with a situation that is as seriously unbalanced as is the present one.

Recognition of the existence of important individual differences that affect how people respond to organizational policies, procedures, and designs is not enough. We need to develop ways to structure organizations that take these differences into account. Unfortunately, not many have been developed (Lawler, 1974). Traditional wisdom has suggested dealing with this problem through better selection practices. For a number of reasons this has proved to be only a partial solution. Simply stated, organizations almost always have greater differences among people than they have among jobs, even when 'good selection procedures' are used. As was mentioned earlier, one reason for the similarity among jobs undoubtedly is that the technology in most organizations is similar throughout and this leads to similar job designs and supervisory practices in all parts of the organization.

Several strategies for individualizing organizations in specific areas have already been suggested and tried. These need to be mentioned to highlight the kinds of developments that need to be made. Several organizations are using systems which give employees the opportunity to choose the rewards they want. In one company a cafeteria-style fringe benefit programme has been installed which allows employees to choose which fringe benefits they receive. This plan was installed because the existing fringe benefit package did not fit 90% of the employees. The new one fits 100% because every individual receives what he or she wants. In another company workers are given a production standard; when they reach this standard they can either go home or continue to work and earn a pay bonus. Some workers choose to continue working, others to go home. This approach has a direct relationship to the flexible hours approach to the work day and to the recommendation of Drenth and associates (Chapter 14) about experimenting with different hours for shift work since they allow people to decide when they will work.

It is also possible to give individuals choices about the kinds of jobs they have. For example, there is a plant in the United States where workers are given the opportunity to work on either an assembly line job or a bench assembly job which produces the same product. If this organization had done what most organizations do, the product would be produced in the same way by all the workers and many workers would be denied the opportunity to work on jobs which fit them. In some Volvo plants workers are given the choice of being part of an autonomous work group, of working on an enlarged job, or of working on a traditional assembly line job.

The pay and job design individualization strategies which have been mentioned so far depend on individuals selecting their own work environment. There is a good reason for this; individuals usually are the best judges of what they want. However, in order to make good choices they must have realistic choices to make and they must have valid data upon which to make choices. This suggests that the whole nature of the selection process in most organizations needs to be changed. Much greater emphasis needs to be given during the process to providing the job applicant with the information he or she needs so that a good job choice or self selection decision can be made. Of course this alone cannot be sufficient; we still need to have greater variety within and between organizations so that realistic choices can be made.

There are areas where organizations probably have to do more than simply offer people choices about which of several ways they will be treated. For example, a number of leadership styles can be used. It may not be realistic to expect that individuals can actually choose which leadership style they will be subject to. This probably has to be decided on the basis of a joint decision process between the supervisor and the subordinate. A similar process is probably needed in deciding which kind of training programmes an individual should attend. This decision can often be improved by outside assessment of the person by professionals, but it is probably best made on the basis of a joint decision by the individual and the organization.

Other examples of individualization can be mentioned. For example, in some firms husbands and wives are sharing the same job based on their preferences about work hours. Still, the point remains that we are woefully short of strategies for organizational design which take into account individual differences. Basically what we need is 'development engineering' directed toward discovering practical ways for having a wide variety of jobs and practices within a single organization. Further, we need ways of ensuring that people end up in jobs that fit their needs and abilities. It is possible that unless we work actively to develop new approaches little variety will exist in the jobs that are offered. Technological developments have been and will continue to be a strong force towards homogeneity in job and organization design. They can only be countered by a combination of innovative new designs and valid data to show their effectiveness.

Finally, the answer to all three of the questions we have tried to answer is the same: a lot. We know a lot, we don't know a lot, and we need to know a lot.

References

Hackman, J. R. and Lawler, E. E. (1971). Employee reactions to job characteristics, *Journal of Applied Psychology*, 55, 259–286.
Lawler, E. E. (1971). *Pay and Organizational Effectiveness: A Psychological View*, McGraw-Hill.
Lawler, E. E. (1973). *Motivation in Work Organizations*, Brooks/Cole.
Lawler, E. E. (1974). For a more effective organization—match the job to the man, *Organizational Dynamics*, 3, 19–29.
Porter, L. W., Lawler, E. E. and Hackman, J. R. (1975). *Behavior in Organizations*, McGraw-Hill.
Quinn, R. P., Staines, G. L. and McCullough, M. R. (1974). Job satisfaction: Is there a trend? *Manpower Research Monograph No.* 30, United States Department of Labor.
Work In America (1971). Report of a special task force to the Secretary of Health, Education and Welfare, The MIT Press.

1.

2.

3.

16

Conference Review: Issues of Value

David Elliott
The Open University, England

Value-related issues were, not surprisingly, frequently raised both in the formal and informal discussions of the conference. Opinions, beliefs, value judgements, theories about the nature of man and the desirability and efficiency of various organizational prescriptions were constantly introduced and debated.

Faced with this mass of material, I decided to structure this review of value-related issues in terms of some of the questions used by work-study analysts, that is: Who? What? Where? How? Why?

Whose Values?

Values do not exist on their own in the abstract; people hold them and operate according to them. So the first question is: whose values were referred to? The values of two distinct groups were constantly mentioned, those of (i) the professional, studying social systems or implementing changes in them, and (ii) the people in the social system under study; in the industrial context this means both the managers and the work force.

While some people suggested that the values of these two groups might in fact be different, a number seemed to believe that there existed a monolithic consensus, a homogeneous set of opinions, assumptions and attitudes that could be lumped together as the values of society. This unitary view has many limitations which could render difficult any action to implement change by the professional.

It is obvious that many professionals have values, attitudes and broadly speaking a 'culture', which is very different from that of their clients, whether these be the employing managers or the work force. For example since the professionals are insulated from many of the environmental and economic pressures on the work force, they may be incapable of acting successfully on their behalf. A similar problem arises for a different group of professionals, the town planners. Some of these 'are becoming increasingly conscious of the limitations as guides to what they should seek to achieve, of their own middle-class, values' (Senior, 1973, p. 126).

Quite apart from this split between professional and layman, there are, in society, many other divisions, factions, and conflicting sets of values and beliefs. Cherns (Chapter 1), Davis (Chapter 5) and Vansina (Chapter 6) all point out that discontinuities exist between various sub-systems in society, between different age groups, classes, elites and other interest groups, each of which may have a different definition of reality.

This recognition of discontinuities is a considerable advance on the traditional assumption of many earlier psychologists and sociologists, with their simplistic and unitary models of primarily 'economic man' (scientific management) or 'social man' (human relations school). However, the crucial question still remains as to whether all these sub-systems, and the interpretations or values held by them, have equal power and legitimacy in the pluralistic interaction.

Some values are more powerful than others, or, to avoid reification, some peoples' values are more powerful than others. There is a set of dominant values which essentially uphold and legitimize the *status quo* and which are transmitted through the institutions of society. Perhaps Marx's dictum that 'the ruling ideas are, in every age, the ideas of the rulers' does indeed hold some truth. If it does, then it is vital not to treat social values as unitary and automatically generated, but to study the way the authority and power structure of society affect the orientations and values of its members. To quote Parkin (1973, p. 84), we should 'acknowledge that moral and political rules hold sway not because they are self-evidently "right" but because they are made to seem so by those who wield institutional power'.

This line of analysis has obvious relevance to the question of why the 'subordinate' sub-groups in organizations have legitimized the overall distribution of power and authority, rarely challenging it except at the margins. One conclusion is that the advocate of radical change in values must contrive to break through this fatalistic accommodation to the *status quo* (Elliott 1974).

What Values?

What are these dominant values? In the industrial context, they centre typically around the sub-division of labour, hierarchical control, tight profit awareness and a belief in the rational application of the scientific method to all aspects of organizational management. Such values were referred to at the conference almost unanimously in a perjorative sense, as nasty, brutish and short-sighted. Typical key words were 'scientific management', 'cost–benefit analysis', 'productivity', 'technical efficiency', all of which, if taken as the only goal of organizational design, were assessed as in some way outmoded or counterproductive.

Much more highly valued were social goals such as job satisfaction, the design of technology to suit people, the provision of the opportunity for autonomy, personal growth, actualization, ethical awareness and social justice: goals with a strong humanistic, altruistic or liberal flavour.

The former set of goals were associated with value judgements about man, technology and society of the type enshrined in the 'economic' model of man or the technological determinism thesis. We were told by some that these values are being replaced by the new, liberal values. It is the latter that the professionals, the OD men, the job designers, those seeking to improve the quality of working life and so on, were trying to implement, through action research and the introduction of techniques such as work structuring. Their argument is that they can in this way successfully change the nature of organizations and the quality of life within them. This is particularly so since it has been demonstrated that there is, in fact, considerable organizational and technological choice; the structural options are not totally determined by the technology or the environment.

Where?

If we now ask where are these new values being introduced, their precise nature should become more apparent. The most obvious changes are those occurring in organizational structure. New forms of organization design and motivational structure are emerging which rely on new models of human behaviour and new assessments about human capacity and needs. Heavy emphasis is laid on autonomy, self-regulation, adaptation, flexibility and so on, in the prescriptions for middle-management 'project teams' and autonomous work groups on the shop floor. These organizational forms differ sharply from those associated with conventional bureaucratic prescriptions and the scientific management view of motivation. There is evidently much room for change here, and it is in this area that the OD approach seems to be making progress.

However, it is usually stressed that technology limits what can be done in the way of job design and organizational flexibility. Technology tends to be accepted as a given, but in many cases it is the technology that encapsulates the values that must be changed. The logic of mass production flow lines is the very logic that must be challenged if one really wants to improve the quality of working life. That managerial values are implicit in the design of production technology is now becoming increasingly acknowledged. The choice of a particular production technology is made not only on engineering logic but according to managerial concepts of worker motivation and control.

As revealed in a study by Davis, Canter and Hoffman (1955) of US job design practice, the criteria for choice were explicitly the scientific management concepts of narrow subdivision into repetitive tasks, tight pacing of the workers by the machine and the minimization of skill. Davis *et al.* concluded that these 'policies and practices in job design are inconsistent with programs and policies in human relations and personnel administration' (p. 11). Lest it be thought that the traditional managerial values are only reflected in the arrangement and coordination of the machine system and not in the actual technology itself, it is well to consider some specific technological choices.

For example, one group of production engineers, discussing automation, have expressed what seems to be a common belief, namely that when 'examining suitable projects for automatic assembly, . . . operations requiring skill should be given the first priority. They are always bottlenecks of production cost and quality' (Jenkins and Desmond, 1968, p. 28). Another engineer (Tipping, 1969) has argued that we should 'continue with the use of machinery to ensure that the human staff do not slip back into their ways before they had machines. This could easily happen, and the best insurance against it is to continue (product) designing to suit machinery'. Implied here is the conscious use of technology to de-skill, control and pace the worker.

The values that can be inferred here are, as Davis admits, diametrically opposed to those preferred by the modern job design school, but they are deeply entrenched. Technological choices are constantly being made according to these traditional values. If the OD man or job designer wishes to make any lasting impact on the quality of life in the organization, then it is apparent that he must become involved at the earliest stage of production technology choice and design, since these choices, and the implicit value judgements, tend to control all others. Cotgrove (1973, p. 71) has pointed out that 'it is the designers of the production technology who largely determine the extent to which work is satisfying'.

This viewpoint was accepted by many at the conference. As Davis (Chapter 5) puts it: 'The new view alerts us to look at the design process of production technology itself to see which social system planning and psycho-social assumptions were considered in the design of various technical system alternatives. Further, we have learned that we need to have made explicit what economic and social as well as technical factors were included in the decision process of choosing a technological form' (see page 70).

Now while it is relatively easy to seek to influence organizational design and man-management style, there is likely to be much stronger opposition from management to attempts to alter the basic production technology philosophy. So although there is considerable opportunity for 'organizational choice', the more crucial problem of 'technological choice' seems less tractable. Nevertheless many people at the conference were convinced that it was possible to bring about change in managerial criteria and values in all these areas, given time. The next question is, then, how?

How?

There were a number of views about how these changes could be facilitated. It is useful to make a distinction between 'ends' and 'means' here. Some advocate the fundamental redirection of organizational goals, that is new ends, while others talk simply of modified means used to reach unchanged goals. For example, some people are resigned to, or willingly accept, the continued control of systems by the existing management structure with no meaningful change in ends, and only minor adaptations of policy or means to ensure the maintenance of the *status quo* (for example by re-structuring jobs so as to reduce worker dissatisfaction and unrest).

This is to suggest that some consultant social scientists would be happy, in van Strien's words to 'become a tool of management in the service of the powerful' (Chapter 8), or in Baritz's terms 'to supply the techniques helpful to managerial goals' (Baritz, 1960, p. 194). Few people at the conference saw themselves in this light, as merely 'servants of power'. Some claimed that managers' and workers' goals overlapped more than was commonly recognized, but many professed themselves committed to the introduction of both new means and ends, and believed that radical change was both feasible and desirable. Two basic approaches were discernible as to *how* such change might occur, namely spontaneously and by professional change agents.

Spontaneously

New managerial values may be generated automatically as a response to the autonomous action of groups within the system, usually subordinate groups responding to changed environmental conditions. Many examples of direct action and self-help by interest groups both inside and outside organizations were referred to: action by disenchanted workers, disaffected members of the community, irate consumers and so on. Most of these were applauded as signs of societal value changes which would help to change organizations.

Bennis and Thomas (1972, p. 21) draw attention to the fact that 'the contemporary organization must necessarily adapt to change by constantly monitoring the relevance and legitimacy of its present goals', while Daniel and McIntosh (1972, p. 57) argue that industry must 'make its policies and practices consistent with social values outside industry'. There is, of course, the question of whether management need respond to changes in a firm's environment; after all, as was emphasized many times, the manager has considerable strategic organizational and technological choice. He can choose to ignore some pressures in pursuit of other goals.

Child (1973, p. 240) has written that 'decision making about organizations is not simply a matter of accommodating to operational contingencies. It is equally a political process into which other considerations, particularly the expression of power-holders' values, also enter'. There is some evidence that industry does adapt to societal pressure, particularly when faced with increased labour turnover, absenteeism and unrest. But the reassessments of values and priorities that result in an increased emphasis on job enlargement, work structuring and fundamental changes in technology, are usually only made with an eye to the unchanged superordinate goals of stability, profitability and efficiency, now perhaps interpreted in a somewhat broader way. Most threats seem to be contained without the need to make fundamental changes in goals or even means. Whether the manager will 'spontaneously' adopt new radical goals is therefore an open question.

Professional change agents

Faced with this situation, there are many who opt for change implemented by professionals acting as change agents within the organization. It is suggested that the OD man could gradually bring about a change in managerial orientation or workers' aspirations. There were disagreements as to precisely how this should occur, and not all conference members thought in quite these terms. Two basic proposals were that one should try to:

(a) Permeate from above, that is work with the top level of management who make the crucial policy decisions which determine the nature of the shop floor environment.
(b) Stimulate change from below by minor adaptations at the shop floor level, the experience of which would lead to pressure for more radical change in higher level policy and practice.

A central value emerges here, that it is the overall aim to improve the lot primarily of these at the bottom of the industrial hierarchy. The quality of life of the shop-floor worker is assessed as significantly more in need of improvement than that of any other organizational member. The debate is largely about how best to improve this, from above or below, slowly or quickly, by force or by choice, on a small scale or on a large scale.

Some people believed that, in general, the professional change agent could intervene successfully to produce fairly basic changes, although it was felt that certain types of change could not (or should not) be induced by external stimulation. It might, for example, be inappropriate to try to stimulate a desire to participate by devious motivational means, since for participation to be meaningful it cannot be manipulated. In the same way Rowan (Chapter 7) suggested that in the long climb toward ethical awareness, there came a point where external aid was inappropriate. Self-actualization in the end must be independently sustained.

These reservations apart, there was little doubt that the professional could inject new values and bring about beneficial changes in both means and ends — 'beneficial' defined of course in the professional's own value terms. But who is to judge whether these values are indeed truly desirable? One man's view of 'benign advance' could be another's 'technocratic manipulation'. Vansina (Chapter 6) stressed the conflicts which this can generate in practice, and the need for a gradual process of learning.

The change model alluded to seems to bear strong similarities to Galbraith's (1967) dream of a radical technostructure, a 'liberalizing elite', a layer of benign technocrats implementing radical changes on behalf of society. Many proponents of this view suggest that the change agent is free to make meaningful changes, that he is not constrained, in his organizational role, by the people who employ him. He can introduce radical new 'means' and perhaps even 'ends' without coming into conflict with the power structure.

While it does seem possible in certain situations to make limited changes, it seems unlikely that any truly meaningful change can be implemented in this way unless some attempt is made at the same time to alter the balance of power. The change agent or action groups may succeed in winning minor changes at the margin, especially if, by reducing friction, these ensure short term stability and therefore maintain the *status quo*. But what if a major prop or goal of the system is attacked, seriously infringing managerial discretion and prerogatives?·

As Fox (1973, p. 219) has written in an examination of trade union pressure for change: 'The discussion may be about marginal adjustments in hierarchical reward, but not the principle of hierarchical rewards; about certain practical issues connected with the prevailing extreme subdivision but not about the principle of extreme subdivision of labour; about financial (extrinsic) reward for greater efficiency but not about the possibility of other types of (intrinsic) reward with some sacrifice of efficiency; about measures which may achieve company expansion and growth but not about the benefits and costs of company expansion and growth; about how the participant interests can protect and advance themselves within the structure operated by management to pursue its basic objectives but not about the nature of those basic objectives'.

In the same way, increased worker participation is, usually, limited to those areas where managerial prerogatives and values are not threatened and the aim often seems to be to *reassert* managerial goals and values rather than to challenge them or introduce new goals. Some limited changes may, perhaps, be worthwhile in themselves but equally they may, by relieving the symptoms but not the cause, reinforce managerial control and, temporarily at least, re-affirm and legitimize the *status quo*. Herzberg, Mausner and Snyderman (1959, p. 137) have suggested that what is being offered by job enrichment is '... more latitude ... to individuals to develop their own ways of achieving the ends that are presented to them by centralized authority'.

It is conceivable that by gaining more control over 'the means', the workforce might develop an appetite for control over higher levels of policy, or the 'ends', but it is doubtful whether management would relinquish such control without a considerable struggle. This struggle would be between the organized work force and the management. Any meaningful change would have to be won through collective action, through a change in the balance of power, a process which the professional consultant could aid (or oppose) but which could not be instigated by him alone. It is interesting, in this context, to note that the Lucas Aerospace Combine Stewards' Committee, which has set up a Science and Technology Advisory Service to provide early warnings and assessments of new technologies proposed by management, intends to call on the services of experts from outside (*New Scientist*, 1974).

In such a situation, it would be naive for the OD man to believe that it will be easy, or even possible, for him acting as a change agent radically to redirect the goals or practices of an organization. As van Strien (Chapter 8) pointed out, it is more likely that the professional will simply be used only to provide the means to reach ends chosen by those in power.

Baritz (1960, p. 195) has suggested in a similar vein that 'The technician's role was literally forced upon industrial social scientists by the nature of their industrial positions. Hired by management to solve specific problems they had to produce . . . Demanding that the social scientists in their employ concentrate exclusively on the narrow problems of productivity and industrial loyalty, managers made of industrial social science a tool of industrial domination'. Now, it may be objected that the modern OD consultant is more free than is depicted here, that the range of problem areas is now much wider and that the industrial social scientist has transcended Munsterberg's dictum that 'industrial psychologists should concern themselves with means only, not with goals, aims, or ends, which could and should be determined only by the industrial managers' (Baritz 1960, p. 199).

It was frequently argued at the conference that the consultant was in some way capable of independent action. However, as van Strien (Chapter 8) noted, 'sponsors tend to refrain from giving new assignments to social scientists who have become too exacting or annoying, or even kick them out in the middle of a project'. This suggests that the consultant must accommodate himself to the organization's goals. Also, as Baritz (1960, p. 16) comments, 'companies began social science research not a minute before they were convinced that this was an effective and relatively inexpensive way to raise production and increase profits'.

Techniques like job enrichment have been accepted by management, in part because (although perhaps erroneously) they have 'been promoted as a panacea for all management's problems', as a way to 'make workers compliant and deferential, seduce them away from trade unionism and from the pursuit of their interests where these are in conflict with the interests of management' (Daniel, 1972). Surely there is a great danger that the industrial social scientist will be used to implement this type of programme.

Despite attempts to reassert the professional ethic of service to the society, the old adage 'he who pays the piper calls the tune' seems appropriate. Certainly few people would suggest that the hired consultant social scientist is free to implement whatever he likes; he is definitely 'on tap but not on top'. The independently funded researcher is even more likely to have his project constrained or curtailed if he strays from the norm acceptable to the company.

This is not to suggest that organizations, either by mistake or for instrumental reasons, will never admit consultants with radical goals, but it seems unlikely that such a consultant would survive long in an organization if he tried to stimulate radical changes beyond those sanctioned by management, for example, if he attempted to encourage the union to press for involvement in decision making about the basic choice and design of the production technology.

Of course, the professional may be content to limit himself to introducing marginal changes, or he may believe that although he cannot redirect the ·organization's 'ends' immediately, the values encapsulated in the new means are subtly subversive of the traditional ends. However, it would seem equally likely that his efforts could result in no more than manipulation and co-option, aiding management to 'regain control by sharing it' (Flanders 1970, p. 172). Certainly this would appear to be a major danger faced by professionals seeking to implement organizational change.

Why?

So the final question is addressed to the OD man and job designer: why are you trying to introduce new values into organizations? Is it in the hope of ensuring the stability of the *status quo*, by adopting new means to reach existing managerial ends, or in the hope of fundamentally changing organizational goals and values as well as means? Or is there a third, intermediate position? Certainly many OD people, action researchers and so on, claim that their aim is to change the organizational world. The central question being asked here is whether such attempts can be successful, except in the most minimal sense. Is the minor relief from unpleasant work good in itself, even though this may divert attention from the need for fundamental change? Can some worthwhile changes be made that do not require a shift of power? Or, in order to make any truly meaningful improvement in the quality of working life, is it necessary to introduce changes that lead to, or at least are made in conjunction with, radical changes in the basic balance of power and the *status quo*?

References

Baritz, L. (1960). *The Servants of Power*, Wesleyan University Press.
Bennis, W. and Thomas, J. (1972). *Management of Change and Conflict*, Penguin.
Child, J. (1973). *Man and Organization*, George Allen and Unwin.
Cotgrove, S. (1973). Technology and work, *Technology and Society*, **8**, 70–74.
Daniel, W. (1972). Changing hierarchies at work, *The Listener*, **88**, No. 2267, 300–302.
Daniel, W. and McIntosh, N. (1972). *The Right to Manage*, Political and Economic Planning.
Davis, L., Canter, R. and Hoffman, J. (1955). Current job design criteria, *Journal of Industrial Engineering*, **6**, 5–11.
Elliott, D. (1974). The social role of the professional designer, *Design Research and Methods*, **8**, 103–106.
Flanders, A. (1970). *Management and Unions*, Faber and Faber.
Fox, A. (1973). Industrial relations: A social critique of pluralist ideology. In J. Child (ed.), *Man and Organisation*, George Allen and Unwin.
Galbraith, K. (1967). *The New Industrial State*, Hamish Hamilton.
Herzberg, F., Mausner, B. and Snyderman, B. (1959). *The Motivation to Work*, Wiley.
Jenkins, R. F. and Desmond, E. (1968). Product design for automated assembly: The elimination of skill, *Electrical and Electronics Manufacturer*, December, 27–29.

244

New Scientist (1974). Technological self-help, **61**, No. 890, 732.
Parkin, F. (1973). *Class Inequality and Political Order*, Palladin.
Senior, D. (1973). Planning and the public. In P. Cowan (ed.), *The Future of Planning*, Heinemann.
Tipping, W. V. (1969). *An Introduction to Mechanical Assembly*, Business Books.

17
Conference Review: Issues of Change

Andrew M. Pettigrew
London Graduate School of Business Studies, England

Many of the discussions of change at this conference have been abstract and difficult to relate to. A major reason for this is that the subject of change itself is difficult to talk about outside the context and situation in which an actual change is taking place. From my point of view the most vivid conference analyses of the problems of making changes happen have come from informal discussions with some of the practitioners in our group, in particular den Hertog, King, Robertson and Lytle.

In what follows an attempt will be made to amplify and generalize some of the messages communicated by those practitioners and develop some further themes about changing which the conference papers and discussions have only alluded to. We have talked about our understanding of how changes happen but little of how to make those changes happen. Davis (Chapter 5) in his assertion that attempts to improve the quality of working life have so far been trapped in marginalia, and den Hertog's observation (Chapter 4) that work structuring as a broad organizational renewal has not been achieved to any real extent in the Philips concern indicate that we are, so far, talking about very limited change indeed. One might ask why. Perhaps it is because of a preoccupation with equating improvement in the quality of working life with the re-design of jobs rather than systems of work, perhaps because of a lack of diagnosis of the contextual variables which surround individual tasks and limit that re-design in any particular situation, maybe because innovations in the area are self-consciously described as experiments and while praised on all sides, are forgotten as onc-off events, and maybe also because even changes in individual jobs create systems repercussions which severely limit the spread of change.

The analytical core of this chapter will be the problem of transforming drive for change into momentum for changing. The problem is not just of starting change, which in some organizational cultures may be difficult enough, but of maintaining the momentum for change through time. The process of changing will be discussed in terms of the constraints and opportunities created by political behaviour within the firm and also by the success with which the advocates of change, often referred to as change agents or internal consultants, are able to generate and maintain credibility for themselves over time.

Drive and Momentum for Organizational Change

Many change projects in organizations start off with tremendous drive and enthusiasm. If the change is being pushed, as it often is, by a small group of change agents either from a project team or a newly-created specialist department, the specialists are likely to take on some of the characteristic values of an innovative sub-system. The specialists will exhibit and experience high involvement in the task and unit goals, high energy given to the solution of novel and consequential problems, a strong sense of group identity leading to extensive in-group social contact in and out of the work place, the development of group rituals often as ways of socializing new members, and unconventional styles of dress and language (Pettigrew, 1975a). The effect of these rituals and values is to increase the group's level of awareness of itself and its commitment to its task, and at the same time to separate out the group from its environment. Therein lies one of the central dilemmas of specialist-based attempts to create organizational change. The very mechanisms and processes which give initial energy to the changes also create countervailing sources of organizational energy to slow the process of changing down.

The history of many organizations is full of examples of changes which started off with great drive and gradually lost momentum. Such changes can be thought of as high-speed trains picking up momentum out of the station. They are new, glossy, well-oiled and driven by people with tremendous enthusiasm, almost missionary zeal. But something happens on the way down the track; processes are set in motion which derail the train altogether, shunt it off into the side-lines, or reconstitute the formation and crew and set it off in another direction. Left behind are a bitter, frustrated set of internal consultants and cynical managers waiting for the next glossy vehicle to get on the rails and start rolling.

In spite of the attempts in this volume by Davis (Chapter 5), den Hertog (Chapter 4), Cherns (Chapter 1) and in a slightly different way Vansina (Chapter 6) to direct our attention to these problems we have hardly grappled with them. We lack any real coherent body of theory which will allow us to understand

and predict the origins and development of the forces which slow down change processes. The development of that body of theory, which would as a minimum have to explain both the displacement of energy from within the change programme and an increase in countervailing force from other organizational purposes towards the weakening of the change, represents one of the significant lines of future thinking for any theory of organizational change. In more positive terms, the creation of such a theory can also provide the guidelines to prevent the displacement of energy from taking place. Elsewhere (Pettigrew 1975b) I have argued that such a theory has to include more self-consciously an analysis of the internal political forces in organizations which act as both sources of constraint and opportunity for changing. This theme will be picked up and elaborated later in this chapter.

Recently Vickers (1968) and Schon (1973) have grappled with important issues around the problem of why systems stay as they are. Both writers are impressed by paradoxes, Vickers in arguing that it is the very flexibility of some types of organizations which helps them to remain stable, and Schon in talking of 'dynamic conservatism', the tendency of systems to burn up great amounts of energy in order to remain as they are. Schon's system-level defences to avoid change, selective inattention, counter-attack, containment and isolation, compartmentalization and cooption are very close to the interpersonally based delaying tactics described by Pettigrew (1974) and others. But what are some of the more widely based factors, internal and external to the organization, which displace energy from and reduce the momentum of organizational change?

One key factor central to the theme of this conference is the uncertainty in conceptualization and knowledge-base from which the changes receive their direction. The papers by Warr (Chapter 10) and Mitchell (Chapter 11) highlight clearly the amount of differentiation in the way the field of motivation is developing. If the conceptual base of work design has its uncertainties and inconsistencies, and the matching process between the technology of work design and the concepts is also problematic, then there are bound to be major problems in relating that technology to any particular institutional context. [See Daniel and McIntosh (1972) and Cooper (1974).] Such difficulties are likely to be compounded if over-optimistic claims are made about the impact of technology in improving the quality of working life. Cooper (1974) has recently gone so far as to label some of change agents in the field of work design as 'over-zealous proselytisers and uncritical good intenders' (p. 117).

Studies of operational researchers by Doktor and Hamilton (1973) and computer specialists by Mumford and Hedberg (1974) indicate that there are appreciable differences in cognitive style and values between the designers of new systems and their users. These cognitive differences, and especially those which are unconsciously concealed within the model of man that designers and users work with, significantly affect the level of understanding and trust between both parties and therefore the potential for, and limits of, any change.

Reviews of some of the experiments in work design by Daniel and McIntosh

(1972), Wild and Birchall (1973) and Cooper (1974) indicate that inadequate diagnosis of the organizational culture and context in which the change is being attempted can lead to system repercussions of various kinds and a perfunctory end to the change. Contextual factors most often mentioned include the history of labour relations on the change site, the system of wage or salary payments, the particular department or work area chosen to experience the first change, the level of managerial commitment to the change and the success with which the process of handling the change was managed. Other factors likely to affect the initial drive and subsequent momentum for the change will include the extent to which interest groups within the firm perceive their power and status to be affected for the better or worse by the change, the skill with which the change agents are able to anticipate such repercussions and manage the release of political energy which will ensue, and the general economic climate in which the organization finds itself. Few of these contextual variables, all of which are likely to displace energy from any attempt at redesigning work, were really confronted by the conference papers.

Leverage Mechanisms for Changing

One of the strong features of the paper by Cummings and Salipante (Chapter 3) is its clear delineation of three kinds of related information required by decision makers interested in improving the quality of working life. They talk of identifying action levers to create changes, the contingencies or contextual variables which will affect the choice of action levers, and information about the handling of the change process itself. The sparse attention given in this conference to the articulation of contextual variables which are likely to affect the success of any attempt at work design has already been touched on. Here I wish to consider Cummings and Salipante's first category of required information for strategy making and to examine the range of action levers dealt with in the conference papers.

For some time Leavitt's (1964) classification of change leverage mechanisms into the four interrelated factors of Task, Structure, Technology and People has provided a convenient starting point for discussions of what is being changed in any context, why, and with what range of systems repercussions. More recently Handy (1975) has supplied us with a slightly larger list of leverage mechanisms or actionable variables. He splits his leverage mechanisms into two groups of three. The first group of three can be manipulated and may produce changes in the short run, but as the second group is in the short and medium term relatively fixed, it is more realistic to expect changes in these in the longer term. The leverage mechanisms actionable in the short term are people and style, roles and relationships, and tasks and technology. People and style mechanisms include hiring and firing, training and education, personal counselling and reassignment. Roles and relationships could involve the reorganization of reporting relationships and the re-negotiation of systems of expectations between those in related positions. Tasks and technology

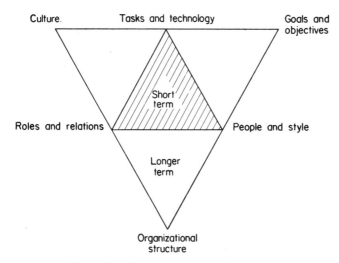

Figure 17.1 Change leverage mechanisms

mechanisms include the re-design of individual tasks and whole systems of technology in factory and white collar environments.

These three types of leverage mechanisms are in their turn linked to a set of variables which may yield action in the longer term. This second set includes the culture of the organization in question, its goals and objectives and its structure. Culture denotes the norms and values of the organization and how they influence systems and procedures through styles of communicating, rewarding and punishing and decision-making. Goals often imply public statements of concern for profit but also involve other forms of organizational purposes such as survival, accountability and growth. Organizational structure is the third of the interrelated set of longer-term leverage mechanisms. Both sets are contained in Figure 17.1.

Using Figure 17.1 as just one possible perspective on leverage mechanisms, it appears that the bulk of the papers at this conference have concerned themselves largely with the area of task and technology, and even then task and technology at the level of the individual and small group. Are these the limits we are to impose on ourselves in questions of understanding and changing in the area of the quality of working life? Those conference papers which ultimately question conventional wisdom in the field of personal goals and work design clearly signify that changes will be required beyond the boundaries of task and technology and outside the limits imposed by conceptual thinking and practical adjustments made from individual and small group levels of analysis.

It is ironic, though intellectually refreshing, to read that Davis (Chapter 5) who earlier challenged the rational-engineering view of organizations and in so doing created part of the language and momentum of job design is now pressing hard to overthrow aspects of the conventional wisdom he has developed. He has argued strongly in his chapter that the job as the 'unit of organization' is not particularly useful for analysis or design. He has even gone so far as to argue that the term and concept of job design should be abandoned in favour of work system design and that analyses of work system design should include reference both to intraorganizational support systems and even organizational environment variables.

Two other detractors from the concern with social psychological variables alone, den Hertog (Chapter 4) and Vansina, (Chapter 6) deal with the limitation imposed on choice of leverage mechanisms by the experimental method and the process of changing itself. Den Hertog argues that the era of small scale experiments in work structuring tied to the dependent variables of satisfaction, absenteeism and quality is now over. What is required is a movement towards system-wide change and a greater concern with the process of change as a mechanism for organizational learning and self-renewal.

Vansina contends that different groups of social scientists have become associated with specific change leverage mechanisms to the exclusion of many others and have in consequence, after planned interventions, left great holes in the development of the organization and confusion for the people concerned. He recommends an integrated approach to organizational change involving micro and macro levels of analysis and a variety of leverage mechanisms clearly articulated for conscious choice. Only in this way, argues Vansina, will the organization start to learn as it changes.

The implications from a research point of view of including variables from the individual, group, organizational and interorganizational levels of analysis in theorizing about work system design and of considering a broader range of leverage mechanisms than task and technology as the point of intervention, are not well understood. The recent volumes on social intervention by Hornstein *et al.* (1971) and Zaltman, Kotler and Kaufman (1972), in cataloguing the forms and processes of intervention, merely add confusion to the fundamental questions: which leverage mechanisms do you start from? do you intervene in sequence, one change lever at a time, culture first and then technology? or in parallel, a new structure, with new or newly trained people and a change in technology? Clearly such questions are unanswerable outside the specific context and contingencies of the organization in focus and even then they challenge the diagnostic ability of most managers and consultants.

However, the most fundamental implications of system-wide changes are likely to be in their reverberations and therefore in increasing the problems of those who design and implement the change itself. Den Hertog (Chapter 4) has whimsically described such reverberations as the 'Anti-Hawthorne Effect', the tendencies of even small scale changes in production systems to threaten and corrode existing power relations between line and staff departments. It is this concomitant of system-wide changes that will be considered next.

Organizational Change and the Release of Political Energy

One of the themes noticeably absent from much of the writing on organizational change is the internal political context of changing. Making changes happen is not only a learning process in the way Vansina (Chapter 6) has described it, but it may also be an influence process as various interest groups within the firm seek to encourage or block attempts at changing the existing system and therefore the resources and relationships which uphold that system.

Considering the organization as a political system directs attention towards the factors which facilitate and hinder change and to the reasons why political energy is often released within the firm at even the prospect, never mind the reality, of change. Political processes within the firm evolve at the group level from the division of work in the organization, and at the individual level from associated career, reward and status systems. Sub-units develop interests based on specialized functions and responsibilities. Individual careers are bound up with the maintenance and dissolution of certain types of organizational activity and with the distribution of organizational resources. At various times claims are made by sub-units and individuals on scarce organizational resources. The scope of the claims is likely to be a reflection of the sub-unit's perception of the criticalness of the resources to its survival and development. The success of any claimant in furthering his interests will be a consequence of his ability to mobilize power for his demands.

It is the involvement of sub-units in such demand and support generating processes which constitutes the political dimension. Political behaviour is defined as behaviour by individuals or sub-units within an organization, which makes a claim against the resource-sharing system of the organization. The point about organizational changes is that to a greater or lesser degree they are likely to threaten the existing distribution of organizational resources as they are represented in salaries, promotion opportunities and control of tasks, people, information and new areas of a business. Additional resources may be created and appear to fall within the jurisdiction of a department or individual who had previously not been a claimant in a particular area. This department or its principal representative may see this as an opportunity to increase his power, status and rewards in the organization. Others may see their interests threatened by the change, and needs for security or the maintenance of power may provide the impetus for resistance. In all these ways new political energy is released and ultimately the existing distribution of power endangered.

These processes are likely to receive their more volatile expression not, as is often imagined, at the implementation of changes but during the decision to go ahead with the change (Mumford and Pettigrew, 1975). Constraints are set during the decision stage which can make resistance and manoeuvre at later stages of the change mere ritualistic gestures. The issue, therefore, is less one of where and when is political energy likely to be released than one of to what extent will it be released within the change process.

It is to be expected that the concern with the existing and future distribution of resources in the firm and the systems of power, status and careers based on those resources will be highly correlated with the extent of the envisaged change. Large scale changes in structure involving the evolution of new departmental groups and the demise of others or the appearance of new technologies may threaten quite fundamentally existing lines of activity and interest. The area of the business affected by the change may also be a significant independent variable when determining the level of concern with the change and the amount of interest group based energy which is released in stopping or slowing the change. One indicator of the amount of political energy released might be the amount of time taken in making the decision to go ahead with the change. In a study of a series of computer purchase decisions in a single organization there was tentative evidence in support of this hypothesis. With each new computer installation the computer technologists gained more influence over the critical as distinct from the peripheral areas of the business. As the technologists moved from peripheral to core areas so they encountered more secure, powerful and vested interests. As they re-defined business activities more within the logic of their approach so the dependency of others upon them increased and their power as an interest group became more visible. Thus the level of political energy within the computer department's sphere of activities increased, both from those in the core areas of the business who wished to slow the computer technologists' progress, and also from within the computer unit itself as different sub-groups attempted to influence the design of each new installation in such a way that their existing control over it was either maintained or enhanced (Pettigrew, 1973).

Additional momentum is likely to be given to these political processes by the amount of slack in the organization at any point in time. It is important to know, for example, whether the changes are being made in conditions of growth or zero-growth. The zero-growth situation resembles rather closely some of the conditions of the psychologists' zero-sum game. If changes are made at the point in time when organizational participants perceive the organizational resource cake to be either fixed or reducing in size, such perceptions are likely to raise people's awareness of the current distribution of resources and therefore what the proposed change can do to that distribution. Conversely the degree of threat created by a change may be less in conditions perceived to be a non zero-sum game or in times of organizational growth when the future might contain the possibilities for increased resources or the same proportion of resources as in the past.

There is, of course, a considerable difference between awareness by an interest group of the impact of change on their position and their ability to translate that heightened awareness into effective action. Consciousness of the implications of a change may have to be tied not only to the awareness that the interest group has of its potential power resources, but also to the tactical manner with which those resources are used in negotiating the parameters of and processes of implementation of change. It has been suggested elsewhere that the power resources of expertise, control over information, political access and sensitivity, assessed stature and group support may be of considerable importance in making and preventing changes from happening (Pettigrew, 1975b).

First line supervisors in some large British process industries offer a pertinent example of a group of people under pressure and yet faced with the systems repercussions of work re-designs in groups interdependent with them. Many supervisors have experienced a considerable loss of autonomy and responsibility in relationship to both managers and workers. Due to considerable over-manning and possibly over-training of middle managers in these large process companies many managers have been probing down the hierarchy as well as up and across in the search for meaningful activity. Supervisors have felt constrained by this encroachment on their responsibilities by managers. They have been frustrated and sometimes embittered both by the increasing weight and credibility given to the shop steward and the effective wage bargaining power of plant operatives.

Although they are becoming increasingly unionized their current bargaining power is weak. They often have poor prospects for job mobility because their skills are specific to their industry or even to a particular factory in it. On top of this there is the current economic climate and the prospect for some firms of zero-growth. Where is the real prospect of an expansion and development of the supervisor's role? Is it realistic to expect them to welcome and encourage further enrichment of operatives' systems of work? Perhaps with these groups of supervisors we will see the strongest manifestations of den Hertog's 'Anti-Hawthorne Effect'.

Summary and Conclusion

The area of organizational endeavour represented by the theme of this conference is one where there has been real progress in applying social science knowledge. If we are to ensure that the increased expectations raised by that progress, not only amongst social scientists but also amongst managers and workers, are not to be frustrated then we must give greater attention to the factors that can influence the range and amount of change.

This chapter has tried to pinpoint some of the variables likely to influence the scope of organizational change in the area of work design. The problem was raised initially in terms of one of the major dilemmas of change, how to translate drive for change into a sustained momentum for changing. In the particular area of job design the summaries of work in progress by Daniel and McIntosh (1972), Cooper (1974) and others indicate that a clear understanding of the context of the change is crucial in determining the amount of change which is possible. The contextual variables they mention, the history of labour relations in the change site and by implication the level of trust between management and worker, the prevailing system of reward and punishment in the factory, even the overall culture of the factory or firm, can all influence the meaning workers and managers attach to the idea of the change and therefore its likelihood of being implemented.

A greater understanding of the interrelationship of these contextual variables in any change site can significantly help the decision about which change

254

leverage mechanisms can be manipulated, and whether adjustments can be made in parallel and/or in sequence, and with what systems repercussions. The other major range of contextual variables mentioned was related to the internal political dimension of the organization and what we know about the release of political energy at the time of decision and during the implementation of organizational changes. Depending amongst other things on the site of the change, the magnitude of the change, the prospects of the firm for growth or zero-growth, so changes are likely to be perceived as affecting the existing and future distribution of organizational resources. Political energy is most often released by the prospect of unscrambling existing distributions of power and status and by the violation of customary expectations about lines of career development. The politics of the firm can exert a significant impact both in limiting and enhancing the prospects for change. In terms of the theory and practice of making changes happen, one area for future development is towards a theory of intervention based more on the political realities of organizational life.

References

Cooper, R. (1974). *Job Motivation and Job Design*, Institute of Personnel Management.
Daniel, W. W. and McIntosh, N. (1972). *The Right to Manage*, McDonald.
Doktor, R. and Hamilton, W. F. (1973). Cognitive style and the acceptance of management science recommendations, *Management Science*, **19**, 884–895.
Handy, C. B. (1975). *Understanding Organizations*, Penguin.
Hornstein, H. A., Bunker, B. B., Burke, W. W., Gindes, M. and Lewicki, R. J. (1971). *Social Intervention: A Behavioral Science Approach*, The Free Press.
Leavitt, H. J. (1964). Applied organizational change in industry: Structural, technical and human approaches. In W. W. Cooper, H. J. Leavitt and M. W. Shelley (eds.), *New Perspectives in Organizational Research*, Wiley.
Mumford, E. and Hedberg, B. (1974). The design of computer systems: Problems of philosophy and vision, *Preprint* 1/74-4, International Institute of Management, Berlin.
Mumford, E. and Pettigrew, A. M. (1975). *Implementing Strategic Decisions*, Longmans.
Pettigrew, A. M. (1973). *The Politics of Organizational Decision Making*, Tavistock.
Pettigrew, A. M. (1974). The influence process between specialists and executives, *Personnel Review*, **3**, 24–30.
Pettigrew, A. M. (1975a). Strategic aspects of the management of specialist activity, *Personnel Review*, **4**, 5–13.
Pettigrew, A. M. (1975b). Towards a political theory of organizational intervention, *Human Relations*, **28**, 191–208.
Schon, D. A. (1973). *Beyond the Stable State*, Penguin.
Vickers, G. (1968). *Value Systems and Social Processes*, Tavistock.
Wild, R. and Birchall, D. (1973). Means and ends in job restructuring, *Personnel Review*, **2**, 18–24.
Zaltman, G., Kotler, P. and Kaufman, I. (1972). *Creating Social Change*, Holt, Rinehart and Winston.

AUTHOR INDEX

SUBJECT INDEX

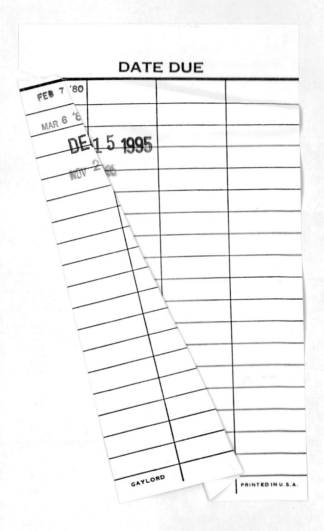

DATE DUE

FEB 7 '80			
MAR 6 '8			
DEC 1 5 1995			
NOV 2			
GAYLORD		PRINTED IN U.S.A.	